CABELL
CENSUS
LOCATOR

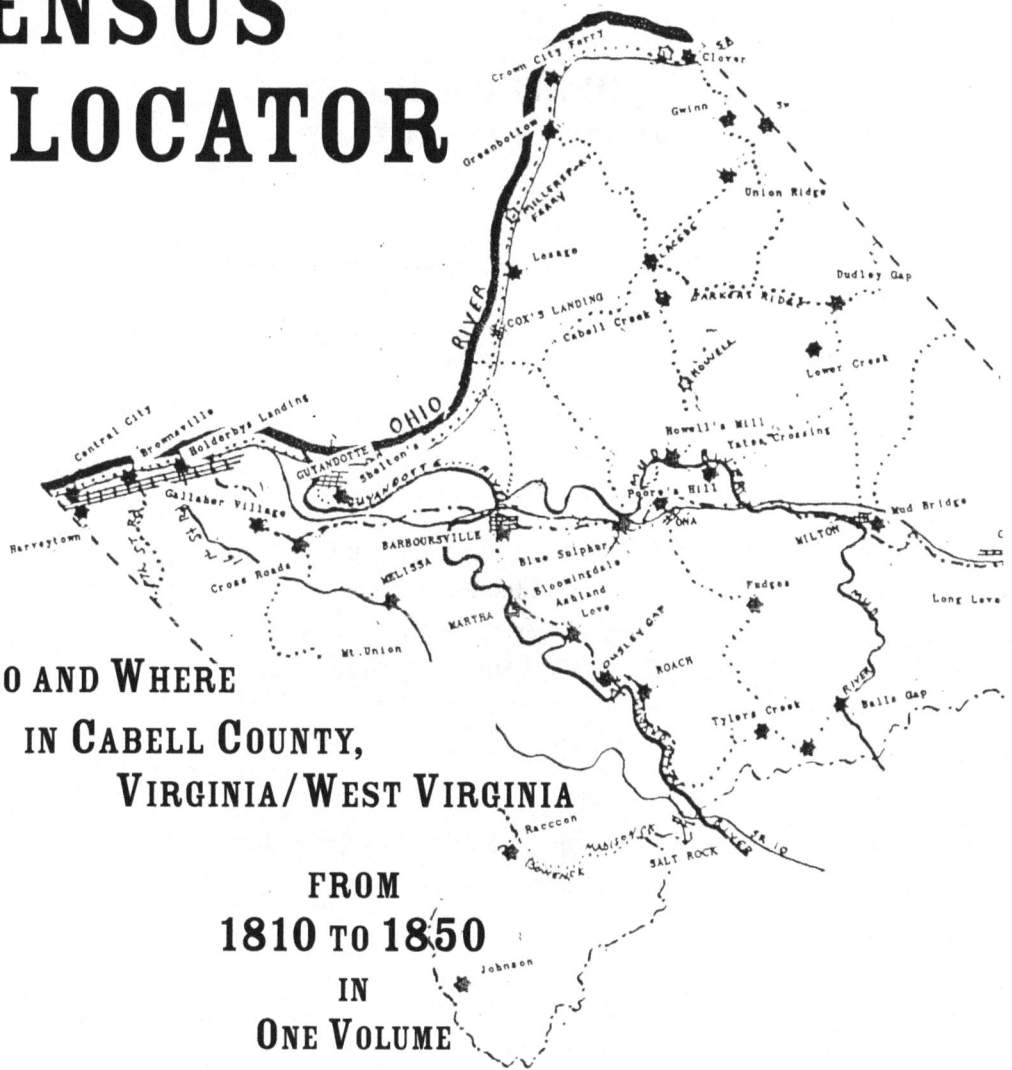

WHO AND WHERE
IN CABELL COUNTY,
VIRGINIA / WEST VIRGINIA

FROM
1810 TO 1850
IN
ONE VOLUME

Carrie Eldridge

Heritage Books
2024

HERITAGE BOOKS

AN IMPRINT OF HERITAGE BOOKS, INC.

Books, CDs, and more—Worldwide

For our listing of thousands of titles see our website
at
www.HeritageBooks.com

A Facsimile Reprint
Published 2023 by
HERITAGE BOOKS, INC.
Publishing Division
5810 Ruatan Street
Berwyn Heights, MD 20740

International Standard Book Number
Paperbound: 978-0-7884-2938-5

CABELL COUNTY COURT HOUSE #1855

NE corner of Center & Main

BARBOURSVILLE

Special thanks to a tireless computer entry person,
my son, Mike Eldridge.

TABLE OF CONTENTS

ILLLUSTRATIONS and GRAPHS

1850 CENSUS LOCATOR-CABELL COUNTY

SOURCES
ABBREVIATIONS

Cabell County,West Virginia was Cabell County,Virginia
from its creation in 1809 until its separation in 1863
A Virginia county if not otherwise marked.

cc -Cabell County Marriages
CCA -Cabell County Annals and Families
DD -Diary of William Dusenberry 1855
EPP -Eunice Perkins Proctor-Newspaper articles
FR -personal family records of my family CE
GAoh-Gallia County,OH Marriages
Gb-Greenbrier County Marriages
GpKy-Greenup County,KY Marriages
KCM -Kanawha County Marriages
LCoh-Lawrence County,OH Marriages
MM -Mason County Marriages
SO -Sigfus Olson-early historian
w/o -wife of--widow or widower of
s/o -son of dau-daughter
cem#--Reference to 3 volume Cabell Cemeteries by this author.

Wayne County was separated from Cabell in 1842,but there
are no recorded marriages until 1853.

A Census Introduction

The United States Population Census is the primary
tool for anyone doing historical or genelogical research;
and it has been this researcher's wish to be able to
compare all of the census at the same time. This study
brings all the census of the first fifty years of Cabell
County together in one book and attempts to locate their
residences.

Almost everyone studying local history or genéalogy
has used some part of the U.S.Census. Begun in 1790 in
order to get an idea of how many people lived in the new
nation, the first census was just a list of the heads of
the household and their taxable property. Each census taken
since that date has added more information and given us a
greater research tool. The census should be your first
research material. If you have a name or location then your
family is before you; if you have no idea where to look
then a family name can be located by searching different
census. Like"footsteps in the sand" the trail may be
indistinct, but it will lead someplace.

The state of Virginia,from which West Virginia
originated, had the misfortune to lose both the 1800 and
the 1810 Census during the War of 1812. Although much of
the information was recovered from county tax lists; there
is no single publication like the census and the lost
information can never be completely recovered.

This study has begun with the 1850 census, with its
household members, and worked backwards through the 1840
census(also taken by household), the 1830 and 1820
alphabetical censuses and the 1815 and 1815 Cabell taxes
lists. By comparing all this information a clearer picture
of the people and their life in Cabell County has begun to
emerge. The annotation provided is only that information
which can be verified from public or private information.
Much about Cabell's people is still unknown or the
information is unclear and hopefully the reader will use
this as a place to start and add his or her own verified
information to complete a family study.

CABELL COUNTY SURNAMES IN RELATION TO POPULATION

1820   included Cabell, Lincoln, Wayne
                and Logan area (see 225)

           POPULATION   4,910

           SURNAMES   410

1830   included Cabell, Lincoln, Wayne

           POPULATION   5,884

           SURNAMES   367

1840   included Cabell, Lincoln, Wayne

           POPULATION   5,954

           SURNAMES   570

1850   included Cabell, Lincoln

           POPULATION   5,710

           SURNAMES   539

A Census Introduction

The United States Population Census is the primary tool for anyone doing historical or genelogical research; and it has been this researcher's wish to be able to compare all of the census at the same time. This study brings all the census of the first fifty years of Cabell County together in one book and attempts to locate their residences.

Almost everyone studying local history or genealogy has used some part of the U.S.Census. Begun in 1790 in order to get an idea of how many people lived in the new nation, the first census was just a list of the heads of the household and their taxable property. Each census taken since that date has added more information and given us a greater research tool. The census should be your first research material. If you have a name or location then your family is before you; if you have no idea where to look then a family name can be located by searching different census. Like"footsteps in the sand" the trail may be indistinct, but it will lead someplace.

The state of Virginia, from which West Virginia originated, had the misfortune to lose both the 1800 and the 1810 Census during the War of 1812. Although much of the information was recovered from county tax lists; there is no single publication like the census and the lost information can never be completely recovered.

This study has begun with the 1850 census, with its household members, and worked backwards through the 1840 census(also taken by household), the 1830 and 1820 alphabetical censuses and the 1815 and 1815 Cabell taxes lists. By comparing all this information a clearer picture of the people and their life in Cabell County has begun to emerge. The annotation provided is only that information which can be verified from public or private information. Much about Cabell's people is still unknown or the information is unclear and hopefully the reader will use this as a place to start and add his or her own verified information to complete a family study.

1850

HOUSEHOLDERS AS ENUMERATED

1	Margaret Maupin	53	William F.Joy	108	John T.Morrison
2	C.W. Maupin	54	Andrew J.Cox	109	Washington Morrison
3	John Templeton	55	William Cox	110	John Morrison
4	Harvey Templton	56	Henry Knight	111	Anderson Bias
5	Jacob H.Sexton	57	Wiliam Small	112	A.N.Wiliams
6	William B.Yates	58	George W.Deer	113	John Porter
7	Andrew H.Sexton	59	Peter Hagley	114	Jewel S.Porter
8	Abraham Stevens	60	Mary A.Hagley	115	Millington Adkins
9	James Miller	61	James Crum	116	Tandy Nipps(Coock)?
10	Jacob Bryant	62	David Trowbridge	117	Nancy Nipps
11	Andrew Gwinn	63	Benjamin Cornell	118	Burton Cremeans
12	Vincent Newman	64	Samuel T.Cornell	119	Jimimah Paul
13	William Newman	65	Henry Jefferson(Sr	120	Sanders Cremeans
14	Stephen Poor	66	Benjamin Winters	121	Hiram Cremeans
15	Elizha Poor	67	Henry Jefferson	122	Samuel Porter
16	Jessee A.Templeton	68	Richard A.Perry	123	William Parsons
17	Henry A.Houching	70	Jessee Ferguson	124	Rhodie Miller
18	Nancy Adams	71	Sarah Ferguson	125	John Johnson
19	John Arthur	72	John Kyle	126	Samuel Hunter
20	William Adams	73	Joseph Ferguson	127	William Elkins
21	John M.Miller	74	John Woods	128	William Porter
22	William Love	75	William Pully	129	Merritt Johnson
23	Andrew Sheff	76	James Ferguson	130	Randolph Adkins
24	Andrew Martin	77	Polly Perry	131	William Adkins
25	Isaac Arthur	78	Harrison Collins	132	Wiliam B.Adkins
26	David Smith	79	Calvery Harvey	133	Charles Tooley
27	Nelson Thomas	80	John W.Holdryed	134	Malinda Bowen
28	Samuel H, Davis	81	Martin Moore	135	John E.Adkins
29	William Bowen	82	Martin Moore Jr.	136	Price Adkins
30	Benjamin R.Jewel	83	Epps Johnson	137	William Turner
31	Ambrose L.Doolittle	84	Tandy Tooley	138	Milford Mayab
32	Martin L.Doolittle	85	Royal childers	139	Samuel Booth
33	James A.Poteet	86	William L.Childers	140	Henry Miller
34	Jacob Baumgardner	87	Thomas Childers	141	James McComas
35	Jacob Harshbarger	88	James F.Bias	142	Thomas McComas (Sr)
36	Wiliam P.Yates	89	Thomas R.Swan	143	Thomas J. McComas
37	Preston Hodge	90	Leven Swan	144	John Booth
38	William Chapman	91	Michael Wintz	145	James McComas
39	John Sexton	92	John R, Swan	146	Solomon Midkiff
40	Margaret Merritt	93	James Nicely	147	Spencer M.Childers
41	John Merritt	94	Daniel Bias	148	Sacheryal Nicely
42	John Bumgardner	95	Emmerson Turley	149	Nelson B.Heth
43	James Bumgardner	96	Jonathan Fielder	150	James H,Roffe
44	Robert Kile	97	John Smith	151	Willam C.Bramlette
45	James D.Barbour	98	John collins	152	James R.Bias
46	Charles Collins	99	Elias Collins	153	William Harrell
47	David H.Colins	100	Robert Ross	154	William Knight
48	William Collins	101	Alexander Porter	155	John Dundas
49	William Carpenter	102	Linsey Gue	156	Benjamin S.DAvis
50	Madison Collins	103	Roland Bias	157	Henry Chapman
51	John Bugky	104	James Bias	158	Mary Reese
52	Thomas Farley	105	Anderson Jenkins	159	Octavius Church
		106	Wiliam Hinchman	160	William Merritt
		107	Ransom Dial	161	Thomas Joy

162	Ansel Knight	216	Thomas Arthur	270	John M.Rece
163	Thomas Jefferson	217	James Arthur	271	America Thomas
164	James Knight	218	Jeremiah Blake	272	Abia Rece
165	William King	219	Charles Latton	273	James Reynolds
166	George W.Knight	220	Ricahrd P.Bexfield	274	Samuel E.C.Wilson
167	Abner Knight	221	Howard Clark	275	Jarman Chapman
168	Jacob Winters	222	Nathan Cremeans	276	Warren P.Rece
169	David Poor	223	Isaac Blake	277	Charles H.Bruce
170	Penel Blake	224	Lawrence Briant	278	Thomas Kilgore
171	Martin Nancel	225	Nimrod Briant	279	George Kilgore
172	John Kleninger	226	Wingit Cremeans	280	Francis J.Duffen
173	George Beecham(Burcham)	227	Sarah Cremeans	281	Thomas W.Kilgore
174	Preston Guthrie	228	Thomas R.Riggs	282	John Morris
175	William Guthrie	229	Cary Jenkins	283	Sarah Morris
176	Robert Guthrie	230	Andrew Wallace	284	Andrew Bilup
177	Chapman M.White	231	Ruben Cremeans	285	Mourning Hudson
178	Thomas J.Jenkins	232	David Hamrick	286	Eraetmus Hanley
179	William Jenkins	233	John Hamrick	287	Josiah B.Poage
180	Joseph B.Scott	234	Anderson Jenkins	288	Hezekiah Hudson
181	Alexander Box	235	Andrew McCallister	289	Joseph McCallister
182	Thomas Brandon	236	Elizabeth Cremeans	290	Lewis Mays
183	Thomas W.Reece	237	Henry Dial	291	Malcolm McCallister
184	James M.Sulivan	238	James Legg	292	James McCalister
185	Jacob R.Brandon	239	James H.Estes	293	Bartholomew Roberts
186	John Hannan	240	Russell Newman	294	Michael G.Comen
187	Edwin Pillow	241	Andrew Black	295	Fairfax W.Nelson
188	David B.Lacy	242	James H.Duncan	296	John Smallridge
189	Robert Wiley	243	James Mathew	297	Jonathan Hensley
190	Robert Chambers	244	Griffin Reynolds	298	James Templeton
191	Sterling Davis	245	Ruth Blacke	299	Moses Beckett
192	Lylan P.Emmerson	246	Thomas Smith	300	Willis Legg
193	John Jack	247	John McClasy	301	John Chapman
194	Leonard Goff	248	Richard Walsh	302	Sampson Hanly
195	Lisbon Goff	249	Frances McWarter	303	William Howard
196	Ludwill Goff	250	Thomas C.Wallace	304	James J.Herndon
197	Jessee Spurlock	251	David Black	305	Porter Wallace
198	Benjamin Emmerson	252	Cathrine Conrad	306	Sarah Everett
199	Thomas Spurlock	253	John W.Smith	307	Charles mays
200	Sarah Bowen	254	Joshua Lunsford	308	William Morrison
201	Ezekiel Bowen	255	Peter Wallace	309	Thompson Morrison
202	Daniel Spurlock	256	Parthena Wallace	310	Henry Hatfield
203	Stephen Spurlock	257	Benjamin Wallace	311	George Hatfield
204	John Oliver	258	Edmund Wallace	312	Hamilton Mays
205	John Perry	259	James McClasky	313	John Stanley
206	William L.Perry	260	William Chapman	314	Hezekiah Swan
207	Joseph Files	261	Green B.Chapman	315	Alexander McComas
208	Joseph Gill	262	Isaac M.Ball	316	Thomas J.Cowens
209	Charles W.Miller	263	Henry Ball	317	Isaac Hatfield
210	Henry Sprecher	264	Andrew Jordan	318	Glouchester Hatfield
211	Godfried Scheiltine	265	Thomas Gibson	319	Everett Feasle
212	John Kheuszenski	266	Chapman Jordan	320	Henry Peyton
213	Anna Luckwaski	267	William Jordan	321	Atha F.Turley
214	James Felix	268	Edmund C.Rece	322	John Vaughn
215	Waldimir Kryszonowski	269	Jessee Wade	323	Harrison Paine

324 David McComas	378 William Derton	432 Harrison Peyton
325 Stephen Paine	379 William Stroupe	433 Armstead Howell
326 Abel Sansum	380 Joseph Wintz	434 Archibald Peyton
327 Edward Franklin	381 Rufus Leonard	435 Mary Casey
328 Simon Paine	382 Elia A.Jenkins	436 Morris L.Ford
329 Parker Lucas	383 Thomas Dundas	437 James M.Ford
330 Aaron F.McKendree	384 Andrew Warren	438 Nathaniel F.Burrel
331 James Cowens	385 Joseph Newman	439 Patrick Keenan
332 Joseph Atkins	386 Henry T.Dundas	440 William M.Williams
333 John G.Atkins	387 Mathew Lusher	441 Elisha Shelton
334 David McComas	388 John W.Blake	442 Harvey Johnson
335 William McComas	389 Sarah Blake	443 Christopher Sites
336 Eliza Adkins	390 John King	444 Sarah Sites
337 John Eplen	391 Lucinda Dodd	445 Burwel Johnson
338 Brison Atkins	392 Joseph W.Roffe	446 Smoot Johnson
339 Christopher Sites	393 Patrick H.McCullough	447 Olly Johnson
340 Sarah Adkins	394 Archibald Vickers	448 John Sites
341 Benjamin Spears	395 Charles L.Roffe	449 Gottlob Scites
342 William Spears	396 William C.Dusenberry	450 Andrew Johnson
343 Joseph Adkins	397 William F.Duseberry	451 Sampson Johnson
344 Harrison Davis	398 John Thompson	452 Andrew Chapman
345 Henderson Drake	399 Benjamin Bowman	453 Bird Hensley
346 John Campbell	400 Andrew Dodson	454 Andrew McComas
347 John L.Baker	401 Elisha Dodson	455 Eli H.Walton
348 Bailey Conley	402 James Meacham	456 David Shelton
349 James Hatfield	403 Clark Thruston	457 Andrew Shawns
350 William Smith	404 Samuel Childers	458 Nicholas Messinger
351 James Smith	405 William Rogers	459 Abel Rock
352 Ballard Smith	406 William Thompson	460 Jerome Shelton
353 Lewis Adkins	407 Patterson Thompson	461 Jerimiah Witcher
354 Rice Elkins	408 Watson S.Davis	462 John W.Peyton
355 Harvey Elkins	409 Chelsey Davis	463 Thomas Dial
356 Fernadez Hatfield	410 John Peyton	464 Joiner Dial
357 Harvey Smith	411 Mary Reins	465 John Dial
358 Samuel Parsons	412 Waldon Beach	466 Abbot Rowe
359 Willam Johnson	413 James Wilkes	467 Emily Terry
360 George Hager	414 Mary Peyton	468 Thomas Parsons
361 James Beckelhimer	415 Richard Lunsford	469 Henry Eplin
362 Thomas Stephenson	416 William Lunsford	470 Samuel Harris
363 Anna France	417 Joseph Stanley	471 Edward Parsons
364 Alonzo Kitchen	418 John Morrsion	472 Benjamin S.Davis
365 Armstonrg Stephenson	419 Charles Peyton	473 William Mays
366 George Stephenson	420 Calvary Swan	474 Sherwood Shelby
367 John T.Adkins	421 John McKeand	475 George Douglas
368 Richard Adkins	422 Josiah Swann	476 Calvin Lucas
369 Lickins Adkins	423 William Williams	477 William H.Harless
370 John L.Franklin	424 James Morris	478 John McComas
371 Jesse W.McComas	425 Rolen Bias	479 John Peyton
372 Isaac McComas	426 William B.Mitchell	480 Lewis Midkiff
373 Harrison McComas	427 Andrew Burns	481 Abraham Coobs
374 Daniel McMillon	428 Andrew J.Hatfield	482 Spencer Midkiff
375 Elijah Turley	429 Adam Hatfield	483 Jessie Paine
376 Harvey Newman	430 Moses Hatfield	484 James Beckett
377 Joseph Montgomery	431 Thomas Dial	485 John Stanley

486	Isaac McCalister	540	William Holstein	594	John McComas
487	Robert Ervin	541	James Smith	595	Alcey Ashworth
488	Jospeh Sidebotton	542	John M.K.Smith	596	William Beck
489	James McComas	543	Andrew Holly	597	John Ashworth
490	Richard McCalister	544	Samuel Kinder	598	Pleasant Roberts
491	Thomas McComas	545	David Burns	599	Zachariah Martin
492	John McCalister	546	Nancy Roberts	600	George Keyton
493	Preston McCalister	547	James T.Carrol Jr.	601	Elijah Cyres
494	Charles Beckett	548	James C.Black	602	James Cyres
495	Mourning Williams	549	Joseph L.Sexton	603	Wilis Mays
496	Andrew J.Smith	550	Andrew H.Ashworth	604	John Murdock
497	Absolum Bias	551	Zilla Burns	605	Madison Johnson
498	John Bias	552	William T.Garrett	606	James Conner
499	Benjamin L.Perry	553	Philip Powel	607	John Chapman
500	Henry S.Hawkins	554	Samuel Powel	608	William Conner
501	Elijah Hawkins	555	Alexander Griffith	609	Ryland Keyton
502	Alexander McCalister	556	Archibald Egner	610	John S.Nicholas
503	Obadiah Bias	557	James Ballard	611	John Nicholas
504	William Ray	558	James King	612	William Smith
505	David Ray	559	Peter Smith	613	William Wheeler
506	Andrew Johnson	560	James Roberts	614	William Porter
507	William Johnson	561	Marine Sanford	615	Miriam Porter
508	Wesley Johnson	562	Nancy Moore	616	James Brown
509	Perry Johnson	563	Thomas T.Adkins	617	Andrew Roberts
510	John Johnson	564	Samuel Carroll	618	James Becket
511	Larkin Bias	565	Dicy Barrett	619	David Porter
512	Winston Nowell	566	Samuel Smith	620	Adolphus A.Newly
513	William Mahone	567	Harvey Barrett	621	Nancy Pine
514	James T.Carroll	568	Samuel Bragg	622	Franklin Curry
515	John Fary	569	Joseph Holten	623	Benjamin B.Wilkinson
516	James Webb	570	Alexander Roberts	624	Squire Johnson
517	George W.Zircle	571	William N.Roberts	625	Lewis Johnson
518	Cynthia Miller	572	Washington Payly	626	Jane Person
519	Nicholas Lake	573	Robert Alford	627	Hiram Curry
520	James B.Snodgrass	574	Burwell Spurlock	628	James Johnson
521	James H.Rece	575	George Morrison	629	Jesse King
522	Rachael Adkins	576	Fredrick Chambers	630	Creed Wysong
523	Timothy Adkins	577	Jacob May	631	Catherine Wysong
524	Polly Bragg	578	Alexander Spurlock	632	Henry Ashworth
525	Silas Cooper	579	James Wheeler	633	John Forth
526	Frances Adkins f	580	Edward Wheeler	634	Harrsion Roberts
527	Francis Adkins m	581	William Ott	635	William Webb
528	William Holly	582	Eli Wheeler	636	John Jordan
529	Charles Holton	583	William Moore	637	Thomas Vickers
530	Allen J.Holstein	584	George Holton	638	James Roberts
531	James A.Holly	585	Ralph Ganne(Gunnoe)	639	Jessee Harbour
532	Francis Johnson	586	Thomas Cooper	640	John Collins
533	Parker Adkins	587	James Rogers	641	Thomas Harman
534	Michael Rogers	588	Henry Wallace	642	George P.Collins
535	William Person	589	Peter Fizer	643	Ezekiel Reynolds
536	Simon Person	590	James Garrett	644	George Brown
537	George A.Holton	591	Gabriel Roberts	645	Simon Reynolds
538	William Kincard	592	William Burton	646	Morris Jordan
539	Samuel Tincher	593	Job Burns	647	Peter Burns

648 Elkana Henkley	702 John Ward	756 Elizabeth Derton
649 Livingston Henkley	703 Thomas Ward	757 Robert McKendree
650 Robertson Patton	704 Thomas Scales	758 Cornwelsey Simmons
651 James Burns	705 Mathew Butcher	759 Edmond McGinnis
652 Andrew Burns	706 John Smith	760 John Derton
653 Isaiah Burns	707 Sarah Cook	761 Madison Thompson
654 Thomas L.Brown	708 Solomon Cook	762 Thorn Dusenberry
655 William Legg	709 Thomas C.Cook	763 Cyrus M.Campbell
656 George W.Summers	710 Henry W.Shelton	764 Allen McGinnis
657 Wesley G.Wooton	711 James Dodd	765 Robert Holderby
658 George Gallaher	712 Enrichy Underwood	766 Henry Clark
659 John Gwinn	713 Albert Huffman	767 William Partlow
660 Washington Gwinn	714 Soloman Thornburg	768 John Everett
661 Hery Johnson	715 Albrecht Becker	769 Isaac Ong
662 Lewis Fullerton	716 John Mills	770 James Emons
663 John J.Nash	717 Thomas Kyle	771 Edward Nixon
664 Benjamin Sandridge	718 John Baumgardner	772 Lewis Sexdinger
665 John Malcolm	719 Greenville Harrison	773 Jesse Dodson
666 Asa L.Wilson	720 Irvin Lusher	774 Erastus Wellington
667 James Gibson	721 John Reacy (Lacy)	775 Noadiah Wellington
668 Beverly W.Maupin	722 Thomas Hatfield	776 Jacob Hiltbruner
669 Edward Malcolm	723 Thomas Thornburg	777 William Hurd
670 John Denison	724 Sanford Scott	778 Nathaniel Adam
671 Alexander Newman	725 Orson Long	779 Elizabeth Gardner
672 Peyton Newman	726 Oscar W,Mather	780 Lewis Peters
673 William Jones	727 John Samuels	781 Ezra Flowers
674 Patrick Morrison	728 Henry J.Samuels	782 Bushrod W.Kensolving
675 James butcher	729 William C.Miller	783 Thomas Dunkle
676 Charles K,Morris	730 Sidney Bowden	784 Peter Clark
677 William J.Harris	731 John G.Miller	785 Joseph C.Wheeler
678 William Messinger	732 Christopher S.Miller	786 Sanders Arhtur
679 Ralph Smith	733 Robert Allen	787 Cyrus Andrews
680 Hannah Jenkins	734 John Lewis Keller	788 Charles Chapder
681 James Morrison	735 John Hibbins	789 Perceval Smith
682 Abram Childers	736 James Pennell	790 Gracey Stone
683 John Hensley	737 Arnold Kraes	791 James Vanderver
684 Samuel Hensley	738 Johnson Lusher	792 Henry H.Miller
685 Matthew Knight	739 Littleton Whitten	793 John W.Hite
686 Jacob Smith	740 William Agers	794 Thomas Christian
687 Henry Smith	741 Susan J.Mathers	795 Augustus S.Woolcott
688 Peter Smith	742 James J.Mahone	796 A.M.McCorkle
689 Edmard Elmore	743 James Parish	797 Victor Latulle
690 Abram Lions	744 Absalom Holderby	798 James Elzey
691 Martin Dillon	745 Henry B.Maupin	799 Dudley D.Smith
692 Eliza Davis	746 Elisha W.McComas	800 James Todd
693 John Deboy	747 Edward Vertigans	801 W.Caspelman
694 William Jenkins	748 Wilson B.Moore	802 Lucy A.Emmons
695 Paulina Hughes	749 Abner W.Wingo	803 Kental Hezeltine
696 Paul Davis	750 Thomas A.Shelton	804 Joseph S.Bradbury
697 John Coburn	751 Benjamin McCune	805 James Barnet
698 John Dolen	752 George F.Miller	806 Girard C.Ricketts
699 Abner Cook	753 George Proctor	807 E.Ricketts
700 John Cook	754 George W.Fulweler	808 Andrew S.Keenan
701 Alexander Roberts	755 Anthony Shelton	809 Fredrick Nichoff

810	Burgess Stewart	864	Thomas Bates	919	Albert Laidley
811	John B.Hite	865	William Topping	920	Noah Fuller
812	Mary McMahone	866	Ira Blankenship	921	John B.Farrel
813	Jacob Miller	867	Isiah Ray	922	Wiliam Seamonds
814	James Stewart	868	William Dillon	923	Philip Bumgardner
815	Henry carter	869	John Topping	924	John Ward
816	Thomas I.Hayslip	870	William M.Blankenship	925	James H,Walker
817	Randolph Dietz	871	William Ray	926	Daniel Dunkle(Samuel)?
818	Franklin Chapder	872	Samuel Balnkenship	927	Overton H.White
819	John Ong	873	Dennis Obrien	928	Edward Wright
820	Sarah Windon	874	Adam Seamonds	929	Isaac Crump
821	Gilbert Stephenson	875	John Thompson	930	William Harrison
822	Enoch D.Blankenship	876	Effy Owens	931	Lewis Arthur
823	Francis Hite	877	David Sullivans	932	Absalom Roberts
824	Charles Dietz	878	John Plybourn	933	George W.Stephenson
825	George W.Grass	879	Mary Beckner	934	Frances Chapman f
826	George Chapman	880	John Roberts	935	Morgan Mays
827	James Woods	881	John Adams	936	Andrew J.Stephenson
828	James W.Ward	882	George Hagen	937	Henry Miller
829	Alfred Whitney	883	Melville McGinnis	938	Robert Denton
830	A.Jogney	884	William Burks	939	James McCorkle
831	nancy Walker	885	James W.Hanly	940	Hannah Stephenson
832	Jacob Hite	886	James Sulivan	941	Calvary Stephenson
833	Robert Stewart	887	Elllen Hollenback	942	Mark Stephenson
834	Melcor Ansel	889	Manoa Cardwell	943	James Gallaher
835	Jacob Ansel	890	John R.Flowers	944	F.G.L.Beuhring
836	Jacob Coffe	891	Patterson Roberts	945	Aaron Sulivan
837	Jacob Rake	892	John Houghland	946	David McAlavy
838	Abram Pennel	893	Joseph Neubacker	947	Burwell Wilkes
839	Daniel Clark	894	Hery Medlin	948	George Chadison
840	James Files	895	Ann Arnet	949	Alexander Johnson
841	George J.Grimes	896	William Cosey	950	Rufus P.Balser
842	Epineter Wallet	897	Stephen Kelly	951	William Peters
843	Benjamin Files	898	James Fortune	952	William Gallaaher
844	Michael Floyd	899	James Piat	953	Thomas Bradshaw
845	William McComas	900	Martin Hull	954	David A.LoveJoy
846	Ephraim Thornburgh	901	Ann Poage	955	Michael Shultz
847	Willam Smith	902	Sarah Hull	956	Jesse Crump
848	Whitfield G.Bryan	903	John McCormack	957	Malinda Stephenson
849	Adam Kelly	904	William Burkett	958	James J.mays
850	John W.Griffith	905	Gilbert Stephenson	959	Real Ferguson
851	James C.Wilson	906	Rebecca Kelly	960	John Kelly
852	Andrew Conner	907	John Morgan	961	Peter C.Buffington
853	Sylvester Fuller (Sr	908	John Belaney	962	James Holderby
854	Oliver W.Fuller	909	Absalom Yates	963	Janes Ayslis
855	Sylvester Fuller	910	Floyd Pine	964	Christopher Peters
856	Archilles Fuller	911	William Johnson	965	Samuel Hunter
857	Edward Shy	912	James Johnson	966	Michael Staly
858	Lafayette Stephenson	913	James hawkins	967	Joseph Staly
859	Skellton Poteet	914	Samuel W.Johnson	968	Henry Paine
860	William Wentz	915	Henry W.Hollenback	969	Beverly B.Burks
861	Adam Keller	916	Ansel A.Adams	970	John Harden
862	Hiram Carter	917	John W.Allen	971	Charles Burks
863	Nancy Bates	918	Nancy Large	972	William Paine

973 James Graham
974 John Duke
975 Park Wynn
976 William Wynn
977 William Buffington
978 St. Mark Russel
979 William Douthet
980 Jacob Plydon
981 John S.Everett
982 Thomas turner
983 Joseph Turner
984 Nanthaniel Turner
985 Andrew J.Dunkle
986 Samuel A.Walker
987 James Shelton
988 David W.Thornburg
989 John Merritt
990 Elizabeth Turner
991 Melchor Merritt
992 Joseph Webb
993 William L.Maupin
994 John A.Everett
995 James Newman

996 William Black
997 Adam Black
998 Gerthard Henri
999 Prospire Deliniere
1000 Francis Dupin
1001 John L.Chapman
1002 William Chapman
1003 Daniel Lake
1004 Thomas Merritt
1005 John Turley
1006 Harrison Defore
1007 Stephen Davis
1008 David Harshbarger
1009 Elizabeth Harshbarger
1010 Winston Wotten
1011 John Laidley
1012 Daniel Love
1013 Edmund H.Hill
1014 John Wotten
1015 William Irby
1016 Isaac Johnson
1017 John Tinchen

THE 1850 CENSUS

There is a wealth of information in the census if a person takes the time to extract it. Although Cabell County was not formed until 1809, some of the early settlers were here much earlier and can be found in the Kanawha County census of 1800 or even the Montgomery County census of 1790.

The 1850 census supposedly listed everyone who lived in Cabell County,household by household. The enumerators appear to have gone from house to house and hollow to hollow, although there is some indication that part of the count was reported. Much information is available from this format that can not be obtained in an alphabetical listing for it is actually possible to locate communities and confirm interrelationships of various families from the location of their homes. Take the time to study the census information. Take the names,ages and occupations and add to that other information you can provide and slowly a picture of life begins to emerge.

Just as today, there are mistakes in the 1850 census. Families were bypassed, names and dates were given incorrectly and sometimes people were included that were not in the household. Just imagine the approach of the census taker. It was difinitely the most important event in your life. As he walked or rode into the yard, all the children would appear. Did he ask them to line up according to age ? Probably. If the neighbors' children happened to be present, they were also counted and a difference of names noted.(It happened at least twice.) If the whole family was not home then a single person had to name everyone and give all their ages and birth places. There was plenty of room for mistakes and mistakes were made in collection, in recording and in reproduction when the various lists were combined.

THE 1850 CENSUS (con't)

The enumerator's route was determined by the settlement pattern of Cabell County, which in turn was determined by terrain as well as fertile soil. The topography of Cabell County is different from most of the state called West Virginia because it contains a fair amount of arable land. A map shows three river valleys, the Ohio, Guyandotte and Mud rivers, as obvious areas of settlement, but the best land in the county is an ancient river bed of the prehistoric Teays River. This area is fertile, well-drained and easily traveled, as opposed to the swampy river valleys. Teays Valley became the home of the most prominent people in the early county, the site of the county seat and site of the James River Turnpike, a state highway from Richmond, Virginia to Lexington, Kentucky.

Earliest settlement was at a stream juncture of the rivers and then up that stream to its head. Although the extent of elevation in the county is only 700 feet from the Ohio River to Barkers Ridge, the ridges and valleys are narrow and numerous. This terrain often determined who the people saw or knew and many marriages were made in "your hollow or the next." This "terrain determined settlement" becomes obvious as the settlement pattern from the census develops.

There were five primary settlements in the county. Guyandotte, a riverport, developed at the mouth of the Guyandotte River and was one on the main ports on the Ohio River between Pittsburg and Cincinnati. Barboursville, at the jucture of Mud River and the Guyandotte River, was less prone to flooding than Guyandotte and served as the county seat from 1814 to 1887. Salt Rock was located at a major salt deposite on the Guyandotte River. The second falls of Mud River was a prime mill site known by many names including Doolittle's Mill and Howel's Mill. The fifth site was called Mud Bridge(today's Milton) and was located were the James River Turnpike crossed the Mud River where the river turned south. As the population of the county increased, communities developed about every two to three miles and provided some service such as a store or church, but no major community(Huntington) developed until the advent of the railroad after the Civil War.

Settlement was delayed in this section of Virginia until after the Indian Treaty of Greenville in 1795, because the Indians used the Kanawha, Guyandotte and Big Sandy Rivers as raid route into eastern Virginia. However, once safe, people entered the area looking for choice home sites and mill sites. Many of these earlist settlers became the core of later communities and by locating them with the census, a picture of life in Cabell County begins to develop.

ORIGIN OF POPULATION
other than Virginia

UNITED STATES		OUTSIDE UNITED STATES	
Connecticut	12	Canada	1
District of Columbia	1	East Indies	1
Georgia	2	England	35
Illinois	6	France	5
Indiana	24	Germany	51
Kentucky	74	Ireland	8
Louisiana	2	Poland	12
Maine	11	Santo Domingo	1
Maryland	36	Scotland	10
Massachusetts	14	South America	1
Mississippi	1	Switzerland	13
Missouri	3	Wales	4
New Hampshire	8		
New Jersey	3		
New York	41		
North Carolina	18		
Ohio	197		
Pennsylvania	66		
South Carolina	2		
Tennessee	24		
Vermont	6		

The remaining population of 5,017 either listed Virginia or no location.

CABELL COUNTY CENSUS 1850
page 1-3 July 1850   C.W. Maupin Asst.Marshall -District 10

```
1-1                                                    YATES CROSSING
      Margaret Maupin      72    Va -cem#50-(2nd w/o Thomas-Albemarle Co.
1-2
      C.W.Maupin           39    Va farmer(Chapman W.)           -cem#H10
      Matilda              25    Ky   (Hope MM 1845)             -cem#H10
      Fanny C.              4    Va
      Thomas M.             2
      Lucy M.            5/12
2-3
      John Templeton       54    Va farmer
      Jane       .         50    Ky
      Hamilton             21    Va
      Mary H.              18
      Jane                 16
      John                 14
      Edward               10
  3-4                                                  LAWRENCE RIDGE
      Harvey Templeton     30    OH farmer                       -cem#34
      Mary A.              30    Va   (Whitten 1839)             -cem#34)
      John L.               8
      Ranson M.             6         (?mMary A.Bryan 1867-SO)   -cem#34
      Isaac                 5         (?mMary A.Bateman 1878-SO)-cem#34
      Eastham T.           3m         (?mFanny Bryan 1875-SO)
      William M.            2                                    -cem#34
      Sarah J.           3/12
      Andrew J.HANLY        3
      Napleon D.HANLY       3
4-5        (see 22)
      Jacob H.Sexton       31    Va
      Acantha              22         (Hinchman-m 1848cc)
      Sarah J.           8/12
      James SEXTON         49
5-6                                                    YATES CROSSING
      William B.Yates      28    Va farmer
      Rebecca A.           23         (Reynolds-m 1848cc)
      Juliet               24         (m Robert Malcolm  1852cc)
      John                 20         Labourer
      Ezra W.            4/12
      Lucretia              3
6-7
      Andrew H.Sexton      41    Va farmer
      Mary         "       21
      John S.      "       19         labourer
      Joseph M.    "       17         labourer
      William A.   "       14
      Mary E.      "       11
      Margaret C.  "        9
      Telithia C.  "       7f
      Peter B.     "        4
      Charles H.   "        2
      Abraham W.   "        1
page 2
(7-8)
      Abraham N.(Stevens) 41  (bad copy)(Stevenson ?)
      Mary         "      35
      Sarah A.     "      13
      James W.     "      11
      William H.   "     8/12
```

```
8-9
    James Miller         62    Va farmer
    Mary                 60
9-10                                                          LOWER CREEK
    Jacob Bryant         46    Va farmer
    Lucy                 36       (Ball-1831cc)
    William P.           16       labourer
    Martha A.            14
    Nancy M.             11
    John W.               8
    Sarah C.              6
    Frances M.           3f
    Chapman M.           1m
10-11                                                         LOWER CREEK
    Andrew Gwinn         55    Va farmer                     -cem#49
    Rachel               43       (Harshbarger- 1827cc)      -cem#49
    Henry                20
    Andrew               17
    Elizabeth            16
    Madison             14f
    William              12
    Mary                 11
    America               9
    Louisa                8
    Emily                 5       (?mJohn Morris-SO)
    Jefferson             2
11-12
    Vincent Newman       44    Va farmer
    Sarah                39       (Elmore- 1826cc)
    Wesley               19       labourer
    John                 17
    Leroy                13
    Herman               11
    Mary J.               9
    Nancy A.              7
    Eliza A.              5
    Emily                 2
    Harrison D.        6/12
12-13
    William Newman       21    Va
    Elizabeth            21       (Perry-1849cc)
Page 3
13-14                                                         POORE'S HILL
    Stephen Poor         34    Va carpenter (w/o Elizabeth)-cem#50
    Sarah                49
14-15                                                         POORE'S HILL
    Elisha Poor          40    Va
    Lucy                 40       (Conner- 1832cc)
    Martha A.            16
    William              14
    Alfred               11
    Stephen               8
    Mary E.               5
15-16
    Jessee A.Templeton   24    Va farmer
    Sarah A.             19
    William H.            1
    Matilda               6
```

```
16-17
    Henry A.(Houching)   47      Va farmer (Henching ?)
    Classey              38
    Francis J.           21
    Rebecca              17
    Elizia P.            14
    Susan C.             12
    William H.           10
17-18
    Nancy Adams          35      Va
    Martha               18
    William H.           16
    John J.              12
    Sarah J.             10
    Franklin              7
    Thomas                3
    Virginia              1
18-19
    John Arthur          28      Va farmer
    Sarah A.             28
    William               6
    John                  3
19-20
    William Adams        35      Va farmer
    Elizabeth            40         (Arter-1835cc)
    Francis M.           1m
20-21
    John M.Miller        40      Va farmer
    Martha J.            29         (S.McCallister-1841cc)
    Mary J.               8
    Emily F.              6
    James T.              4
    Eliza                 2
Page 4                                             HOWELL'S MILL
21-22            (mother ? Susannah Childs Cem#13-1stw-Susanna Brown-CCA
    William Love         69      Va farmer (?s/o Charles-SO)   -Cem#13
    Elizabeth            58      NC        (Hampton-1829 GpKy)
    Daniel A.           17      Va laborer
    Cynthia A.          20
    Minirva HANLY       11
22-23                                              HOWELL'S MILL
    Andrew Sheff         50      Va farmer            -cem#13
    Mary                46
    Caroline            23
    George              22         boatman(m Susan Maupin 1852cc)
    James               20         labourer
    John H.             17         labourer
    Dianna              19
    Sarah E.            15
    Catherine A.        12
23-24
    Andrew Martin        27      Va farmer
    Eliza               24
    Romaine A.           2
24-25                                              CABELL CREEK
    Isaac Arthur         38      Va labourer
    Rebecca             41
    Elizabeth           17
    Sarah               16
    Thomas              14
```

```
24-25 Arthur(con't)
     Edward              13
     Everline            12m
     Clarissa            11
     Cinthia             10
     Ambrose             5m
     Tabitha F.          3
25-26
     David Smith         43    Va farmer
     Sinia (Asena)       45         (Jarrett-1829cc)
     Mary P.             20
     Martha              18
     Sarah M.            16
     Jacob J.            15
     David J.            13
     William J.          11
     Margaret F.         10
     Benjamin T.          9
     Lucy C.              7
     Eliza C.             5
     Nancy V.             3
     Eli J.B.             2
page 5
26-27
     Nelson Thomas       44    VA farmer
     Susan               38
     Mary                20
     Nelson              17         laborer
     Nancy                5
27-28
     Samuel H.Davis      25    Va farmer
     America             25         (Arthur    1847cc)
     Thomas W.            3
     Joseph             4/12
28-29
     William Bowen       30    Va farmer
     Adalaide            26         (Templeton- 184cc)
     Jane A.              4         (?m Dekalb Hughes-Mason Co.-SO)
     Sarah E.             3         (?m Abraham Keithly-SO)
     Ezekiel              1         (?m Melissa Michael of Iowa-SO)
29-30                                                       BARKER'S RIDGE
     Benjamin R. Jewel   54    Va farmer (Juel ?)      -cem#31
     Sarah A.            50              (bur-Guyandotte-cem#H4
     Sarah               20
     Catherine           17
     Louisa              14                              -cem#H4
     Matt                12
     Emily T.C.           9
     Gauteir             6m
30-31                                                       HOWELL'S MILL
     Ambrose L.Doolittle 50    Pa manufacturer          -cem#13
     Sarah               51    Va (Brown- 1821cc)
     Ellen V.            23    OH
     Amanda F.           16    Va
     Mary A.HARSHBARGER  28    Va (M.Ann Doolittle w/o John  1832cc)
     William L.    "      5
     Henry C.POTEET      20         laborer               -cem#H10
```

```
31-32                                                      HOWELL'S MILL
    Martin L.Doolittle  36    NY sawyer(lawyer ?)
    Amanda P.               23    OH
    Ambrose L.              1     Va
32-33
    James A.Poteet      47    Va merchant(?1w/Lucinda Turner-1829cc)
    Mary                   28
    James M.               14
    Eliza                  16
    Adalaide V.            6
    Francis A.             3
Page 6
33-34
    Jacob Baumgardner   54    Va farmer
    Mary                   55
    John W.                31
    Rebecca                25
    Barbery                21
    Henry                  19         laborer

    James M.               16
    Isabelle               12
    Arianna                10
    Nancy M.BAUMGARDNER    23
    Rebecca BOWEN          17
34-35                                                      MUD RIVER
    Jacob Harshbarger   35    Va farmer
    Elizabeth              31        (?Blake-SO)
    Adaline                11        m William Hanley FBL
    Eveline                9
    John P.                7
    Henry                  5
    Eliza                  3
35-36                                          YATESMONT-HOWELL'S MILL
    William P. Yates    65    Va farmer            -cem#15
    Elizabeth             55        (Lillard-CCA)     -cem#15
    Margaret A.          22        (m-James O.Cox)   -cem#15
    Martha A.            20        (Mortace Wilson 1850cc)
    Elizabeth            18
    Caroline             17
    William             13
    Silas CARTER         8
36-37
    Preston Hodge       33    Va farmer
    Susan                34
    Charles T.H.         12
    Amanda C.            6
    Theodore H.          5
    Zerilda              2
    Elizabeth            1
    Elizabeth HODGE      62
37-38
    William Chapman     60    Va farmer
38-39                                          YATE'S CROSSING
    John Sexton         46    Va  farmer  (w/o Louisa Ann -cem#50
    Elizabeth SEXTON    69
    Horotio H.           8
    Henry B.             4                             -cem#50
    James T.             1
```

```
39-40                                        MUD RIVER & MERRITT'S CREEK
    Margaret Merritt    86        Va  (Cooper-w/o William-[Strupe Rev.Pen.])
    George W.           68            manufacturer(?w/Levina Turley-1826cc)
                                              (Margaret      -cem#17)
40-41 (not written)
   -41                                        MUD RIVER & MERRITT'S CREEK
    John Merritt        21        Va miller
    Margaret            21
Page 7
40-42                                      east/o Guyan at MUD RIVER
    John Bumgardner     42        Va farmer                -cem#18
    Malinda             31           (Lusher 1835cc)       -cem#18
    Trianna B.          11
    John P.              9
    Margaret E.          6
    William W.           3
    Fredrick L.          1                                 -cem#18
41-43                                      east /o Guyan at MUD RIVER
    James Bumgardner    43        Va farmer
    Elizabeth           30           (Wilson-1836cc)
    Henrietta           11
    Arronetta            9
    Henry J.             7                                 -cem#H10
    John A.              4
    William T.           1                                 -cem#23A
    Samuel WILSON       13
    Samuel WILSON       65
42-44                                        OHIO RIVER at LITTLE 7 MILE
    Robert Kile         49        Pa farmer
    Rebecca             44        NC    (Pull 1830 GpKy)
    Sarah               19        Ky
    Samuel              17
    Elizabeth           15
    Missourie           12        Va   (m Samuel Kile 1856cc)
    Virginia             9
    Robert               7
    Lewis                3
    George              13
43-45
    James D.Barbour     40        Va farmer
    Frances             47
    Susan E.            22
    Martha A.           20
    Mary F.             14
    Charles W.T.        18            laborer
    Malinda IRBY        26
44-46                                                     LITTLE 7 MILE
    Charles Collins     55        Va farmer
    Mary                24
    Polly J.            17
    Martha J.           15
    Ellen               10
    Wesley D.            9
    Mortimer T.       3/12
  (-47)                                                   LITTLE 7 MILE
    David H.Collins     19        Va farmer
    Madison             31            carpenter
    Miranda J.          26
    Rebecca B.           2
    Artemus B.           2
```

page 8
46-48
LITTLE 7 MILE

William Collins	66	Va farmer	cem#17B
Sylvie	41	NY (Zilphia Conner 1837cc)	
Nathaniel	18	Va (Mary J.Woodyard 1852cc)	
Mahala	13		
Nathan	11		
Patience	7		
Ruth	5		
Aaron	5	(m-Susan Cremeans -cem#17B)	

47-49

William J.Carpenter	24	VA farmer	
Mary J.	16	(Collins 1849cc)	
Mary F.	1		

48-50

Madison Collins	22	Va farmer
Mary Ann	19	(Perry-1849cc)

49-51

John Bugky	52	Va farmer
Rebecca	49	Ky
Radolphus	24	Va laborer
Isaac B.	21	laborer
John W.	16	
Sarah J.	15	(m-Phillip Farley 1853cc)
Agnes	10	

50-52

Thomas Farley	45	PA farmer
Margaret	41	Va
Philip	20	OH laborer(Sarah Bughy 1853cc)
Minerva	17	OH
Thomas	14	
Harvey	10	
Selick H.	7	Va

51-53
OHIO RIVER above COX'S LANDING

William F.Joy	33	Va farmer
Minerva	33	
John W.	12	SC
James M.	10	Va
William E.	9	
Joseph O.	7	
Mary	5	
Buena Vista	3	
Chapman W.	2/12	

52-54
COX'S LANDING

Andrew J.Cox	35	Va farmer
Margaret(Mary Ann)	28	(Hite 1839cc)
Henrietta H.	7	
Sarah J.	6	
Mary E.	2	
Priscilla G.HITE	15	

page 9
53-55
COX'S LANDING

William Cox	60	Va farmer Rockingham Co.-SO
Sarah	54	(White-1813cc)
James C.	24	farmer (m-Margaret Yates -cem#15)
Nelson	23	farmer
John A.	21	laborer -cem#28
George W.	17	(m-Sarah Ann Maupin-cem#23D
Joseph	11	-cem#23D

OHIO RIVER above COX'S LANDING

```
54-56
    Henry Knight        48    NC farmer
    Margaret            34    Va    (Bryant 1831cc)
    John H.             15         laborer
    Partina             13f
    William             11
    Nimrod               8
    Lafayette            6
    Cathren              3
    Sarah                1
55-57
    William Small       37    Va farmer
    Susan               23
    Adeline              4
    Susan                3
    Ruth                 2
                                    (Deer Pen Rd ?)
56-58
    George W.Deer       43    Pa
    Mary J.             22    Pa
    Cathrin              5    Ky
    James                3    Va
                                                    7 MILE
57-59
    Peter Hagley        26    Va farmer
    Mary E.             22         (Perry-1847cc)
    Polly                1
                                                    7 MILE
58-60
    Mary A.Hagley       75    Pa
    Polly               22    Va
    Peter                2
    Jacob WENTZ         71         laborer  (brother ?)
59-61
    James Crum          60    Va
    Penlipe             50
    Ruth                31
    Polly               29
    James               22
    Penelope            17
    Matilda             15
    Lucinda             14
    Elizabeth           13
    Julian              11
page 10
60-62
    David Trowbridge    46    Va farmer
    Elizabeth           40    NY         (Knight-1831cc)
    Parthene            15    Va
    Herman              14
    Lucinda              9    OH
    John W.              7
    William              5
    Isabella             1
    Isabella HENWOOD     3    Ill.
61-63
    Benjamin Cornell    68    Vt farmer
    Percilla            69    Vt
    Emma M.             42    NY
    Louisa              39    NY
    Martin J.           31    Va
```

```
62-64
     Samuel T.Cornell    34    NY farmer
     Miranda S.          30    Va
     Charles W.           8
     Mary F.              7
     Margaret E.          5
     Nancy E.             4
     Pricilla A.          2
63-65                                                      7 MILE
     Henry Jefferson     72    Va gunsmith                 cem#9c
     Elizabeth           65
     America             22
     Washington          18       farmer
     Mahala              16
     Jackson             24
64-66
     Benjamin Winters    26    OH farmer
     Elizabeth           26    Va        (Jefferson-1846cc)
     Henry B.             4
     Daniel L.            2
page 11
65-67                                                      7 MILE
     Henry Jefferson     26
     Mary A              21
     Mahala               2
66-68
     Richard A.Perry     56    NC farmer
     (Hidon)Anne         43    Va   (Kyle to George Hagley  1832-
                                     Kyle/Hagley to Perry 1849cc)
     Adriadre HAGLEY     17
     Julian        "     15
     Harrison      "     10
     Henry         "     12
     Joseph        "      6
67-69
     Joseph Hagely       38    Va farmer
     Jane                26
     Polly T.             4
     Joseph               2
     Henry F.             1
68-70                                                      7 MILE
     Jessee Ferguson     32    Va
     Hannah              35 (2 Hagely/Kyle-Hagley to Samuel Kyle-1831cc)
     Samuel KYLE         18       farmer  (Missouri Kile 1856cc)
     Elizabeth "         16
     Peter       "       14
     Rebecca     "       12
     Margaret M.          7
     Polly                4
69-71
     Sarah Ferguson      75    Pa
     William             26    Va laborer
     Sarah               24
     Mary                 8
     Polly KYLE          17
```

```
70-72                                                        7 MILE
    John Kyle              Pa laborer
    Jane                   TN           (Woods-1845cc)
    Thomas
    Sally
    Rebecca
    Ann                                                      7 MILE
71-73
    Joseph Furguson    41  OH farmer
    Sally              41  Va           (Turley-1833cc)
    Minerva            16
    Viney              14
    Cynthey T.         12
    James T.            9
    Ada F.              7
    Everline           4f
    Jessie             1
72-74
    John Woods         22  Va laborer
    Nancy              50
    George H.           5
73-75
    William Pully      45  Va coal digger
    Julian             40
    Margaret           10
    John A.             8
    Melissa             6
page 12-16 Jul 1850
                                                             7 MILE
74-76
    James Ferguson     36  Va farmer              cem#9B
    Martha A.          36
    William H.         18
    John L.            14
    Benjamin F.        12
    Jessee              6
    Eliza A.            4         (m-Joseph Hagely-      cem#23
    Mary E.             3
    Martha A.           1
75-77
    Polly Perry        40  Va    (Ansell-w/James Perry-18 mar 1876-CCM)
    Haney F.           17f
    Melachu A.         15m
    William H.          9
    Jacob               9
    Sarah A.            7
76-78
    Harrison Collins   31  Va.
    Martha             23
    Amanda              8
    William             7
    Allen W.            2
    Eliza SYRUS        16         (m Presly Woodyard 1853-cc)
77-79
    Calvery Harvey     27  Va.
    America            24
    John W.             1
```

```
78-80                                                    BLUE  SULPHUR  RD
   John W.Holdryed      62   Va                               cem#15c
   Sarah               50           (Chapman 1819 cc)
   Olivia              30           (Wm.P.Sheff 1863 cc)
   Elizabeth           27
   Marian              18
   Lewis               15
   Caroline            13
   Allen               10                                  cem#15c
   Sarah V.             6
   James W.HOLDRYED     60
79-81   (see 748-762)                                    POORE'S HILL
   Martin Moore        75   Va    (d nov 1850 DD)
   Mary                57
   Frances             13f
80-82                                                    POORE'S HILL
   Martin Moore Jr.    24   Va
   Sarah               23      (Everett-                   cem#16
   Samuel               3
   Elizabeth            1         m  John Douthet   FBL
81-83
   Epps Johnston       40   Va
   Anna W.             29
   Amos                16
   Emma V.             14
   James O.            10
   Joseph O.            7
   Peter                5
   Henry                3
   Elizabeth            2
82-84                                                    SMITH CREEK
   Tandy Tooley        35   Va
   Cynthia A.          24      (Bias 1840 cc)
83-85   (see 87)
   Royal Childers      45   Va
   Nancy               47      (?Midkiff-SO)
   Greenville A.       22      (Mary Wheeler  1852cc)
   Telithia            20
   Elizabeth A.        18
   Benjamin A.         16
   Sarah A.             9
   Royal B.             7
   Itha MIDKIFF        83f
84-86                                                    HICKORY RIDGE
   William L.Childers  23   Va                            cem#s78
   Elizabeth           22
85-87
   Thomas Childers     84   Va   farmer                   cem#s34A
   Elizabeth           75   !
   Nancy               49
   Thomas              31        farmer
   Melvil              23        farmer
   Ann                 21
86-88                                                    ( 7 MILE ?)
   James F.Bias        25   Va   farmer                   cem#23
   Sarah               22
   Emily T.             3
   Cornelius           10/12
```

18

```
87-89
   Thomas R.Swan        74   Va   farmer
   Lize                 60
88-90
   Leven Swan           36   Va   farmer
   Susan A.L.           32             (Roffe   1841cc)
   Shelbey(Jackson)      7                                  cem#S47A
   John K.               5                                  cem#S48
   Martha A.             3
   Joseph W.             1
88-91                                  (Mike & son died 1854 Madison Ck)
   Michael Wintz        28   Va            buried B'ville)   cem#17
   Isabella             25             (Swann 1843cc)
   Robert M.             5
   William W.            3
   Mary A.               1
page 14
89-92                        R#10-Merritt's CK
   John R.Swan          38   Va   farmer
   Nancy B.             35             (Adkins 1833cc)
   Elizabeth            16
   Angeline             14
   Isabelle N.          12
   Hester M.            10
   Nancy B.              8             (m-Canaro Sharity  -cem#s47A)
   Enoch A.              6
   William               5
   Reason               3m                                  cem#S47A
   John                  1
90-93
   James Nicely         26   Va   farmer
   Elizabeth            22             (Stanley 1845cc)
   Sarah E.              4
   James H.              2
   Henry C.              1
   Jane JENKINS         55
91-94
   Daniel Bias          42   Va   farmer
   Janetta              42
   William C.           16
   Nancy A.             14
   Julia A.             12
   Thomas A.             8
   Sarah E.              6
   Daniel B.             4
   Janetta               2                                  near Martha
92-95
   Emmerson Turley      40   Va   farmer
   Polly(Mary Ann)      39             (Russell 1829cc)
   Elizabeth            23
   Samuel               16
   Mary F.              12
   Susannah              9
   Amazelta              7
   Floyd                 3
   Elizabeth RUSSELL    60
93-96      (see 92-95)
   Jonathan Fielder     21   Va   farmer
   Eliza                20
   Emmerson              1
```

94-97
  John Smith   31   Va farmer
  Martha   19
  Amanda   1
page 15
95-98
  John Collins   54   Va farmer
  Nancy   43   (Curtis 1823cc)
  Anna   24
  Elizabeth   22
  William   17
  John W.   15
  Madison   12
  Margaret   10
  James M.   8
  Martha J.   6
  Hezekiah   4
  Clarissa   1
95-99
  Elias Collins   36   Va farmer
  Mary E.   19
  Merritt   6/12

                                          MADISON CREEK
96-100
  Robert Ross   36   Va farmer
  Elizabeth   37   (Adkins 1840cc)
  George   8
  Elihu   6
  Jane   4
  Nancy   1
                                          MADISON CREEK
97-101
  Alexander Porter   39   Va farmer
  Harriet   36
  Frances J.   11f
  Cyntha   9
  Felaida   8f
  John L.   6   cem#S44A
  Elvira   3
  Elisha   8/12
                          DOG FORK of MADISON CK
98-102
  Linsey Gue   36   Va farmer
  Nancy   26   (? Nicely SO)   cem#S76A
  Daphney   10
  James   6   (? Mary Turley SO)
  Julemima   5
  Samuel D.   4
  Powhatton (Tany)   3m   cem#S76A
  Lucy A.   2   cem#S76A
  Paulina   4/12
page 16 - 17 Jul 1850
                          TRACE CREEK of TYLER
99-103
  Roland Bias   50   Va farmer (1-Dicy Brumfield 1813cc)#S62A
  Martha   31   (Mitchell 1839cc)   cem#S62A
  America   17   (mSolomon Midkiff 1850cc)cem#s98B
  Hugh   14
  Margaret   12
  Emerline   10f
  William   8
  Drusilla   5   (m-Alex McKeand 1859 cc)
  Mears   3m
  Adele   7/12

```
100-104    (see 103)
    James Bias (B.)      34   Va  farmer                    cem#S73B
    Polly                26                                 cem#S73B
    Criesby              10m
    Dicey                8        (m Rowsey                 cem#s73D
    Lavinia              7
    Rolind               5m
    Clarissa             4
    Angeline             2
    William B.JENKINS    4
101-105                                   (moved ?)  -DUDLEY GAP
    Anderson Jenkins     33   Va  farmer                    cem#44
    Polly(Marritha)      36        (Cremeans 1842cc)        cem#44
    Silas E.             11
    Gendry               7m
    John J.              5
    Elizabeth            1
102-106     (s/o Wm & Mary-SO)                    east/river ROACH
    William Hinchman     49   Va  farmer(1-Elizabeth Seymour-SO) .
    Elizabeth            46        (?Hatfield d/o Adam SO)
    George S.            23        (m-Elizabeth Swann 1851cc)
    William R.           19
    Leander H.           15        (d1859-SO)
    Lewis F.             10        (m Eliza McKeand 1866cc)
    John W.              9         (d1861-SO)
    Adam                 7         (m Martha Hatfield SO)     cem#S45
    Susannah             6         (m John Templeton  SO)
    Wesley               5         (m Margaret Morrison SO)
103-107                                          east/river  ROACH
    Ransom Dial          76   Va  farmer
    Nancy                64        (McComas 1810cc(d/o John&Cat.)cem#s46A
    John                 26   farmer
    Elisha               23   farmer
    Nancy                21
104-108                                          east/river ROACH
    John T.Morrison      34   Va  farmer
    Nancy                29        (Peyton SO)
    Mary A.              9
    Martha A.            8
    Nancy                4
    John T.              2
    Margaret             3/12       (m Wesley Hinchman SO)
    Wills BRUCKS         31    laborer
page 17                                   (possible river ford)
105-109                                           TYLER CREEK
    Washington Morrison 34   Va  farmer                     cem#S74
    Margaret             31                                 cem#S74
    James L.             8
    Patience W.          7
    John W.J.            5
    Eliza A.             3
106-110                                          east/river SALT ROCK
    John Morrison        30   Va  farmer                    cem#s70
    Elizabeth            19        (Deatley(b-Wisconsin)    cem#s70
    Mary E.              1
```

```
107-111      (see 103)
   Anderson Bias        37
   Nancy                27              (?Bias So see 152)
   Enos                 16
   William              13
   Evermont             11
   Linville              7m
108-112
   A.N.Williams         30    Va   farmer
   Mary                 25
   Thomas J.             3
   Walter              10/12
109-113                                               SALT ROCK
   John Porter          75    Va   farmer                    cem#S90
   Sarah                75                                    cem#S90
   James                25
   Sarah MOOMAN         56
110-114                                               SALT ROCK
   Jewel S.Porter       42    Va   farmer
   Judith               32
   Sarah                14         (m-Roberts)               cem#S90
   Adeline S.           12
   Jacob G.             10                                   cem#S90
   James S.              7
   Melsenner P.          4m
   Nancy A.              1
111-115                                               MADISON CREEK
   Millington Adkins    31    Va   farmer
   Clarissa             33         (Gilkerson 1840cc)
   Emmerine              9
   Parker                8
   Reecey                6f
   Nancy                 5
   Leander               3m
   Frances             10/12f
   A.RONNIAS(RENNIAS)   33    Ky   farmer
   Hester               26    Va       (probably Adkins)
   Rebecca               7    Ky
   John E.               5    Ky
   William H.            1    Ky
page 18
112-116
   Tandy Coock(Nipps)   24    Va   farmer (overwritten Cppck ? ?
   Jemimah              24
   Emmerine              1
113-117
   Nancy Nipps          52    Va
   Samuel               14
   Rosanna              11
   Charles              10
114-118                                        MOUTH of LONG BRANCH
   Burton Cremeans      62    Va   Wheelwright (Polly Adkinson 1811 CCM)
   Nancy                20
               Burton bur cem#S95A(many field stones-his is marked)
115-119
   Jimimah Paul         35f   Va   (Cock-to Jesse Paul 1824cc)
   Amasiah              18m         farmer
   Lewen                16         farmer
   Goodwin L.           13
   Louisa               11
   Susannah             10
```

```
116-120
   Sanders Cremeans      31   Va  farmer
   Sarah                 31           (Curtis 1837cc)
   Eliza J.              13
   Parker                11
   Edissy                 8f
   Joicy                  7
   Joseph                 8
   Ruben                  3
117-121                                           MADISON/BOWEN CK
   Hiram Cremeans        39   OH  farmer                  cem#S80
   Cathren               40           (Cook 1834cc
   Lewis                 18
   Cyntha                15
   Minta                 13f
   Cathrin               11
   Hiram                  9
   Wesley                 7                               cem#S80
   William                5
   Burton                 2
                                                  RACCOON
118-122
   Samuel Porter         21   Va  farmer
   Sarah                 20           (Johnson   1848cc)
   Letha                  1
page 19
                                                  RACCOON
119-123
   William Parsons       62   Va  farmer
   Susanna Parsons       62           (William Johnston  1841cc
   George                15       laborer
   Nancy J.              10
120-124
   Rhodie Miller         54   Va
   Henry                 21       laborer
121-125
   John Johnson          45   Va  farmer
   Elizabeth             36
   Polly                 18
   Lurissa               16f
   Lugkey                15f
   Linville               8m
   Franklin               6
   Melitta                4
   Isham                  3
122-126
   Samuel Hunter         63   Va  farmer
   Margaret              63
   John PORTER           18       farmer (m Sarah A. Clark  1851cc)
   John PORTER           22       laborer
123-127
   William Elkins        33   Va  farmer
   Elizabeth             27       (? 1-Dudly 1840-2-Eplin  1846cc)
   Samuel                 6
   Margaret               2
   Wesley               9/12
                                                  RACCOON
124-128
   William Porter        20       farmer
   Lucy                  20
   Margaret               1
```

```
125-129
   Merritt Johnson      34    Va  farmer
   Rhodie               40        (Adkins 1834cc)
   Maxwell              15        laborer
   Polly                14
   Betty                12
   Nancy                 8
   Zerelda               5f
   Francis M.            1m        (m Spicy Adkins SO)
   Margaret JOHNSON     12
126-130                                                    RACCOON
   Randolph Adkins      40    Va  farmer
   Elsey                32        (Polly Johnson  1833cc)
   Sylvester
   Ballard               4m
   Charity               2
   Anderson ADKINS      22        laborer
page 20   19 Jul 1850
127-131
   William Adkins       55    Va  clergyman
   Elizabeth            54
   James                29(idiot)
   Sarah                23
   Nancy                21
   Rebecca              18
   Mathew A.            16
   Thomas               16
   Ephram                3
128-132
   William B.Adkins     28    Va  farmer
   Ann                  33        (Douglas   1845cc) 2nd ?
   Re--- D.             13f       blurred
   Jacob                 4
   Letha                 2
129-133                                                 MADISON CREEK
   Charles Tooly        48    Va  farmer
   Elizabeth            44
   James                24
   George W.            19
   Milly A.             16
   Obadiah J.           14
   Charles T.           12
   Elizabeth            10
   Sarah                 8
   John                  5
   Polly                 4
130-134
   Malinda Bowen        37        (w/o Richard Bowen SO)
   Nancy J.             11
   Elizabeth             8        (m David W.Franklin 1859cc)
   Amanda J.             2
131-135   (see 133)                                     MADISON CREEK
   John E.Adkins        29        farmer
   Nancy                26        (Tooley 1843cc)
   Elizabeth             6
   George W.             3                                 cem#S95
   Julian A.             1
```

```
132-136
   Price Adkins          35        farmer
   Eliza (beth)          34           (Cremeans 27 dec 1832 CCM)
   Polly                 15
   Cenilda               12f
   Lucinda                8
   Cassa                  6
   Abigail                4
page 21
133-137                                     FALLS  of GUYANDOTTE
   William Turner        43    Va   lumberer
   Rebecca               33           (Hull -SO)
   Elizabeth             18    Ill    (m Gordon Midkiff 1850cc)
   Eliza S.              16    Va
   Susannah              13
   James M.              11
   Joseph                10
   George M.              7
   Nathaniel              5
   Lucy A.                3
   Amanda                 1
   Leonard TURNER        25        lumberer(oldest child 1st mar.?) cem#13
134-138
   Milford Mayab         43        laborer
   Elizabeth             40
135-139
   Samuel Booth          47        farmer
   Rachael               45           (R.Monroe Spurlock 1831cc)
   Mercy                 25f
   James                 23
   Ballard               12
   Martha                18
   William                4
136-140
   Henry Miller          40        farmer
   Toysee                27           (Cremeans 1840-1cc)
   Polly                  7
   Hudene                 5m
   Lucy                 6/12
137-141    (see 335)
   James McComas         45    Va   farmer
   John                  23        laborer
   Elizabeth             21
   Equella               19f          (m Addison McComas 1851cc)
   Alexander             13
   David                 11
   Cyntha A.              8
138-142
   Thomas McComas        71    Va   farmer
   Mary                  71
139-143                                              SALT ROCK
   Thomas J.McComas      32    Va   farmer
   Catherine             32
   Mary A.               15           (mGodfrey Scites(#443) cem#S99A
   Thomas F.             14
   James P.              12
   Martha A.             10
   Julia A.               8
   Sarah E.               6
   Blackburn              4
   David                  2
```

page 22
140-144
```
    John Booth            26    Va   farmer
    Elevey                28
    Nancy                  1
```
141-145   SALT ROCK
```
    James McComas         49    Va   farmer         cem#s99D
    Emily                 38                         cem#S99D
    Frances               18f
    David                 16         laborer
    Elisha                13                         cem#S99D
    Elvira                 8
    Arnold SULZBACKER     17
    N. McCOMAS            76f
```
142-146   SALT ROCK
```
    Solomon Midkiff       45    Va   farmer(1 Sarah McComas SO)   cem#S73A
                                    (2 America Bias 1850cc)Sol & Am   cem#S98B
    William B.            21
    Gordon C.            19          (Elizabeth Turner  1850cc)
    Itha J.              17f      (Joseph Hill  1852cc)Silas Perry-cem#S62
    Adaline              11
    Cynthia A.            8          (Elijah Perry              -cem#S73A
    Emily                 5          (William Dick SO)
    America               1f
```
143-147
```
    Spencer M.Childers   22    Va   farmer
    Elizabeth            21          (McComas 5 aug 1849 CCM)
    William F.          2/12
```
144-148
```
    Sacheryal Nicely     28    Va   farmer
    Elizabeth            21
    James A.              1
    Lucinda              2
```

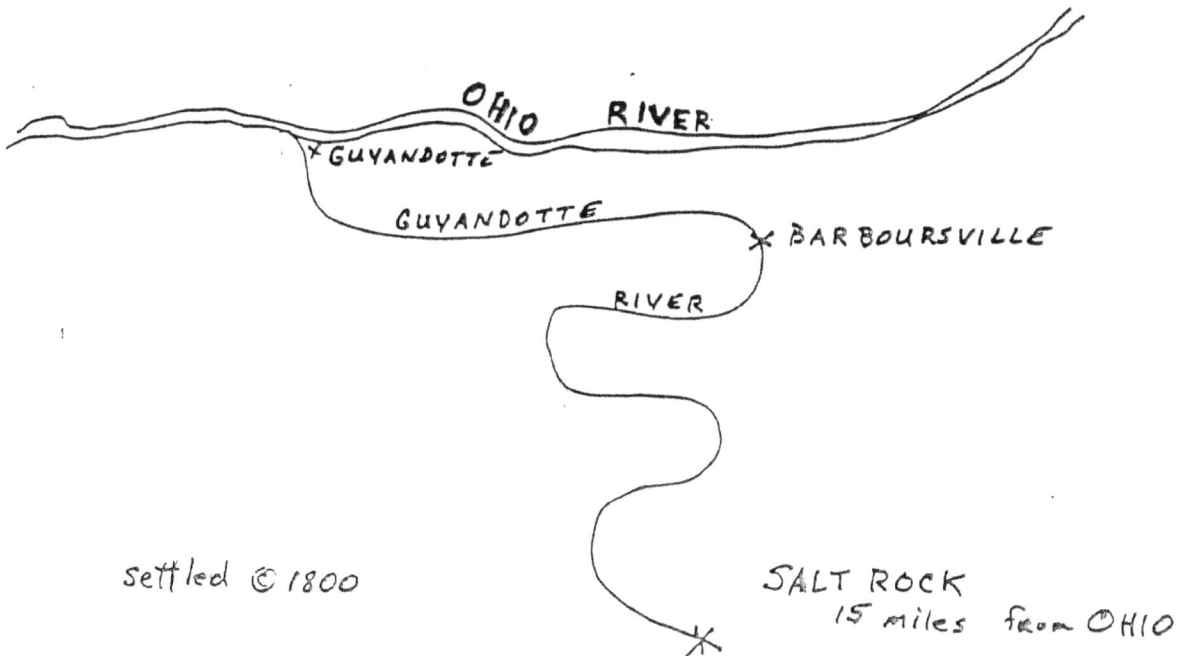

OHIO RIVER

Guyandotte

Guyandotte River

Barboursville

settled © 1800

SALT ROCK
15 miles from OHIO

```
145-149                                                          HEATH CREEK
   Nelson B.Heth        31    Va  farmer
   Sarah                32            (Porter 1838cc)
   Josuah K.            11
   Julia A.              9
   John M.               7
   Eliza B.              5
   William B.            3
146-150
   James H.Roffe        34    Va  farmer
   Mary                 34            (Swan 1837cc)
   Mary J.              12
   Susan J.             10
   Louisa F.             5
   Aminta                1
147-151                                          R#10 north/SMITH CREEK
   William C. Bramlette 25    Va  School Teacher        cem#S47
   Amelda               21
Page 23 - 20 July 1850 - Cabell Co.
148-152
   James R. Bias        53    Va. (w/o Mary Bryant SO)
   James A.             20
   Mary A.              12
149-153                                             HOLLAND BRANCH
   William Harrell      43    Tenn. Farmer
   Nancy                28    Va.
   Amanda ELKINS         5    Tenn.
   Merian BIAS (f)      25    Va.
   Thomas A.BIAS         2    Va.
150-154
   William Knight       36    NC Farmer(1 Mary E.Ansell 1838cc)
   Sarah                36    Va.      (Cardwell 1835cc)
   James E.             13
   Ann                   7
   America               5
   Adella                3
   Homer                 1
151-155  (see 383-386)                       MUD RIVER at BLUE SULPHUR
   John Dundas          52    D.C.
   Ann                  43    Va                            cem#s51
   Eliza A.             19         (m-Jonathan Turley 1852cc)
   Mary V.              17
   Frances              15f        (m-John Merritt 1862cc)
   Mareya               13f                                 cem#S51
   Lucy                 12
   Susan                10
   Sarah                 8         (Napoleon Johnson 1865cc)
   Thomas                3


152-156
   Benjamin L.Davis     37    Va  corder
   Harriet              35
   Joseph M.            11
   William W.           10
   John S.               5
   Mary H.               3
   Elizabeth         10/12
```

```
153-157                                              TURNPIKE-EAST
   Henry M.Chapman      31    Va  farmer
   Mary                 25
   John M.               8
   Susan E.              6
   Lewis H.              4
   Mary M.               3
   Pecky HUNTERS         1f
154-158
   Mary Reese           65    Va
   John B.              30        farmer
   Albert G. DAVIS       4
page 24
155-159                                      MERRITT CREEK at MUD
   Octavius Church      35m   Eng farmer                      cem#17
   Margaret             34    Va    (Merritt 1830cc)
   John W.               8
   Henry L.              6
   George                4
156-160                                            MERRITT CREEK
   William Merritt      37    Va  farmer  (s/o Wm.SO)
   Deborah              35        (Bumgardner 1832LCoh)
   John F.              16
   Sarah E.             15
   Thomas J.            12
   Mary W.              10
   Eliza V.              8
   Theresa               7
   James S.              5
   Phillip N.            4
157-161   (see 166,167)                       OHIO above 7 MILE
   Thomas Joy           45    Va  farmer
   Mary                 40    NC    (Polly Knight 1832cc)
   Ann                  17    Va
   Ellana               14
   James                11
   Sarah                 8
   Elizabeth             6
   Thomas                4
   Victoria              1
158-162                                  OHIO RIVER near GOOSE RUN
   Ansel Knight         25m   Va  farmer
   Matilda              24
   Lenard                5m
   Harriet L.            4
   Ann C.                1
   John McCRUMM         26        lumberer
159-163                                       OHIO  at 9 MILE
   Thomas Jefferson     35    Va  farmer
   Pathena              30
   Elizabeth            10
   Margaret              3
   Lewis                 1
160-164  (see 161-165-166-167)               OHIO about 9 MILE
   James Knight         64    NC  farmer
   Ann                  48    Ky    (Clark 1833 LCoh)
   Abner                16    Va  farmer
   Angeline             13
   Lucinda              12
   Harriet               9
```

28

161-165
```
    William King      37   Va   farmer
    Elizabeth         39             (Knight 1840-1cc)
    Nancy              9
    James              8
    Anslom            5m
    John W.            3
```
162-166
```
    George W.Knight   36   NC   farmer
    Mary              36   Va
    Sarah A.          14
    Mary E.           13
    John              11
    Pattina           8f
    George W.          6
    William H.         3
    Margaret F.     2/12
```
OHIO RIVER about 9 MILE
163-167
cem#26B
```
    Abner Knight      46   NC   farmer
    Margaret          25
    Preston           14
    Hamilton          17        farmer
    Mary              12
    Sarah M.           9
    Nancy              8
    Susannah           5
```
164-168
```
    Jacob Winters     52   Va   farmer
    Hester            48   NY
    Daniel            22   OH
    George W.         14   Va
    Mary               8
    Lemuel             6
    Martin             4
```
GOFF HILL
165-169
```
    David Poor        37   Va   Farmer
    France L.         23             (Louiza Goff 1847cc)
    France M          1f
```
GREENBOTTOM
166-170
cem#26
```
    Pennel Blake      49   Va   Farmer (s/o Isaac SO)
    Nancy             25             (Knight 1842cc)     cem$26
    Fredrick           5
    Mary E             3
    Margaret A         1
```
167-171
```
    Martin Nance(1)   65   Va  Farmer
    Hannah            57
    Cathrin           25
    Malachai          21
    Sarah             17
    Abraham           14
    Mahale            11
```
168-172
```
    John Kleninger    44   MD
    Margaret          43   Va
    John H            20        cooper
    Margaret A        16
```

168-172 Kleninger (con't)

Name	Age	State	Occupation
Joseph P	15		farmer
Thomas P	13		
Mary A	10		
Sarah E	8		
Catilia (f)	6		
Eustachia (f)	2		

169-173

Name	Age	State	Occupation
George Beecham	38	OH	farmer (Burcham ?)
Mary A.	30	Va	
Elisabeth	14	OH	
John	10	OH	
Melvina	9	OH	
Sampson S.	7		
Amanda	4		
Andrew	1		

170-174

Name	Age	State	Occupation
Preston Guthrie	34	Va	Farmer
Elvira	25		
Charles	2		
Mary	2		
Frances(f)	1		
John GUTHRIE	38		farmer (m Hannah Ancel 1852cc)
James GUTHRIE	36		farmer

171-175

Name	Age	State	Occupation
William Guthrie	35	Va	farmer
Mary	35		
Abigoe	5f	OH	
Almida	2	Va	
William H.	1		

172-176

Name	Age	State	Occupation
Robert Guthrie	72	Va	farmer
Frances	66		
Almeda	26		(Guthrie marriages at Gallipolis)

173-177

Name	Age	State	Occupation
Chapman M. White	40	Va	teacher
Rebecca	40		
John C.	17		farmer
James C.	15		
Benjamin	13		
Mary C.	9		
Joseph C.	7		
Virginia M.	4		
Sarah J.	1		

174-178 (s/o 179)

Name	Age	State	Occupation
Thomas J.Jenkins	23	Va	farmer(m Susan Holderby 1856cc) cem#H10

(Family cemetery on Ohio moved to Spring HIll-HTGN

175-179

Name	Age	State	Occupation
William Jenkins	63	Va	farmer (w/o Rachel McNutt CCA-Rockbridge)
William A.	21		physician(Julia Reed-CCA cem#H10
(A.J.) at Harvard)			(CSA General)

176-180

Name	Age	State	Occupation
Joseph B.Scott	32	NY	manager(overseer at Greenbottom)cem#5
Mary	22	Va	
Eliza V.	2	Miss	

177-181

Name	Age	State	Occupation
Alexander Box	50	Va	laborer
Temperance	27		
Charlotte J.	8	OH	
Melissa	5	OH	
John H.	3	OH	

```
178-182
   Thomas Brandon      42    Va    laborer
   Nancy M.            28
   Sarah A.            10
   John F.             7
   Elizabeth           4
   Emily J.            3
   George E.           1
   Enoch REED          20
179-183
   Thomas W.Reece      40    Va    Lawyer(sawyer ?)
   Martha A.           29          (Defoe 1839MM)
   Allan W.            10                                        cem#S54
   James T.            8
   James WHITE         48          laborer
180-184
   James M.Sullivan    29    Md    lawyer
   Martha              29    Va    (Toney 1841cc)
   Margaret A.         7
   John W.             6
   James T.            4
   Steven V.           1
181-185
   Jacob R.Brandon     39    Va    Wood Dealer
   Lois W.             28    OH
   Misouri E.J.        3     Va
   Charles T.          2
   Anna V.             6/12
182-186                                OHIO RIVER at MASON CO.line
   John Hannan         67    Va    farmer  (s/o Thomas SO)        cem#1B
   Nancy G.            57          (White 1812cc)
   Jesse W.            36          tanner
   Thomas V.           33
   John H,F.           26          lumberer
   Benjamin F.         23          trader
   Jenista             20f
   Milton McCOY        25          physician
   John McCUNE         53          laborer
page 28
183-187
   Edwin Pillow        38    Va    blacksmith
   Mariah              36
   Sarah A.L.          7
   William T.          4
   Thomas J.           4
   Mary A.             2
   May PILLOW          55
184-188  (See 179)                     OHIO RIVER at MASON CO. line
   David B.Lacy        50    Va    brickmason
   Eustacia :          46          (Jenkins 1834cc)(dau/William)cem#27C
185-189
   Robert Wiley        40    Pa    joiner
   Elizabeth           31    Va    (Hannon SO)
   Nancy               12
   William             9           (m Anna Sweetland SO)
   Margaret            6           (m Franklin Day SO)
   Lucinda             3
   Frances             1/12f        (m Thomas Reese SO)
```

```
186-190
   Robert Chambers      45   Va   farmer
   Moses McCOY          50   Pa   shoemaker (?w/o Hannah Lawson 1824GpKy)
187-191
   Sterling Davis       36   Va   farmer
   Elizabeth            34             (Conrad 1837cc)
   Adison              10m                                        cem#11
   Emily                11
   Martha                9
   Charles               5
   Jessee                3
188-192
   Lylan P.Emmerson     28   OH   farmer
   Elizabeth            22
   Sylvester             1
189-193
   John Jack            42   Pa   laborer
   Louvinia            41   Va
   Mary E.               8   Pa
   Martha A.            16   Va
   Lewis P.             14
   Louisa                7
190-194                                       GOFF HILL at GREENBOTTOM
   Leonard Goff         48   Va   farmer
   Nancy                40
   Mariah               14
   Charles              12
   William               8
   Joseph                6
   Leonard               3
191-195   (see 192)
   Lisbon Goff          27   Va   farmer
   Sarah                24             (Emmerson 1848cc)
   William H.            1
page 29
192-196                                       GOFF HILL at GREENBOTTOM
   Ludwill Goff         24   Va   farmer
   Margaret             20             (Winters 1849cc)
193-197
   Jessee Spurlock      35
   Margaret             28
   Simon                 7
   Thomas B.             1
194-198   (see192,195)                                         GWINN
   Benjamin Emmerson    66   Maine farmer
   May                  52   OH
   Lavina               16
   Benjamin             11
   Jane FUREL           17   Va
195-199                                                        GWINN
   Thomas Spurlock      39   Va   (w/o Minirva Hannan 1831MM)cem#2
   Daniel E.            18
   Sarah E.             14
   Eliza                 6
196-200                                                        GWINN
   Sarah Bowen          53   NC
   Sylvester            14   Va
   Jefferson            12
   Zazy                  8             (wife Catherine Joy-bur. Cem #26B)
   Susannah             18
```

```
196-201
   Ezekiel Bowen       26   Va  boatman
   Ann                 22
   Margaret TEMPLETON  24                              SPURLOCK CREEK
197-202
   Daniel Spurlock     65   Va  farmer
   Sarah               44
   David TURNER        40   Eng teacher
   Ellenopine TURNER   12   Eng
198-203                                            SPURLOCK CK at GWINN
   Stephen Spurlock    25   Va  farmer
   Jane A.             25
   Elizabeth            3
   William              1
199-204
   John Oliver         49   Va  farmer
   Rebecca             49   Md
   John                13   Pa
   Rebecca              8   Va
   Griffin              6
   George A.F.          4
   Clemens SULLIVAN    23   Md  boatman
page 30
200-205
   John Perry          45   NC  farmer
   Lucy                45   Va       (Toney 1826cc)
   William W.          19       farmer
   Thomas H,GRAVENER   28   Pa  laborer
201-206
   William L.Perry     55   NC  farmer   (Nancy Toney 1838cc)
   Nancy               29   Va       (Wyatt 1840cc)
202-207
   Joseph Files(Fife)  37   Va  farmer
   Hannah              35            (Ansell 1835cc)
   Sarah E.            10
   Jacob                8
   Daniel               6
   Amanda H.            4
   Emily                2
   Virginia          5/12
203-208 (family must have moved-buried at SALT ROCK-living GWINN area)
   Joseph Gill         43   Eng  Engineer              cem#S99
   Mary A.             32                              cem#s99
   Joseph              14
   William             12            (m-Emma D.)       cem#S99
   Mary A.             10
   George               9                              cem#S99
   Charles J.           4
   John              11/12                             UNION RIDGE
204-209
   Charles W. Miller   30  Ger(Sexony) farmer
   Luana K.            30
   Luana E.             9
205-210
   Henry Sprecher      30  Switzerland   farmer
   Augusta             18  Ger
   Henry ADAMS         14  Va.
```

```
206-211
   Godfried Scheiltine  29 Switzerland   Merchant
   Conred RUED          19 Switzerland   Clerk
207-212 (Koreuszenski)
   John Kheuszenski     43 Poland    farmer
   Zeophta              35     "
   Wiadeston            15m    "
   Sophia               13     "
   Senon                10m    "
   Edward                8     "
   Ludmilla              3f    "
   Matilda              3/12 Va
208-213
   Anna Luckwaski       35   Poland   (Lukowski)(different spelling)
   Wladislow            15        "
   Clementina           10        "
   Adolphus              8        "
209-214                                              UNION RIDGE
   James Felix          45   Switzerland   surveyor      .
   Julia                40
   Julias               11m
   Walter               10
   Arnold                6                       (bur. Cem.#6)
   Werner                8
   Gustav A.GULDIN      39
210-215
   Wladimir Kryszonowski  32  Poland    farmer
   Wibold KALUSOWSKI      10m France
211-216
   Thomas Arthur        62   Va   farmer
   Elizabeth            40
   Thomas M.            17
   Lafayette             4
   Eliza TEMPLETON      13
212-217                            CABELL CREEK RD at HOWELL'S MILL
   James Arthur         35   Va   farmer              ( Cem #11)
   Elizabeth(Ann)       33        (Beckett  1845cc     .Cem #11
   Annie M.              8
   Emily M.              6
   Thompson              4
   James                 1
213-218
   Jerrimiah Blake      56   Va   farmer
   Margaret             46
214-219
   Charles Latton       40   Conn   carpenter
   Jane A.              39   NY
   Margaret E.          15   NY      (m James Thompson 1851cc)
   David O.             12   NY
   Charles A.            6   OH
215-220
   Richard P.Bexfield   24   Eng.  farmer
216-221
   Howard Clark         46   NH   Physician
   Lilly R.            36   NY
   Philip F.            18   Oh   farmer
   William F.          12   Pa
   Philina M.          11f  Pa
   Johanna              9   NY
   Frances              7f  NY
   Virginia H.          1   Va
```

```
217-222
   Nathan Cremeans      36   Va  farmer
   Elizabeth            38   Va       (Jenkins 1838 CCM)
   Louisa               10   OH
   Mary E.               7   OH
   Virginia              9   OH
   Martha J.             5   Va
   John W.               1   Va
page 32
218-223
   Isaac Blake          37   Va  farmer
   Johannah             30            (King SO ?)
   James M.              9
   Christian             7
   Albert C.             3
   Jeremiah              2
219-224                              BRYAN CREEK off UNION RIDGE
   Lawrence Briant      29   Va  farmer            ( Cem #5A)
   Mary E.              22        (Hinchman  1845)       Cem#5A)
   William P.            4
   Mary A.               2
   Cathrin             5/12
   Fredric LEWIS        14
   Rebecca LEWIS        16
220-225                                        BRYAN CREEK
   Nimrod Briant        27   Va  farmer              (.Cem#5A)
   Nancy               23            (Spurlock 1847cc)    Cem#5A
   Matlida               2
   Sarah C.            9/12
   Cathrine BRIANT      70   (Shope w/o John 1805 GpKy )   .Cem#5A
221-226
   Wingit Cremeans      44   Va  farmer
   Mary                38            (Lynn 1838MM)
   Frederic             14
   Charles              13
   Luther               10
   Marritha              8
   Delila                6
   Sarah A.              3
   Isaiah              7/12
222-227
   Sarah Cremeans       67   Va
   Elijah               22        laborer
   Sarah                19
223-228                              MASON CO.line/east of GWINN
   Thomas R.Riggs       39   Va  farmer                  cem#29
   Celia                38
   Charles C.           16        farmer
   Elizabeth J.         12
   Easton M.            7m
   Albert P.             5                               cem#29
   Thomas J.             2
224-229                              JENKINS BRANCH near DUDLEY GAP
   Cary Jenkins        81m   Va  farmer
   John                 25
   Elizabeth            14
page 33
```

```
225-230
   Andrew Wallace        33    Va   farmer
   Elvira                33
   Jane A.                2
   May L.              6/12                        DRY RIDGE east/DUDLEY GAP
226-231
   Ruben Cremeans        91    Md  (b 1759)
   Elizabeth             85    Va  (Tackett KCM-@ 1808)(not 1st)
   Polly C.              22
   Alexander             19
   Asa L.S.              16
227-232
   David Hamrick         35    Va   farmer
   Lavicy                30              (Cremeans 1838 CCM)
   Neah J.               6m
   Burton F.J.            4
   Elijah C.M.            2
   Elias V.            4/12
228-233
   John Hamrick          65    Va   farmer
   Nancy                 36
   William M.C.C.         7
   James M.               5
   Eliza A.E.             3                         JENKINS BRANCH n/o DUDLEY GAP
229-234
   Anderson Jenkins      69    Va   farmer
   Telitha               25
   Eliza A.E.             7
   Emily                  5
   John J.                2
   John JENKINS          51         laborer
230-235
   Andrew McCalister     50    Va   farmer      (1-Minny Cremeans 1838cc)
                                                (2-Frances Ford 1841cc)
                                                  3-?
   Neoma                 26
   Richard               10
   Sarah M.               8
   Miranda                8
   Nathan                 2
231-236
   Elizabeth Cremeans 55       Va                              DRY RIDGE
   John A.               19         laborer
   Amanda                30
   Baily                22m
   Elizabeth              8
   William                6
   Wesley                 6
   Abia C.              11m
   Nancy J.               4
page 34
232-237
   Henry Dial            36    Va   farmer
   Rutha                 38              (Chapman  1836cc)
   John F.               14
   Emeletta S.          11f
   Cornelius E.          9m
   Cad C.                 8
   Martha L.              5
```

```
233-238
   James Legg          50    Va   farmer
   Veletta             50
   Esther              16
   Thomas              14
234-239
   James H.Estes       27    Va   farmer
   Elizabeth           21              (Newman  1848cc)
    Virginia            1
235-240
   Russell Newman      74    Va   farmer (w Sarah Harbour  1828cc)
   May                 20
   Eliza               19
   Martha              18
   Albert              18         laborer
   Addison             16         laborer
   Amanda              14
   Malinda             12
   John                 9
   Milton               7
   Edna A.              4
236-241
   Andrew Black        25    Va   farmer
   Hulda               27              (Smith  1846cc)
   Mary A.              3
   Margaret             1
   Joseph TONY         22         laborer
237-242
   James H.Duncan      22    Va   farmer
   Mary E.             22
   Charles H.           1
238-243
   James Mathew        63    Md   farmer
   Martha              56
   Sarah J.            21
   George F.           17         farmer
   James W.            15         farmer
   Sarah F.             5
page 35
239-244
   Griffin Reynolds    50         cooper
   Elizabeth           47
   Eliza               20              (m Emerson Chapman  1851SO)
   Nancy               19
   John                17         laborer
   Harding             15         farmer
----245
   Ann Blacke          24    Va   (Reynolds ?)
   Ruth                 5
   Mary E.              3
   John J.              1
240-246
   Thomas Smith        64         farmer
   Mary                66              (Deal  1819cc)
   Eda LEGG            20    (Edith) (m-Joel Toney  1851cc)
                                        LEFT FORK of FUDGE CREEK
241-247
   John McClasky       51    Va   stonemason(?1-Arie Roberts 1818KCM)
   Emeline             35
   Floyd                2
   Nancy J.          8/12
   Lemrions            9m
```

```
242-248
   Richard Walsh        43    Ireland school teacher
   Sarah T.             22
243-249
   Frances McWarter     55f   Va      (w/o James d1849 SO)
   James                24          roadmaker
   Henry                22          laborer
   John                 17          farmer
   William              16          farmer
   Floyd                14
   Albert                8
244-250
   Thomas C.Wallace     31    Va  farmer
   Elizabeth       .    28            (Jordan 1841cc)
   Jonathan J.           8
   John M.               6
   Mary A.               5
   Lavanus              3m
   Evira                1f
245-251
   David Black          27          farmer
   Lavicy A.            27
   Mary                  8
   Katy                  6
   Adam K.               4
   Sarah E.              2
   Emberson              1
245-252
   Cathrine Conrad      29          (Black w/o DAvid 1838MM)
   Francis M.           10    Va
   Joanna                7
   Elizabeth             4
page 36
246-253
   John W.Smith         37          farmer
   Margaret             22            (Chapman  1846cc)
   William H.            3
   Victoria             1
   Sarah J.FERRELL      19    OH      (David Smith 1853cc)
247-254
   Joshua Lunsford      34    Va  farmer
   Sarah                30            (Wallacines 30 aug 1838 CCM)
   Susannah             10
   William J.            9
   Mary E.               5
   George W.            1


248-255
   Peter Wallace        34    Va farmer
   Nancy                30
   Martha A.             9
   Mary M.               7
   Love C.(m)            5
   Sarah A.              3
   Mount E.(m)           2
```

```
249-256
   Parthena Wallace    39f    Va
   Margaret             9
   Tabitha              6
250-257
   Benjamin Wallace    60     Va    farmer
   Letty               54
   Jessee              24           farmer
   Hugh M.             20           larborer
   Susan               15
   Washington          13
   Amanda              10
   Mary JOHNSON        18
251-258
   Edmund Wallace      26     Va    farmer
   Mary A.E.           20
   Susan F.             3
   Charles L.           7
   Mariah MATTHEWS     45f
   Elizabeth MATTHEWS  10
                                              FUDGE CREEK
252-259
   James McClasky      31     Va    laborer
   Nancy               30
   Robert A.            3
   Hamilton             1
page 37                                LEFT FORK of FUDGE
253-260
   William Chapman     54     Va    farmer        cem#S52
   Elizabeth           39                         cem#S52
   John                13
   Leffaner            12
   Mary J.             10
   Nehemiah            10m
   Minerva F.           8
   Martha               5
   Cenantha E,          5f              (2 sets of twins ?)
   America M.           3
   James H.K.         2/12
254-261
   Green B.Chapman     34     Va    laborer
   Lucy                34
   Milton              12
   Rutha               10
   Willis               8
   Sophia               7
   Martha               6
   Warren               3
   John                 1
   Jackson            2/12
   Susan SHOEMAKER     10
   William H.SHOEMAKER  9
   Nancy J.SHOEMAKER    6
                                              BALL'S GAP
255-262
   Isaac M.Ball        46     Va    farmer(w/Sarah Hand 1832cc)
   Nancy               80
   William P.          16           farmer
   Jerremiah           14
   Neoma               13
   Francis M.          11m
   John H.              8
   Amanda               3
```

256-263   BALL'S GAP
   Henry Ball   52   Va farmer
   Telitha   23
   Lafayette   16   farmer
   Hetty A.   12
   Martha   9
   John D.S.   6/12   MUD BRIDGE(Milton)

257-264
   Andrew Jordan   65   Va farmer
   Mary   65   (Polly Chapman 1802 KCM)
   Mary M.   25
   William J.FORTH 15   farmer

258-265
   Thomas Gibson   28   Va Farmer
   Sarah   31
   Nancy A.   11
page 38   MUD BRIDGE(Milton)
259-266
   Chapman Jordan 36   Va shoemaker
   Mariah   32   OH
   John M.   10   Va
   Mary M.   5
   James M.   1   MUD BRIDGE(Milton)
260-267
   William Jordan 34   Va farmer
   Esther   33   (Trippet 1836cc)
   Samuel   13
   Andrew J.   11
   Mary E.   9
   Delila A.   7
   John W.   4
   Henry A.   1   MUD BRIDGE(Milton)
261-268
   Edmund C.Rece   30   Va Joiner   cem#S54
   Sophia P.   36   cem#S54
   Charles A.   12
   Lois A.   5
   Theodore H.   3
262-269
   Jessee Wade   54   Va tailor
   Lucy   45
   Samuel   21   carpenter
   Jacob   15   laborer
   Jane   8
   Jessee   7   MUD BRIDGE(Milton)
263-270
   John M.Rece   36   Va merchant   cem#S54
                           1w-Lucretia A.Love-2w Marian A.
   Joseph A.   6
----271
   America Thomas 31   Ill   (w/o John H.Thomas SO)
   Mary J.   12   Va
   Susan S.   6
264-272   MUD BRIDGE(Milton)
   Abia Rece   66   Va farmer   cem#S54
   Elizabeth   68   (Harmon 1808 SO/KCM) Cem#S54
   John C.   32   (m-Margaret   cem#S54
   Joseph A.   21
   David MORRISON 50   insane
   Martha TARRETT 55
   Elizabeth JOHNSON 29

```
265-273
   James Reynolds      47    Va   farmer
   Dorothy             49                                    cem#S54A
   Jeremiah C.         18
   Joseph M.           16
   Louisa              13
   Nancy               11
   James C.             8
page 39
266-274
   Samuel E.C. Wilson  42    Md   farmer
   Sarah               38    Va
   Thomas              18
   Allan               15
   Louisa              12
   Charles              7
   Margaretta           5
   Malinda              3
267-275
   German Chapman      31    Va   farmer
   Catharin            29              (Hambrick 1838cc)
   Martha              10
   Nancy L.             8
   Frances J.           5f
   Rufus                1
268-276
   Warren P.Rece       28    Va   farmer
   Elizabeth           22
   Marion            5/12
```

```
269-277
   Charles H.Bruce     33    Va   farmer
   Martha A.           31
   Frances J.          11f
   Lavinia              9
   Jane C.              7
   Charles H.           5
   Martha A.            3
   Margnis D.L.         1f
270-278                                      MUD BRIDGE(Milton)
   Thomas Kilgore      84    Pa   farmer  (York Co.PA)     cem#S55
   Hetty               68    Va        (Saunders-d1852)    cem#S55
      (sister to Sampson Saunders-her children inherited his property)
271-279                                      MUD BRIDGE(Milton)
   George Kilgore      47    Va   farmer
   Nancy               36
   James               19         farmer
   Malinda             21              (mJames Riggs So)
   William             18         farmer
   Martha              16
   Mary                13
   Sarah               11
   Elizabeth            9
272-280
   Francis J. Duffen   46    Va   school teacher
   Catherine           45
   Eliza A.            21              (mThomas Ervin 1850cc)
   James E.            17         laborer
   Sarah C.            10
   Joseph L.H.          4
   Nancy DUFFEN        75    Tenn
   James ASHWORTH       5
```

Page 40
273-281   east/MUD BRIDGE(Milton)
   Thomas W. Kilgore   28   Va. farmer
   Mary J.   22   (Margaret McCormick CCA-?)
   Joseph C.   2
   Nancy KILGORE   53
274-282   (John Morris of the Valley) TEAYS VALLEY
   John Morris   56   Va (1-Mary Everett 1814-d1816)
   Mary   69   (2-Kinaird 1818cc)
   Mary   18   (m Ira McCunihay 1850CC)
   Ephriam KINNAIRD   14
   William KINNAIRD   16   laborer
   William SOWERY   25   Eng laborer
283
   Sarah Morris   26   Va (Russell mJoseph M. Morris 1844CC)
   John O.   5
   Mary R.   3
   Helen J.   7/12
275-284
   Andrew Bilup   36   Va blacksmith
   Mary   36   (Wilson 1841cc)
   James J.   11
   Charles W.   5
   John   3
   Alexander   2
   Mary WILSON   75   Pa (w/o John)(James-SO)   cem#54A
276-285
   Mourning Hudson   50   Va
   Haney   18
   Quintina   13
277-286
   Erastmus Hanley   43   Va farmer
   Catherine A.   34
   Malvina N.   19
   Virginia P.   17
   Susan T.   15
   John M.   13
   Patrick H.   10
   Augusta A.   8   m Miverva McGinnis d/Allen FBL
   Benjamin F.   6
   Munroe   1
278-287
   Josiah B. Poag   33   Va Minister
   Frances A.   30
   Calvin A.   3
279-288
   Hezekiah Hudson   33   Va Blacksmith
   Mary   28   (m Mays 1838cc)
   Elizabeth J.   11
   Malinda F.   9
   Mary A.   3
   Albert F.   5/12
Page 41
280-289
   Joseph McCalister   31   Va Farmer
   Eliza M.   22   (m McCallister 1845cc)
   Jackson   4
   Albert   1

```
281-290
   Lewis Mays            40    Va   Farmer
   Jane                  41
   Margaret J            11
   John H.               17         Farmer
   James B.              15
   George T.              6
   Virginia T.            1
282-291
   Malcolm McCalister    37    Va   Farmer
   Sarah H.              30
   Charles              10
   Henry                 8
   Edna A.               6
   Margery               4
   Elizabeth             2
   Ison McGEE           55         (black)
283-292
   James McCalister     68    Va   Farmer(1-Mary Smith 1820 cc)
   Olivia               42
   Allen                19
   Isaac                10
   Polly HANLY          55
284-293
   Bartholomew Roberts  39    Va   Farmer (w/o Mary Pollock 1833 cc)
   Henry                46
   Elizabeth            44
   Rhoda ROBERTS        86
285-294
   Michael G. Comen     56    Va   Farmer
   Elizabeth            58
   Manutha              20
   Elizabeth            15
   Johnny R.            13
   Stephen              10

286-295
   Fairfax W. Nelson    26    MD   Labourer
   Mary                 26    Pa.
   Martha E.             5    OH
   Nancy L.              3    Va.
   William L. NELSON    13    Va.
p42
287-296
   John Smallridge      57    Va.  Farmer
   Mary                 49    Ky       (Bell 1820cc)
   John W.              23    Ky   Labourer
   Sylvester W.         16    Va   Farmer
   Elizabeth            18
   Sampson S.           14
   William S.           12
   Mary A.              10
   James A.              8
   Matilda A.            6
288-297
   Jonathan Hensley     36    Va   Labourer
   Delila               30             (B. Griffith 1839 KCM)
   John S.               9    Ind
   James                 6    Ind
   Abraham               2    Va
```

```
289-298 s/o Robert Rev. Soldier of Pittslyvania Co.Va.    MUD BRIDGE
  James Templeton       85    Va (1.Lucy Billups SO)        cem#s54A
  Ann                   55       (2.Frazier 1835cc)
  Adaline               23
290-299                                           south of MUD BRIDGE
  Moses Beckett         49    Va  Farmer(w/Rebecca Wilson 1831cc)cem#55B
  Mary                  29                                   cem#55B
  Emsley    (m)         17        Farmer (Mary Roberts 1855 SO)
  Charles               16
  Louisa                14
291-300
  Willis Legg           30    Va  Farmer
  Rebecca               23        (Chapman 1846cc)
  John H.               9/12
292-301
  John Chapman          79    Va  Farmer
  Molly                 72        (? Abbott SO)
  Polly                 40
  Phebe                 35        Idiot
  Martha                28
  Cynthia               16
  Tazwell    (m)        10    (m-Abigail)                    cem#S59
  Minta                 7
293-302                                           POORE'S HILL
  Sampson Hanly         49    Va  Blacksmith          cem#s51
  Susan                 46        Webster Harman FBL  cem#S51
  Caroline              23        (m-Moses Thornburg 1852 cc)
  Emily                 19
  Frances               18
  Mary                  15
  Wm. H.                13    m Adaline Harshbarger d/o David FBL
  Martha                7
p43
294-303
  William Howard        40    Va  Shoemaker
  Anna                  38
  Ann M.                13
  William M.            11
295-304                                    YATESMONT off HOWELLS MILL
  James J. Herndon      38    Va  Farmer(1.Mary Yates 1834cc)(cem.#15)
  Adaline               34
  John W.               1
  Susan E.              10                              (cem.#15)
  Mary PAINE            9     Eng.
296-305
  Porter Wallace        34    Va  School Teacher
  Caroline              32
  Benjamin O. SUTTLE    27    Va  School Teacher
  Mary WOOTEN           16
297-306                                           POORE'S HILL
  Sarah Everett         52    Va  (Rece-Nathan Everett-EPP) cem#S54
  Mary                  32
  James                 27        (m-Mary V.             cem#S54
  Charles               21         m Frampton FBL       cem#H10
  Peter B.              19
  Mary RECE             86    Pa  (Mother EPP)
```

```
298-307
  Charles Mays         38    Va  Farmer
  Elvira               36
  Melissa A.           15
  Emily J.             15
  America               7
  Joseph A.             4
  Celia E.            2/12
                                                CAVILL CREEK at ROACH
299-308                                              cem#S49A
  William Morrison     62    Va  Farmer
  Ellenar G.           42
  William              13
  Mariah J.            11
                                                CAVILL CREEK
300-309
  Thompson Morrison    39    Va  Farmer
  Mary A.              36                           cem#S49A
  Valeria              15
  Thomas               13                           cem#S49A
  Elizabeth            11
  Albert                8                           cem#S49A
  John                  6                           cem#S49A
  Calvin                4                           cem#S49A
  Mary A.               1
p44
301-310
  Henry Hatfield       41    Va  Farmer              (cem.#S45)
  Catherine            36        (Dial 1832)    (unmarked)cem#S45
  David J.             16
  John L.              14
  Andrew W.            12
  Nancy A.             10
  Polly E.              8
  Catherine M.          6
  Henry M. (Martin)     4                           cem#S45
  Emily C.            9/12
  Julia SNELL          18
                                                    ROACH
302-311
  George Hatfield      49    Va  Farmer
  Eliza A.             32        (Beckett 1841)
  Elizabeth            22
  Louisa               18
  Editha               15
  Emizetta             12
  Josephine             7
  Adam S.               5
  James A.              4
  Eliza C.              1
                                                CAVILL CREEK
303-312
  Hamilton Mays        30    Va  Labourer
  Nancy (Mary)         30        (Stanley-1841 cc)
  Elizabeth             8
  John T.               5
  Cathrin F.            4
  Matilda               3
  Hezekiah S.           1
  Jane STANLEY         15
  David STANLEY        16        laborer(mAdeline Butcher 1853cc)
```

```
304-313
  John Stanley         54    Va farmer
  Elizabeth            51
  Robbin               13
305-314
  Hezekiah Swan        52    Va farmer
  Catharin             47        (Hatfield 1819cc)
  Isaiah C.            22
  Ballard S.           21
  Henley C.            19
306-315
  Alexander McComas    35    Va farmer
  Julia A.             24        (Ann Swan 1844cc)
  Andrew                3
p45
307-316
  Thomas J.Cowens      35    Va farmer
  Viney                36        (Elvina Turley 1838 LCOM)
  Mary                 10
  James                 7
  Willis                5
  Henrietta             3
  Hester A.          6/12
308-317                      (s/o Isaac)
  Isaac Hatfield       47    Va farmer  (1-Rachael Drake 1827cc)
  Elizabeth            23        (2-Moore 1843cc)
  Caperton             21
  Arminta              20
  Overton              18        (m-Emily Hatfield 1856cc)
  Joseph               14
  Susan                10
  Dingus                8
  Fernadez              6
  Driezella             4
  Rufus                 2
309-318
  Glouchester Hatfield 22    Va farmer
  Julietta             19        (Hatfield 1848cc)
  Sarah V.           6/12
310-319
  Everett Feasle       24    Va lumberman
  Amicetta             16
311-320
  Henry Peyton         32    Va farmer
  Margaret             26
  Cynthia               1
  Margaret             50    Va
312-321
  Atha F.Turly(m)      62    Va pauper
  Martha               68
  Zophera(f)           21        (m William Fielder 1852cc)
  Louisa               16
313-322
  John Vaughn          26    Va farmer
  Lucy A.              24
  Andrew                2
  Jane CURTIS          68
```

```
314-323
  Harrison Paine        62    Va farmer (m Polly McComas 1813cc)
  Joseph A.             18
  Mary                  14
315-324
  David McComas         49    Va farmer
  Eudocia               38    TN (Drake-SO)
  Henderson G.          15       (m Cynthia Cummins-SO)
  Lewis                 10       (m Minerva Adkins SO)
  Dike                   8       (m Elizabeth Lawrence-1846cc)
  Arminda                4       (m Joe Burger-SO)
p46
316-325
  Stephen Paine         28    Va farmer
  Lucy A.               28       (Ann McComas 1846cc)
  Velera                 2
  Mary J.            10/12
  Charles               16    laborer
317-326
  Abel Sansum           33    Va farmer
  Julia A.              27
  Edward                13       (m Laura Cummins-Boone Co.SO)
  Rhoda                  9
  Amanda                 7
  Mary A.                5
  William                3
  Malinda                1
318-327
  Edward Franklin       58    Va farmer
  Christina             54
  William M.            26       farmer
  Malinda K.            23
  Eliza M.(m)           20       farmer
  Oliver G.             17       farmer
  David W.              15       farmer
  James W.              11
319-328
  Simon Paine           34    Va farmer
  Polly                 38
  Eliza A.M.            12
  Nancy D.               7
  Julia E.               6
  Judith E.              4
  Mary                   1
320-329
  Parker Lucas          36    Va farmer (marrriages show Lewis)
  Cloa                  41       (Dial 1834cc)
  David                 14
  Mary                  12
  John                  10
  Charles A.             8
  Rebecca                6
  James                  5
  Minerva                2
321-330
  Aaron F.McKendree     45    Va farmer  (b-Franklin Co. SO)
  Catharine             33       (Grubbs -SO)
  Samuel P.              9
```

```
321-330 McKendree (con't)
   Margaret J.            8
   Charles A.             6
   Evelina                5
   Robert S.              2
   James ADKINS          32  laborer
p47
322-331
   James Cowens          29  Va   boatman   (2-Sarah Butcher 1855DD)
   Hester                29             (1-Ester Turley 1844cc)
   Thomas J.              5             (m-Lou Reynolds SO)
   Elizabeth McGETTES     7  Ky
323-332
   Joseph Atkins         33  VA farmer
   Elizabeth             38
   Stephanus(m)           8
   Cosby(f)               6
   Mary A.                4
   Oscar                  1
   George L.              2
324-333
   John G.Atkins         35  Va farmer
   Letty                 27
   Letty                  8
   Clara                  6
   Caroline               4
   Frances(f)             3
   Albert G.P.            1
----334
   David McComas         56  Va Judge S.C.L.&C.(s/o Elisha)
   Cynthia               47             (French SO)
325-335
   William McComas       59  Va farmer
   Elizabeth             48
   Emberson              25     farmer
   Mary                  22
   Addison               16     farmer(cem#14-m-Auilla McComas 1851cc)
   William               11
   Sarah                  6
----336
   Eliza Adkins          28  Va
   Louisa                30
   Sarah F.            2/12
326-337
   John Eplen            37  Va farmer   (Epling)
   Julia                 33             (Parsons-1834cc)
   Henry                 17
   Oliver                13
   Archa(m)              10
   Almeda                 4
   Blackbourn             4
   Alonzo              2/12
327-338
   Brison Atkins         66  Va farmer
p48
328-339    (s/o 443)
   Christopher Sites     38  Germany  farmer
   Bety                  24  Va   (Elizabeth Peyton 1844cc)
   Henry                  5
   Mary                   3
   Hiram                  1            (m Margaret Price SO)
```

```
329-340
   Sarah Adkins          46    Va
   Thomas                12
   Polly                 10
330-341
   Benjamin Spears       26    OH farmer
   Anna                  25
   Rhoda                 10
   Sally                  8
   Henry                  5
   John                   1
331-342
   William Spears        39    Va farmer
   Sally                 30
   Willie                12
332-343
   Joseph Adkins         26    Va laborer
   Margaret              37        (Bragg 1842cc)
   Susan                 16
   Melvina                7
   Sarah A.               5
   Daniel D.              2
333-344
   Harrison Davis        27    Va farmer
   Louisa                19        (Drake 1848cc)
   Henderson C.           1
   Frances DRAKE(f)       2
334-345
   Henderson Drake       43    TN farmer (m Amacetta Hatfield 1852cc)
   Nancy Drake           63    Md     (Atkins-m-James 1797 Mont.Co.SO)
   Penelope              17    Va
   James                 15        (m Emmarine Brumfield 23 mar 1859cc)
   Guy                   11
   Blackbourn(m)          8
   Osbourn(m)             5
335-346
   John Campbell         50    Md farmer
   Elizabeth             56        (Carter 1829cc)
   Francis HUMPHREY(m)   15        farmer
336-347
   John L.Baker          36    Va farmer
   Arminda               38    TN
   James McCOMAS         16
   Elizabeth DRAKE        2        (see 345)
337-348
   Bailey Copley         26        Farmer
   Adaline               21         (Hatfield SO)
p49
338-349
   James Hatfield        59    Va farmer     d1853 SO-(s/o Isaac)
   Zarelda               50    NC    (Dunlap 1822cc)
   Amicetta              28    Va    (m Henderson Darake 1852cc)
   Harriet               23
   James A.              24        farmer (m Marietta Messenger 1871 SO)
   Frances               18
   Andrew J.             16        farmer (m Eleanor Brumfield 1856 SO)
   Eliza P.              15             (m Mary Sanders 1875 SO)
   Martha(Ann)           12
   Emily                 11             (m Overton Hatfield 1856cc)
   America(M.A)           8             (m John foster 1870 SO)
   Samantha O.            3             (m Solomon Burchett SO)
```

```
339-350
  William Smith          67    Pa farmer
  Sarah                  50    Va   (Hatfield 1811cc)
  Elizabeth              25         (m David Burns 1851cc)
  Matilda                21
  Ellener                18
  David F.               21         farmer
  Cynthia A.             17
  Isaac                  27         laborer
340-351
  James Smith            28    Va Farmer.
  Tennessee              29
  Guy                    10
  Mary J.                 6
  Julia A.                5
  Rebecca                 3
  William O.              2
  Addison                 1
341-352
  Ballard Smith          34    Va farmer
  Susannah               19
  David                   2
  Luana                10/12
342-353
  Lewis Adkins           35    Va farmer (2-Emmazetta Brumfield SO)
  Melcina                29         (Hunter SO)
  Evermont               11
  Anderville              7
  Albert                  5
  Hansford                3
  Bartlett ADKINS        18         laborer
  Ida ADKINS             18
p50
343-354
  Rice Elkins            30    Va farmer
  Mary                   45         (Blankenship 1839cc)
  Elizabeth BLANKENSHIP  14
  Ralph BLANKENSHIP      12
344-355
  Harvey Elkins          49    Va farmer (s/o Richard SO)
  Elizabeth              44         (Mays SO)
  Parthena               25
  Milton                 23
  Elenor                 21
  Overton                19         farmer
  Elizabeth              17
  Nancy                  14
  John                   11
  Mary                    8
  Leander                 3
345-356
  Fernandez Hatfield     23    Va farmer
  Mary E.                25         (Franklin 1846cc)
  Julia A.                4
  Elizabeth A.            2
  Adria A.A.           6/12
346-357
  Harvey Smith           32    Va farmer
  Sarah                  28
  Ann T.                 10
  Harrison Z.A.           3
```

```
347-358
  Samuel Parsons          51    Va farmer
  Thurza                  58
  John                    14
  Ehervel (f)             12
  Cynthia                  9
348-359
  William Johnson         24    OH farmer
  Susannah                26    Va   (Parsons 1841cc)
  Louisa                   8
  John W.                  6
  Hannah                   4
  Jonathan                 1
349-360
  George Hager            34    OH farmer
  Rachael                 27    Va   (Johnson 1844cc)
  John                     5
  Wesley R.                4
  Hannah                   1
350-361
  James Beckelhimer       21    Va farmer
  Mary A.                 27          (? Parsons widow)
  Susannah PARSONS         9
  William R.PARSONS        4
  Robertson PARSONS        2
  Margaret PARSONS        64    Pa
  Hannah PARSONS          33    OH
page 51
351-362
  Thomas Stephenson       35    Va farmer
  Malinda                 30    TN   (Hunter 1845cc)
  America                  4
  Adalene                  2
  Francis M.(m)            1
352-363                                     HENRY FRANCE ROAD
  Anna France             42    Va
  James                   16          laborer (m Viola -cem#S20)
  Reny A.(f)              12
  Julia A.               12
  Rebecca A.              8
  Benjamin                5                        (cem#S20)
353-364
  Alonzo Kitchen          26    Va laborer
  Margaret                26          (Hunter SO)
  Eliza S.                 7
354-365
  Armstrong Stephenson    28    Va
  Caroline                19
  Christopher              3
  Frances P.(f)            1
355-366
  George Stephenson       49    Va farmer
  Nancy                   48          (Moore 1824cc)
  Amanda                  14
  Rutha A.                22
356-367
  John T.Adkins           34    Va farmer
  Nancy                   23          (Dial 1848cc)
  Lucretia                13
  William P.              12
```

```
356-367 Adkins(con't)
  Joseph                     10
  Rachael                     8
  Eliza A.                    5
  Susan                       1
357-368
  Richard Adkins             45          farmer
  Lucinda                    50             (Mrs.Hunter 1828cc)
  Alfred                     21
  Samuel                     18
  James                      16
  Nancy                      13
  Lewis R.                    8
----369
  Lickins Adkins             24          farmer (s/o 368)
  Eliza                      22
358-370
  John L.Franklin            33    Va tanner
  Ellenor                    32
  Julia A.                   10
  Elizabeth                   7
  Evermont                    2
359-371
  Jessee W. McComas          24    Va farmer
  Mary E.                    25
  Cynthia                  6/12
360-372
  Isaac McComas              63    Va farmer
  Nancy                      55
  Ballard                    35
  Jefferson                  22
  Andrew                     20
  Isaac                      19
  Wellington G.KENNISON 18             laborer
361-373
  Harrison McComas           36    Va farmer
  Valeria                    27
  Benjamin F.                10
  Nancy                       8
  Blackbourn                  6
  Eliza                       3
  James EDWARDS              60          laborer
  Elisha EDWARDS            55          farmer
362-374
  Daniel McMillon            72    Va farmer
  Margaret                   58
  Daniel J.                  21          farmer
  Clement C.                 20          laborer (m Sarah Matthews 1851cc)
  James W.                   18          laborer
  Rebecca A.                 17
  Margaret                   15
  Amanda                     28
  Gilbert W.                  4
  William                     1
363-375                                    MUD RIVER at BLUE SULPHUR
  Elijah Turley              27    Va lawyer          cem#S51
  Agnes                      24
```

```
364-376
   Harvey Newman          42    Va farmer
   Mary                   42         (Ann Jefferson 1828 cc)
   William A.             16
   Caroline               14
   Albert                 11
   Elizabeth               8
   Lucinda                 5
   Harvey                  1
Pg.53
365-377
   Joseph Montgomery      35    Va farmer
   Charlette              34
   Mary                   12
   Elizabeth             10
   Minerva                8
   Martha                 6
   James                  1
366-378                                 MUD RIVER at MERRITTS CK
   William Derton        40    Va farmer              cem#17
   Sarah                 37        (Wintz 1832 cc)
   Mary A.E.             16
367-379                                 MUD RIVER at MERRITTS CK
   William Stroupe       57    Va farmer              cem#17
   Margaret              51        (Merritt 1817cc        cem#17
   Catherine             62
368-380                                 MUD RIVER at MERRITTS CK
   Joseph Wentz          55    Va farmer
   Mary                  49         (Polly Merritt 1820cc)
   Elizabeth             27
   John W.               18    Va farmer
   Lewis M.               9                       (cem. #23)
   Wm. L.              3/12
369-381
   Rufus Leonard         45        farmer
   Mary                  47         (Elizabeth Wentz 1830cc)
   Cyntha A.             18         (m-A. Jackson Dick 1851 cc)
   Mary E. WENTZ         72
   Joseph DICK           13
370-382
   Elia A. Jenkins  (m)  37    Va joiner
   Lucenda               28
   Hannah                 7
   William S.             5
   Mary E.                4
   Serena DORMAN    (f)  25
   Benjamin PAINE        14    Eng.
371-383                                  Mouth of FUDGE
   Thomas Dundas         51    Va farmer
   Eliza                 55        (sister)            cem#S51
   Sophia M. PEYTON      52
   Mary WATSON           12    La
372-384
   Andrew Warren         30    Va minister
   Mary A.               30
   Marion L.              5
   Clark B.               3
   John L.                2
   Augustus N.         8/12
```

p54
373-385   MUD RIVER
```
  Joseph Newman          47    Va farmer
  Margaret               38
  Mary A.                22
  Nancy                  19
  Jasper                 17       farmer
  Cyrus P.      (m)      14
  Sarah M.               11
  Malinda L.              8
  Joseph A.               4
  Sylvanus T.             3
  Joseph CYRUS           23       LABORER
374-386                              between FUDGE & BLUE SULPHUR
  Henry T. Dundas        47    Va farmer (b-Alexander, Va)
  Margaret               43
  John                   22                            cem#S51
  Elizabeth              17       (m- John Dick 1852 cc)
  Thomas                 16       (m-Martha Turley 1855)
  Virginia               14                            cem#S51
  James                  10                            cem#S51
  Agnes                   9
  Henry                   7
  William                 4
  Charles                 2                            cem#S51
375-387                               east end of BARBOURSVILLE
  Mathew Lusher          36    Va farmer               cem#S25
  Margaret               29       (Blake) (d/o Peter 1841cc)
  Sarah                   7       (m- Wm. Lusher)
  James M.                5
  Mary L.                 4
  Taliaferreo   (m)       1
  Morris                 13
376-388
  John W. Blake          24       farmer
  Nancy                  22       (Kinnard 1846cc)
  Albert E.              41
  Edna                    1
377-389                               east end of BARBOURSVILLE
  Sarah Blake            48    Va   w/o Peter
  Nancy                  22
  Peter                  18       farmer
  Isaac                  15       farmer (m- Mary A. Kilgore 1854cc)
  Martha                 13       (m- Salmon 1855 SO)
378-390
  John King              51    Va laborer
  Catherine              55       (McCOMAS 1822 LCoh)
  Sampson S.             19       laborer
  Mary A.                17       (m- David Payton 1850cc)
  Catherine M. KENNAN    13 (f)
  Sidney M.KENNAN        11
  William KENNAN          9
p55
379-391
  Lucinda Dodd           34    Va
  John L.                11
  Letitia G.              9
  James L.     (?)        8
  Henrietta L.            3
```

54

```
380-392                                      MARTHA east of RIVER
  Joseph W. Roffe        37    Va farmer
  Rebecca                32
  Cynthia A.             13        (m-John Tasson 1852 cc)
  Thomas J.              12
  William D.             10
  Lucretia A.             7
  Charles P.              3
  Eliza F.            11/12
381-393                                      DAVIS CREEK wB'ville
  Patrick H. McCullough  34    Pa merchant              cem#H10
  Rachael W.             29    Va                        cem#S23
  Isadora T.              8
  Julius W.               6
  Louisiana SELLERS      27    La
382-394
  Archibald McVicker     48    Va farmer
  Permalia               43
  Hiliry   (m)           18        farmer
  Pattie                 16
  Rachael                13
  Rebecca                11
  Sarah A.                9
  Almira                  7
  John                    4
  James                   2
383-395                                      MARTHA east of RIVER
  Charles O. Roffe       41    Va Merchant (m-Mary Ruffner of Charleston)
                                              1855DD
  Cyrus MOORE            52    Maine S. Public Works
  Lucinda MOORE          52
  Orson  MOORE           28        Lumberer
  Albert MOORE           25        lumberer
  Ann S. MOORE           20
  Helen H.MOORE          17
384-396                                      MARTHA east of RIVER
  Wm.(C)Dusenberry       57    N.Y. merchant
  Susan                  49    Pa
  Robert                 12    N.Y.
  Samuel                  8
---397                                       MARTHA east of RIVER
  William F. Dusenberry  23    N.Y. dentist             cem#H10
  Cynthia                24                              cem#H10
  Susan                   1
  Ann PANDERLY           18    Ireland
  Andrew PANDERLY        22    Va laborer
  Peter WHITE            30    GERMANY laborer (m-Mary Blackwood 1855cc)
                                  (miller later at Howell's Mill)cem#14
385-398
  John Thompson          45    Va teamster
  Cary B.                30
  Susan                  18
  Isaac                  14
  Jemimah                12
  Mary                    6
  George                  2
```

MARTHA west of RIVER

```
386-399
  Benjamin Bowman        46    Va miller
  Sophia                 45
  Samuel                  7
  Sophia                  5
  Thomas                4/12
387-400
  Andrew Dodson          22    Va farmer
  Mary S.                19
  George W.               2
388-401
  Elisha Dodson          23    Va farmer
  Lucy A.                24
  Elisha W.               1
  Elizabeth              40
  William                10
389-402
  James Meacham          21    Va laborer
  Mary                   18
  Joanna                3/12
390-403
  Clark Thurston         35    Vt laborer
  Evelene                28    Va
  Charles W.            5/12
```

MARTHA

```
391-404
  Samuel Childers        35    Va joiner
  Catherine              30
  Sarah E.               10
  William                 8
  George W.               6
  Patrick H.             11
  John M.                 2
  Samuel                8/12
p57
```

MARTHA

```
392-405
  William Rogers         34    Va farmer
  Clarinda               31       (Bias 1838 cc)
  Fenton       (f)       11
  George                  9
  Wilson                  7
  Thomas M.               5
  Elizabeth               3
  Cynthia                 1
```

MARTHA

```
393-406
  William Thompson       66    Va  farmer
  Margaret A.            49
  Virginia               37
  Patterson   THOMPSON   69
  Rebecca     THOMPSON   62
```

MARTHA

```
394-407
  Patterson W. Thompson  30    Va farmer
  Sarah                  26
  Thadeus                 7
  Patterson W.            5
  Ellen   THOMPSON       64
395-408
  Watson S. Davis        42    Va blacksmith
  Rebecca A.             44
  Jemima F.              17
  Elizabeth              15
```

```
395-408 Davis(con't)
    John W.                 14
    James F.                12
    Robert W.               10
    Richard A.               8
    Frances A.   (f)         7
    Frederick M.             5
    Susan D.                 3
    Watson                4/12
396-409
    Chelsey Davis (m)       19    Va
    Ginetta       (f)       18                          McCOMAS RD-TOM'S CREEK
397-410
    John Peyton             44    Va farmer                (probably cem#S43)
    Elizabeth PEYTON        85
    Milly                   40                               cem#S43
    Elisha                  18
----411
    Mary Reins              25
    Eliza J.                 8
    William                  5
    Elizabeth                2
398-412
    Waldon Beach            51    Va
    Mary J.                 35        (Polly Steele 1831cc)
    Caroline M.             16
    Samuel                  14
    Celia A.                12
    Hannah                   7
    Columbus                 5
    John W.                  3
    Sarah S.                 1
399-413
    James Wilkes            67    Va farmer
    Mary                    54
    Elizabeth               16                          McCOMAS RD at TOM'S CREEK
400-414
    Mary Peyton             52    Va
    William                 26    Va farmer
    Perry                   28       farmer
    Mary J.                 13
    Susannah                 8
    Sabrina WILKES   (f)    36
401-415
    Richard Lunsford        28    OH farmer
    Nancy                   20    Va
    Mary                     2
402-416
    William Lunsford        34    Va farmer
    Martha                  28
    John T.                  7
    Nancy A. K.              5
    William S.            8/12
403-417
    Joseph Stanley          29    Va
    Cynthia                 27
    Eliza J.                 8
    George W.                6
    Samuel                   4
    Margaret                 2
    Charicy REINS (f)       29  (see 411)
```

```
                                                        LOWER TOM'S CREEK
404-418
  John Morrison          65    Va farmer                    cem #S44
  Nancy                  65                                  cem #s44
405-491
  Charles Peyton         60    Va farmer
  Alexander              24       farmer                      ⌄
  Eliza                  21
  Charles                19       farmer
  Elizabeth              16
  William                11
  Mary                    9
  Minerva McCOY          26
                                                        LOWER TOM'S CREEK
406-420
  Calvary Swan           30    Va    (s/o Leven)             cem#S44
  Emily J.               31          (Morrison 1841cc)       cem#S44
  Isaiah                  9
  Ambrose D.              7                                   cem#S44
  Henry                   6
  Mary A.                 4
  Calvery M.              2
  Benjamin F.             1
p54
407-421
  John McKeand           37    Va farmer
  America                36          (McComas 1834cc-d/o Elisha-SO)
  William                14
  Alexander              13
  Sarah A.                6
  Eliza                   4          (m Lewis Hinchman cc)
  Emily                   1

408-422                              (s/o Leven)          OUSLEY GAP
  Josiah Swan            54    Va farmer (1-Edith Maab 1819cc) cem#S44
  Rachael                36          (Morrison 1830cc)
  John T.                19       farmer
  Benjamin F.            17          (m Louisa Hatfield 1852cc)
  Elizabeth              14
  Beverly J.             12
  Amicetta                8          (m William Alger 1858cc)    cem#S44
  Thomas J.               6
  Cynthia A.              4
  Sarah                   2
  George W.            9/12
409-423
  William Williams       50    Va farmer
  Nancy                  31          (Cornell 1836cc)
  John H.                11
  Elizabeth               9
  Mary A.                 8
  Spencer                 6
  Eliza F.                4
  America                 2
  Miriam                  1
410-424
  James Morris           20    Va farmer
  Helen M.               21          (Russell CCA)
  Joseph W.               1          (m Fanny McKendree CCA)
  Moriah MORRIS          18
  Louisa MORRIS          14
```

```
411-425
  Rolen Bias              28    Va farmer
  Matilda BIAS(mother)    43       (Turner ? w/o Linsey Bias SO)
  Emily P.                16
  Jerrimiah               21       farmer
  William                 18       farmer (Elizabeth Burns 1852cc)
  Lindsey M.              16            (m Martha Vickers SO)
                                       (Mary A. Bias 1851cc)
p60
----426
  William B.Mitchell      29    Va farmer
  Elizabeth G.            32
  John J.G.                6
  Lucy A.               6/12
412-427
. Andrew Burns            45    Va farmer (m1829 SO) (s/oPeter&Jane)
  James                   21       laborer
  David                   18       farmer (m Elizabeth J.Smith 1851 SO)
  Elizabeth               17            (m Elizabeth Bias SO)
  Mary A.                 15
  Margaret                14
  Sampson                 11
  Delila                  10
  Seabird(m)               7
  John H.                  5
413-428
  Andrew J.Hatfield       35    Va farmer
  Frances                 32            (Pinnell 1836cc)
  Mary F.                 12
  Benjamin L.             10
  Phoebe P.                3
  America L.R.           3/12
414-429     (s/o Andrew of Orange Co.)              ROACH
  Adam Hatfield           75    Va farmer(w/oMary William 1799)cem#S45
  Andrew L.BECKETT        26       farmer                   cem#S67
  Emily BECKETT           26       (Hatfield 1850cc -Andrew) cem#S45
415-430                                            ROACH
  Moses Hatfield          28    Va farmer            (cem#S45)
  Penina                  29       (Beckett )         cem#S45
  Martha                   6       (m Adam Hinchman )  cem#S45
  Lucinda H.               4
  Albert W.                1
416-431                                            ROACH
  Thomas Dial             32    Va farmer
  Elizabeth               26       (Swan 1840cc)
  Hosena A.(f)             8
  Nancy E.                 6
  Emily A.                 4
  Louisa F.               2
417-432
  Harrison Peyton         29    Va farmer
  Elizabeth               25
  Henrietta                1
418-433                                            ROACH
  Armstead Howell         45    Va miller(bought Howell's Mill)cem# 14
  Frances                 50
  John H.                 17       (m Elizabeth Hatfield 1851cc)
  Sarah KEYTON            10
  James BUTCHER            7
```

p61
----434

Archibald Peyton	30	Va laborer	(cem# 14)
Susan	18		
Sarah C.	6/12		
James GILLENWATERS	92	Va Rev.Soldier	
		(d 15 mar 1856	cem#S44)

419-435

Mary Casey	50	Va
Louisa	19	
Marietta	2	

420-436

Morris L.Ford	38	Va farmer	
Mariah	35		(Bannister 1840MM)
Robert	8		
Mary	6		
Willard B.	3		
Caroline	1		

421-437

James M.Ford	32	Va farmer
Mary A.	26	
Ethelbridge (m)	5	
George	3	
Chesley B. (m)	1	

422-438

Nathaniel F.Burrel	39	Mo Carpenter
Peter EDBEY	43	Mo shoemaker
George PITENZIL	23	NH laborer

423-439   east side SALT ROCK

Patrick Keenan	56	Va farmer	cem#S99E
Rebecca	51	(McComas 1818cc)	cem#S99E
David	21		
Cynthia A.	18		
Nancy	16		

424-440

William M.Williams	37	Va farmer
Matilda	39	(Parsons widow ?_)
James PARSONS	7	

425-441   (s/o John)   SALT ROCK

Elisha Shelton	33	Va farmer	
Elizabeth	32	(Mitchell 1839cc)	cem#S99F
John W.	10		
Sarah F.	7		
Mary F.	4		
Anderson B.	10/12		
Henrietta SHELTON	15	(d/o John)(m John G. 1851 SO)	

426-442

Harvey Johnson	33	Va farmer
America	25	
William W.	5	
Rebecca A.	3	

p62
427-443   (see 444,448,449,339   SALT ROCK

Christopher Sites	64	Germany farmer	
Sarah	62	Va	
Godfrey	28	(Mary McComas 1855cc) cem#S99A	
Mary	23	(m Henry Johnson 1853cc)	

```
428-444
  Sarah Sites              26           (2-?- Bennett Johnson 1854cc)
  Mary F.                   5
  John V.                   1
429-445
  Burwell Johnson          54      Va farmer
  Catherine                18              (m James William 1855-Logan Co.SO)
  Squire                   16
  Benjamin JOHNSON         85           farmer (?Mary McCallister 1814KCM)
430-446
  Smoot Johnson            35      Va farmer
  Minerva                  26
  Nancy                     8
  Eveline                   6
  Columbus                  4
  Iva (f)                   2
----447
  Olly Johnson(f)          48
  Richard                  21           laborer
  Delila                   15
                                                        SALT ROCK
431-448
  John Sites               37      Germany farmer
  Susannah                 35      Va      (Porter 1839cc)
  Thomas J.                11
  Christopher A.            9
  John F.M.                 7
  Charles S.                4
  Catherine S.              2
                                                        SALT ROCK
432-449
  Gottlob Scites           32      Germany
  Catherine                29      Va
  Harriet F.                4
  Elias W.H.                2
433-450
  Andrew Johnson           25      Va laborer
  Lucinda                  18      OH
  Rebecca                7/12      OH
434-451
  Sampson Johnson          27      Va farmer (w/o Emaline Russell 1844cc)
  Christina                20           (Scites ?2nd)
  Cinderella                7
  Melton                 5/12
435-452
  Andrew Chapman           56      Va farmer
  Julia                    50           (McComas 1820cc)
  John                     26      constable(m Malvina Barrett 1850 SO)
  Cynthia                  20
  James                    17
  Elizabeth                15
p63
436-453   (see 683)
  Bird Hensley             39      Va laborer
  Nancy                    38
  Lucinda                  20
  Belinda                  18
  Elizabeth                16
  William                  11
  Mary A.                   9
  Sarah                     6
  Columbus                  3
```

```
437-454
  Andrew McComas          51   Va farmer(w/o Cinderella McComas 1832cc)
  Sarah E.                15
  Emily                   12
  William W.               9
  Mary K.                  7
438-455
  Eli H.Whalton           30   Va merchant
  Susan                   35
  Waldo W.                 5
  Mary                     2
  Lawrence LETULLE        15      clerk
  John LETULLE            13      (see 797)
439-456
  David Shelton           32   Va farmer (s/o John SO)
  Elizabeth               18
440-457
  Andrew Shawns           50   Va laborer
  Sarah                   40
  Prestley                13
  Elizabeth WILLIAMS      16
  George W.WILLIAMS       21
441-458
  Nicholas Messinger      60   Va miller
  Mary                    60        (Williams SO)
  John H.                 10
  George W.                7
  Emily                   14
  Mary J.McCOMAS          20
442-459
  Abel Rock               46   Va lumberer
  Sarah                   42   Ky
  Pauline                  8   Ky
  George                  11   Ky
  Joseph                   5   Ky
443-460
  Jerome Shelton          29   Va blacksmith (s/o John SO)
  Malinda                 22        (Messinger 1843 cc)
  Luzana                   6
  Eliza A.                 4
  Susan                    2
444-461
  Jerimiah Witcher        53   Va farmer
  Polly                   40        (Thompson 1849cc)
  Emily                   12        (m Benjamin Curry 1860cc)
  John                    11
  America                  6
  Valeria                  4
  Sarah WITCHER           86
page 64
445-462
  John W.Peyton           35   Va Physician
446-463
  Thomas Dial             43   Va farmer
  Polly                   43
  William                 21      farmer
  Andrew J.               18        (m Margaret Toney SO)
  Mary                    15
  Thomas S.               14
```

```
446-463 Dial (con't)
   John A.                 12
   Susannah                 8
   Clemetta (f)             7
   Cynthia                  1
447-464
   Joiner Dial (?Triner)   53    Va laborer
   Lucy                    43
   Permelia                17
   Pricy                   15
   Elizabeth               12
   Phebe                    9
   Mary                     7          idiot
   Rhantha(f)      .        5
   William                  2
   Caroline                 5
   William ELLINGTON       80          none
448-465
   John Dial               38    Va farmer
   Caroline                35          (Wilkinson 1838cc-(Willarson/iamson)
   James                    9
   Elizabeth S.             6
   William, W.              5
   George W.                2
   Judy A.                  2
   John W.               4/12
   John A.DIAL             80    Va farmer (s/o James & Nancy SO)
   Mary A.DIAL             76          (Sprinkle-m Stokes Co.NC-SO)
   Willam P.STAFFORD       25    NC
p65
449-466
   Abbott Rowe             40    Va farmer
   Anna                    36
   Almida                  10
   Eldridge                 9
   Parker                   8
   George                   6
   Lewis M.                 4
   Polly                    3
   John                     1
   John ROWE               65    Va farmer
450-467
   Emily Terry             31    Va
   Icabod                  13
   America                 11
   Ferrily (f)              9
   Betsy                    7
   James                    7
   Emily                    3
451-468
   Thomas Parsons          20    Va farmer
   Lydia                   19
452-469
   Henry Eplin             46    Va farmer
   Jane                    46          (Adkins 1823cc)
   William                 22          farmer
   Randal                  21          farmer
   Rhoda                   15
   John                    13
   Julia                   13
```

```
452-469 Eplin (con't)
  Nancy                10
  Polly                 8
  Russell               6
  Charity               4
  Elizabeth             2
453-470
  Samuel Harris        51     Va farmer
  Nancy                48
  Jane                 25     Ky
  Greenville           22     Ky laborer (m Ruth Stephenson 1851cc)
  Henry                18     Ky laborer
  Nancy                16     Ky      (m Ferandez Hatfield SO)
  John                 10     Ky
p66
454-471
  Edward Parsons       50     Va farmer
  Elizabeth            42
  Rebecca              16
  John                 14
  Edward               10
  William               5
  Ballard            8/12
  Guy MILLER           14
  Isham MILLER         10
455-472
  Benjamin S.Davis     66     Va farmer
  Sarah                65     TN
  James                24     Va
  Sarah F.ADAMS        19
  Polly DICK           19
456-473
  William Mays         24     Ky farmer
  Susanna S.           18     Ky
  Dicy A.           10/12 Va
457-474
  Sherwood Shelby      42     Va farmer
  Susanah              41
  Victoria              9
458-475
  George Douglas       28     Va farmer
  Elizabeth            25          (Dial 1844cc)
  William H.            6
  Mary F.               3
459-476
  Calvin Lucas         40     Va farmer
  Rebecca              40
  Daniel D.            18          farmer
  William P.           15          farmer
  Mary E.              10
  Samuel H.             8
  Martha                3
  David PARSONS        79          none
460-477
  William H.Harless    35     Va farmer
  Nancy                35          (Douglas So)
  James H.             15          farmer
  Polly J.             12
  John A.               9
  George W.             8
  Josepha B.(M)         6
  Joseph M.             2
  Elizabeth DOUGLAS    32
```

```
461-478
  John McComas            61    Va farmer
  Mary                    54        (Barnes 1813cc)
  Minerva F.              32
  Elisha E.               24
  James M.                24        farmer
  Sarah A.K.              13
p67
----479
  John Peyton             36    Va farmer
  Judith B.               31
  William H.               7
462-480
  Lewis Midkiff           43    Va farmer
  Elizabeth               41        (Condon 1832cc)
  Lucy                    16        (m Elisha Childers SO)
  Abraham H.              14
  John A.                 13
  Spencer                 12
  Harriett                 9
  Adalene                  7
  Sarah                    5
  Solomon                  4
  Mary M.                  2
  Joseph B.             3/12
463-481
  Abraham Coobs           53    Maine manager
  Moses POOCK             18    Maine laborer
  Elisha F.PEAS           30    Maine cook
  Samuel KELLY            53    Maine ship carpenter
  A.M.KINNON              40    Maine ship carpenter
  Thomas SHERMAN          21    Maine tinker
464-482                                                  SALT ROCK
  Spencer Midkiff         40    Va farmer
  Vitura (Vitoria)        31        (McComas 1839cc)
  Julia                   10
  Sarah J.                 8
  Alexander                6
  Walden                   4
  Emma                     3
  Albert                   1
  Nathaniel Booth         22
465-483
  Jessie Paine            30     Va farmer
  Milly                   28
466-484                          (Montgomery Co.)        FUDGE CREEK
  James Beckett           75    Va farmer               cem#S67
  Hannah                  62        (Lee 1814cc)(Patrick Co)cem#S67
  Lenis C.C.(f)           21
  Lucinda McCALISTER      26
  Hannah A.McCALISTER      2
467-485
  John Stanly             27     Va farmer
  Elizabeth               26        (Mays 1841cc)
  Columbus M.              2
  William F.            3/12
```

p68

468-486

Isaac McCalister	34	Va farmer	
Rebecca	34	(Ervin 1845MM)	
Margaret J.	13		
Richard A.	12		
Susannah	9		
Sarah A.	6		
Mary F.	4		
James A.	3		

469-487

Robert Ervin	32	Va farmer
Sarah A.	24	
William L.	6	
Sarah J.	2	

TYLER CREEK

470-488

Joseph Sidebottom	43	Va Physician	
Nancy	43		
Joseph C.	13		
John	9		cem#S62
James A.	5		

471-489

James McComas	22	OH
Mary A.	22	Eng
George W.	1	OH

472-490

Richard McCalister	58	Va farmer
Sarah	58	
James	15	

473-491

Thomas McComas	46	Va blacksmith
Elizabeth	24	
John W.	1	

Water Gap-FUDGE CREEK

474-492

John McCalister	33	Va farmer	cem#S69
Mariah	24	(Ervin 1842MM)	cem#S69
Martha J.	5		
Preston	4		
Malinda	2		
Isaac	7/12		cem#S69

475-493 FUDGE CREEK

Preston McCalister	26	Va farmer
America	19	
Mary A.	1	

476-494 (Susannah Chapel) FUDGE CREEK

Charles Beckett	23	Va farmer
Susannah	21	
Louisa J.	2/12	

477-495

Mourning Williams (f)	51	Va
Nancy	35	
Louisa	7	

p69

478-496

Andrew J. Smith	20	Va farmer
Mary	19	
Sarah M.	10/12	

```
479-497
  Absolum Bias            30    Va farmer
  Elizabeth               31       (Butcher 1838cc)
  William A.              11
  John N.                  8
  Marietta                 6
  Melvil (m)               4
  James P.                 2
  Broadus D.(m)            2
  Mary A.                 16       insane
480-498
  John Bias               60    Va farmer
  Sarah                   57       (Ray 1819 SO)
  James                   18
  Mary                    16
  Charlotta               12
  William B.              10
481-499                                               TYLER CREEK
  Benjamin L.Perry        42    Va minister          cem#S73A
  Julia A.                43     (Beluah Hawkins by   cem#S73A
  William B.              18       farmer (m Mary A.Ray 1852cc)
  Elizabeth               17         (m Benjamin Morris 1851cc)
  Silas B.                15       farmer (m Zepha Midkiff) cem#S62
  Elijah Hawkins.         13                          cem#S73A
  Peter F.                10         (m Nancy Francis  cem#S62
  Benjamin D.              8         (m Emily V.       cem#S62
  Thomas H.                5
  John James               3                          cem#73A
  Martha J.                1
  Benjamin MORRIS         21       farmer(m Elizabeth Perry 1851cc)
482-500
  Henry S.Hawkins         30    Va farmer
  Elizabeth               22
  Silia C.(f) (Celia)      1
483-501
  Elijah Hawkins          36    Va farmer
  Elias Hawkins           36    Va farmer
484-502                                               ZOAR-BALL'S GAP
  Alexander McCalister    28    Va farmer            cem#S59
  Helen                   28                          cem#S59
  Emily                    4
  Henry M.                 2
485-503
  Obadiah Bias            26    Va farmer
  Martha J.               22
p70
486-504        (s/o Benj)
  William Ray             42    Va farmer
  Julia P.                43
  Mary A.                 20
  Morris                  19
  Andrew                  15
  John                     8
487-505
  David Ray               22    Va    (Wray)
  Catherine               24          (Hatfield  1849cc)
```

```
488-506
  Andrew Johnson          38    Va farmer
  Alcey                   36         (Rutherford 1835cc)
  Harvey                  13
  Jefferson               12
  Rebecca                 10
  Emeline                  8
  William                  4
  Henry                    2
489-507
  William Johnson         34    Va farmer
  Sarah                   31         (Williams   1840cc)
  Thomas J.                9
  John W.                  7
  James G.                 5
490-508
  Wesley Johnson          31    Va farmer
  Senia (Acentha)         26         (Johnson 1845 cc)
  Ritty A.                 4
  Angeline                 1
491-509
  Perry Johnson           39    Va farmer
  Serrena                 36         (Adkins 1833cc)
  Andrew                  16
  Cynthia A.              14
  America                  9
  Lavana                   7       (m-Evermont Brumfield SO)
492-510
  John Johnson            25    Va farmer
  Henrietta               25
  Mary                     3
  James JOHNSON           25         farmer
  Sarah JOHNSON           24
  Mary JOHNSON            64
  Eliza JOHNSON    (f)    27
  Rebecca JOHNSON         20         (m-David Keenan 1851cc)
  Wilson JOHNSON           5
     (Mother-married son/wife/child-3 unmarried -dau-in-law & son??
p71
493-511
  Larkin Bias             50    Va farmer(1-Martha Porter 1826cc)
  Rutha                   48         (Childers 1830cc)
  Lindsay                 17
  James                   13
  Obadiah                 10
  Thomas                   8
  Cornelius                4
494-512                         (Vincent Nowland & Vinson Nowell)
  Winston Noel            49    Va farmer
  Mary                    41
  Angeline                16
  Emiline                 14
  Mary J.                 12
  Wilks                    8
  Matilda A.               6
  Nancy                    3
```

495-513
  William Mahone   23   Va farmer
  Nancy   29   (Carroll 1831cc)
  Mahala F.   7
  Virgil H.   4
  Bennet D.   1
  James REACH   12
496-514
  James T. Carroll   60   Va farmer
  Margaret   56   (? Black SO)
  Cynthia A.   17
  William A.   13
  Nancy CLARK   50   Ky (pauper)
497-515
  John Fary   32   farmer
  Elizabeth   25
  Mary F.   2
  Leatha A.   7/12
498-516
  James Webb   72   Va Rockingham Co farmer
  Elizabeth   69
  Cynthia A. Zircle   8   (granddaughter)SO
499-517
  Geo. W. Zircle   32   Va carpenter
  Elizabeth   31   (Webb SO)
  Andrew J.   8
  James L.   6
  Amanda W.   5
  George W.   2
500-518
  Cynthia Miller   50   Va
  Sarah HOLTON   (F)   62
501-519
  Nicholas Lake   27   Va farmer
  Rachael   32
  Robert A.   6
  Henry N.   4
  Christopher   1
p72
502-520
  James B. Snodgrass   41   Va Farmer
  Mildred   25   Ky (Row 1843cc)
  Mary A.   16   Va
  James H.   14
  Joseph R.   13
  Rebecca M.   12
  George W.   4
  William A.   2
  Nancy A.   10/12
  James SNODGRASS   76   Va farmer
503-521   MILTON
  James H. Rece   39   Va   cem#S54
  Rebecca   30   cem#S54
  Elizabeth J.   10
  James A.   7
  Martha A.   5
  Thomas H.   3
  Rebecca A.   1

```
504-522
  Rachael Adkins  (f)      39    Va
  Elizabeth                41
  Phebe                    11
  Amanda F.                 7
  Alexander J.              4
  Mary F.                   8
505-523
  Timothy Adkins           21    Va farmer
  Mary A.                   20         (Holton 1847cc)
  Nathaniel                 5
  Charles W.                2
  Malitta     (f)        8/12
506-524
  Polly Bragg              25    Va
  Ferrily                   1
507-525
  Silas Cooper             60    Va farmer
  Lucy                     60
  Hudson                   26         farmer
508-526
  Frances Adkins   (f)     30
  Oma                       7
  Isabel                    5
  Judy                      3    (m-Hudson Cooper s/o Silas & Lucy SO)
509-527
  Francis Adkins   (m)     21    Va farmer
  Elizabeth                16
510-528                                            MADISON CREEK
  William Holly            26    Va farmer
  Margaret                 27
  Andrew J.                 4
  Lucy J.                   3
  James F.               3/12
p73
511-529                                   REUBEN BR-MADISON CREEK
  Charles Holton           59    Pa. Miller
  Frances                  63    Va (Holly 1822cc)
  Alfred H.                 8
  Lovicy F.                 6
  Andrew S. HOLLY          16    Va Farmer
512-530
  Allen A. Holstein        33    Va farmer
  Mary                     31         (Hatstead SO)
  Albert                    8         (m- Elizabeth Adkins SO)
  Lettride     (m)          7
  Doliver B.   (m)          5
  Perry F.                  3
513-531
  James A. Holly           30    Va farmer(1-Nancy Holcolm 1843cc)
  Margaret                 27
  David S.                  4
  Warren D.                 3
  Julia A.                  1
514-532
  Francis Johnson          48    Va farmer (1-McClung ?SO)
  Ida E.                   32         (Kelly 1834cc)
  Squire A.                14
  Charles A.               12
  Benjamin A.              10
```

```
514-532 Johnson (con't)
   James A.              7
   Sarah                5
   Martha               3
   Crosby  (f)          6/12
   Caroline ADKINS      20           (Are Adkins 1st family of 533)
   Milton ADKINS        20        laborer
   Mahala ADKINS        14
   Malinda PERSON       14           (see 536 counted twice)
   Lewis PERSON         12
515-533                                          BOWEN CREEK ?
   Parker Adkins        39        Va laborer (m Jane Holt 1824cc)
   Elizabeth            25             (Midkiff 1849cc)
   Charles              10
   Joseph                6
516-534
   Michael Rogers       53        Va farmer
   Frances              46
   John                 26
   Rebecca J.           23
   Catharine            21
   James                17
   Isabel               14
   Nancy                12
   Michael A.            8
   Mary J.               6
   James LAWRENCE       23        Va farmer
p74
517-535    Person=Parson
   William Person       30        Va
   Malinda              24
   Frances (f)           8
   Sarah J.              6
   Nancy                 4
   Ida E.                1
----536
   Simon Person         68        Va farmer
   Malinda              14
   Lewis                12
518-537
   George A.Holton      26        Va blacksmith
   Nancy                25
   John H.               4
   Priscilla             2
   Arispa (f)           3/12
   Woodward HOLLY       27           laborer
519-538
   Willam Kincaid(Kincard)38      Va laborer
   Sarah                38             (Holten 1845cc)
   Simon                14
   Wesley                4
   Cynthia               1
520-539
   Samuel Tincher       30        Va laborer
   Elizabeth J.         29
   John M.               8
   James W.              5
```

```
521-540
  William Holstein        29    Va farmer
  Cynthia                 30
  James R.                 6
  Mary A.                  6
  Addison O.               4
  John W.                  1
  Benjamin HUGHES         23    Va school teacher
522-541
  James Smith             37    Va farmer
  Phebe                   27       (Hilton 1842cc--Holton)
  Nancy                    8
  Betsy                    6
  Martha                   4
  Joseph                   3
  Sarah                    1
p75
523-542
  John M.K.Smith          81    Pa farmer (1 Eliza Fuller 1809cc)
  Sarah                   65        (Brown 1822cc)
524-543
  Andrew Holly            65    Va farmer
  Sarah                   40
  Franklin                21       laborer
  John H.                 13
  Edgar L.                11
525-544
  Samuel Kinder           30    Va farmer
  Nancy                   23
  Madison                  6
  Mary                    4
  Elizabeth                2
526-545
  David Burns             35    Va farmer(? 2-Elizabeth Smith 1851cc)
  Ibba                    37       (Butcher SO)
  Elizabeth               13
  Job                     11
  Robertson                9
  Thomas                   7
  Andrew W.                6
  Taylor                   5
  Mary J.                  3
  Buggy (m)                2
  David                    1
527-546
  Nancy Roberts           83    Va  (w/o Thomas Roberts-RevW)(d 1852 SO)
  Jackson ASHWORTH        22        farmer (grandson SO)
528-547
  James T.Carrol Jr.      23    Va farmer
  Martha                  22        (Roberts 1846cc)
  Adam Z.                  2
529-548
  James C.Black           44    Va farmer
  Lucy W.                 39
  Mary H.                 20
  George A.               16
  Permelia A.             14       (m Wm.H.Meadows SO) Boone Co.
  Adam C.                 12
  Sarah C.                10
```

```
529-548 Black (con't)
  Eliza C.                   6           (m Joseph Lawrence SO) Boone Co.
  John W.                    8
  William                    1
530-549
  Joseph L.Sexton          35      Va farmer
  Lucinda A.               19          (Black 1847cc)
  Malissa A. (f)            1
p76
531-550
  Andrew H.Ashworth        27      Va farmer
  Milly                    19
  Andrew J.                 1
532-551
  Zilla Burns (f)          40      Va  Alford(m Frances Burns 1828 cc)
  Cynthia                  27
  Mary                     20          (m Charles L.Roffe SO-DD)
  Jane                     15
  Virginia                 11
  Cindarella                9
  George W.                 6
  Fredrick G.L.B.           5
  Vermila (f)               2
  Artemica (f)              1
533-552
  William T.Garrett        28      Va farmer
  Carolina                 24
  Elizabeth M.              6
  Mahala C.                 4
  William A.                2
  James P.               5/12
  Mary A.BUTCHER           59
534-553
  Philip Powel             43      Va farmer
  Mary                     46
  Mary                     21
  Elizabeth                16
  Andrew J.                12
  Henry C.                  6
535-554
  Samuel Powel             21      Va
  Mary                     26
536-555
  Alexander Griffith       49      Va farmer
  Sarah                    45          (Welch SO)
  William                  18
  Lorenza D.               16
  Henry B.                 14
  Lewis                    11
  Martha A.                 9
  Joseph                    6
  Adaline                   2
  Julia GRIFFITH           21
p77
537-556
  Archibald Egner          39      Va farmer
  Lany (f)                 39          (Massey 1832-Monroe Co.SO)
  John W.                  17          (m Lucinda Plumley SO)
  William C.               15          (m Jane Adams 1858cc)
  Margaret A.              12          (m Sylvester Plumley 1855cc)
```

```
537-556 Egner (con't)
   Josiah                    10        (m Martha Baisden-Logan Co.SO)
   Archa H. (m)               8        (m Octavia Compton SO)
   Mary L.                    6
   Martha C.                  4
   James M.                   2
538-557
   James Ballard            54     Va farmer
   Mary                     55
   Perry                    26        farmer
   Caroline                 19
539-558
   James King               73     Va farmer
   Mary                     71
   Sarah                    24
540-559
   Peter Smith              46     Va farmer
   Asseanetta               44        (Alford 1828cc)
   Mary                     24
   Marinda                  22
   Cynthia                  21
   Rhoda                    18
   Nancy                    16
   Alfred                   13
   Sarah Jane               11        (m George Alford SO)
   Julia A.                 10
   Louisa                    6
   Christopher               5
   William H.                1
541-560
   James Roberts            38     Va farmer
   Nancy                    23        (Mitchel SO)
   Columbus F.               3
   Oma ROBERTS (f)          74        (w/o Henry Roberts SO)
542-561
   Marine Sanford (m)       31     Va farmer
   Minerva S.               28
   Vanlindon E. (m)          6
   William                   5
   Milton W.                 4
   Robert E.                 1
   Rober SANFORD (m)        18        farmer
   Nancy Ellison SANSFORD   36
543-562
   Nancy Moore              55     Va
   Granderson               28        farmer
   Sarah                    22
   Martin L.                20        farmer
   Samuel                   18
   Rhoda                    15
   Isaiah                   13
page 78
544-563
   Thomas T.Adkins          30     Va farmer
   Christina                30
   Roxalina                 13
   Parthena (f)             11
   Ballard   (m)            11
   John W.                   9
   Samuel L.                 7
   Calvary                   3
   Calahill (m)            9/12
```

page 78
545-564
```
  Samuel Carrol              30      Va farmer (1-Lucinda Swan 1840cc)
  Amanda A.                  18
  William H.                  5
  Charles B.                  3
  John A.                   5/12
546-565
  Dicy Barrett (f)           54      Va (McComas w/o Andrew Barrett 1818cc)
  Malvina                    18
  James                      13
  Alice                       4
  Abraham SEXTON             28      Va farmer
  Lewis SMITH                28         none
  Lucinda ADKINS             20
  Henry ADKINS                2
           (are Adkins of 565-566-567-569 all one family ?)
547-566
  Samuel Smith               40      Va farmer
  Mahala                     40
  Nancy                       6
  Sarah A.                    6          (m Bartlett Adkins SO) Boone Co.
  John                        4
  Alexander                   3
  Harvey                      1
  Jessie ADKINS              16         laborer
  Elmina ADKINS     (f)       9
548-567
  Harvey Barrett             28      Va farmer
  Lucy                       23
  Andrew C.                   3
  Thomas                   8/12
  John ALLFORD               28      Va constable
  Lucretia ADKINS            15
  Sampson ROACH              15         farmer
p79
549-568
  Samuel Bragg               24      Va farmer
  Ann E.                     27         (a.Eliza Holley 1846cc)
  Sophrona J. (f)             4
  Cynthia O.                  2
550-569
  Joseph Holten              53      Pa farmer
  Nancy                      53      Va  (Holley 1822cc)
  Cynthia                    25
  Frances (f)                24

  Nancy                      21
  Andrew J.                  17         farmer
  Joseph                     15         farmer
  William                    11
  William A.ADKINS           19         laborer
551-570
  Alexander Roberts          48      Va farmer
  Susannah                   41          (Lawson SO)
  John L.                    25         farmer
  Dabney M.                  18
  Dolly A.                   15          (m William Miller 1854cc)
  Roxalena                   13          (m Evermont McNeely SO)
```

```
551-570 Roberts (con't)
  Mary L.                11              (m Emsby Beckett 1855cc)
  Ellener J.             10
  Elizabeth M.            6              (m Martin Bennett)Boone Co.SO
  Dorothy D.S.            4
  Bird   (m)              2
552-571
  William H.Roberts      26    Va farmer
  Susan                  24              (Ford 1846cc)
  Elvira                  2
  Andrew P.               1
  Joseph P.ROBERTS       20       farmer  (m Nancy McNeely SO)
553-572
  Washington Payly       38    Va farmer
  Mary                   27
  Lafayette               9
  Serena (f)              6
  Lamira (f)              2
  Sidney (m)              1
554-573
  Robert Alford          36    Va farmer
  Leanza                 28
  George W.              12
  Joseph                 10
  Adam A.                 9
  Aseaneth                7
  Lorenzo D.              6
  Cynthia                 2
  John W.              3/12
p80
555-574                                                    WAYNE
  Burwell Spurlock       33    Va farmer
  Nancy                  22
  Thomas                  2
  Rebecca              7/12
556-575
  George Morrison        53
  Hannah M.              49
  John                   29
  Martha J.              24
  Mary E.                17
  Mariah                 14
  George STEWART         14        farmer
557-576
  Frederick Chambers     37    Va farmer
  Elizabeth              44
  Sylvester M.           20        farmer (m Elizabeth Wheeler SO)
  Edward LAWRENCE        18        laborer
  John STEPHENSON        19        laborer


558-577
  Jacob May              36    Va farmer
  Clarenda A.            25
  Jacob A.                9
  Cynthia                 5
  Octavia                 4
  Elmira                  3
  James                   1
```

```
559-578
  Alexander Spurlock        28    Va
  Mary                      24
  John H.                    4
  Thomas                     2
  Andrew                     1
  Harrison SPURLOCK         21        laborer
560-579
  James Wheeler             67    Va farmer
  Jane                      68        (Nickell SO) Monroe Co.
  David TONNY               37        farmer
  Cynthia TONNY             27          (Lawrence SO)
561-580
  Edward Wheeler            41    Va farmer (w/o Mary Fleshman 1832cc)
  Alexander                 17        farmer
  Elizabeth J.              13        (m Sylvester Chambers SO)Boone Co.
  Lucy A.                    7
  Frances S.                 3
Pg.81
562-581
  William Ott               48    Va farmer
  Michael OTT               77
  Catherine OTT             55
  Simson  OTT               31        farmer
  Julia A. OTT              50
  Elizabeth  OTT            44
563-582
  Eli Wheeler               34    Va farmer
  Rhoda                     32
  Leatha                    10
  Henly                      6
  Venila                     5
  Matilda                    3
  Mary                       1
564-583
  William Moore             26    Va farmer
  Sarah                     26
  Nancy                      4
  Amira                      2
  Granderson               6/12      (see 562)
565-584
  George Holton             35    Va farmer
  Elizabeth                 49
  Clarind C.    (f)         12
  Elizabeth J.               8
  Lucinda LAWSON            15
566-585
  Ralph Ganno               36    Va farmer (Gunnoe)
  Jane                      29
  Julia A.                   9
  Sarah E.                   6
  Mary J.                    4
  John T.                    1
567-586
  Thomas Cooper             51    Va farmer
  Catherine                 37
  Armilda                   21  ?(12)
  Lucinda C.                10
  Sarah                      8
  Thomas                     2
```

```
568-587
  James Rogers          27    Va farmer
  Susan                 30
  Samuel G.              3
  Elizabeth              1
569-588
  Henry Wallace         47    Tenn farmer
  Elizabeth             39    Va
  Levi                  14    Va
  Henry T.              13    Ky.
  John                  11    Va
  Sarah                  9
  Solomon                8
  Daniel                 6
  Susanah                5
  Dicy                   4
  Mary J.             2/12
570-589                                           page 82
  Peter Fizer           25    Va farmer
  Margaret P.           21          (Roberts 1845cc)
  William P.             4
  Moses L.               1
571-590                                                BOWEN RIDGE
  James Garrett         52    Va farmer (w/o Nancy Ray 1816cc)
  James C.              24       farmer
  John L.               15       farmer
  Stephen J.            13
  Robert L.             12
  Albert M.             10
  Alexander B.           8
  Richard J.             7
  Virginia C.            5
  Jeremiah W.            4
572-591     (see 932)                          BOWEN RIDGE-4 POLE
  Gabriel Roberts       51    Va farmer
  Priscilla             52
  Henrietta             25
  Martha                22
  George                15
  Nancy                 11
  Green                 10
573-592
  William Burton        29    Va farmer
  Mary                  31
  Joseph W.              4
  John K.                2
  Ann E.              6/12
  Virginia ASHWORTH     14
  James A.ASHWORTH      12
  William B.ASHWORTH     9
  Abigail JORDAN        29f
574-593
  Job Burns             46       Va farmer
  Sarah                 30
  Julia A.               8
  Elizabeth              5
  Allen                  2
```

78

```
Pg 83
575-594
   John McComas            30      Va farmer
   Lucinda                 25
   Joseph W.                4
   Benjamin F.              3
   Mary J.                  1
576-595
   Alcey Ashworth          53f     Va
   Michael J.              24m         farmer
   Van Buren               20          farmer
   Hellery                 16m         farmer
   Mary                    14
   Alcey J.                11f
   William H.               6
577-596
   William Beck            48      Va farmer
   Sandal                  48
   Dolly                   19
   Abaz                    12m
   Julia                    9
   Eliza J.                 2
578-597
   John Ashworth           50      Va farmer
   Nancy                   39
   Thomas                  18          farmer
   Elizabeth               16
   James                   14
   Joel                    11
   Oney M                   8f
   Nancy                    6
   John W.                  2
579-598
   Pleasant Roberts        58      Va farmer
   Sarah                   46          (Bryant 1829 LCoh)
   Isaac                   19
   Malissa                 18
   Anna                    16
   Rebecca                 14
   Calvin                  12
   Minerva                 10
   Sarah                    7
580-599
   Zachariah Martin        45      Va farmer
   Nancy                   45
   William D.              16          farmer
   Jonathan SHOEMAKER      20          labourer
   Elizabeth J.SHOEMAKER   18          (Martin m 1850cc)
Pg 84
581-600
   George Keyton           44      Va labourer
   Sandal                  38
   M. Harriett             23
   Nancy                   20
   Recey                   19f
   Emiletta                16f
   Mary C.                 15
   John                    13
```

```
582-601
  Elijah Cyres           32      Va farmer
  Margaret               25
  Mary A.                 6
  John E.                 3
  William F.          10/12
583-602
  James Cyres            60      Va farmer
  Sarah                  55
  Nancy                  15
  Matilda                12
  William                 9
  Mary                    5
584-603
  Willis Mays            40      Va farmer
  Margaret               54         (Duncan 1832cc)
  Addison                14
  Margaret               12
  Franklin               10
  Willis                  1
585-604
  John Murdock           25      Va farmer
  Sarah                  25
  Elizabeth               3
  William                 1
586-605
  Madison Johnson        37      Va farmer
  Martha                 30
  Eura                   13
  Lelia                  11
  Almeda                  9
  Elizabeth               6
  Warren W.               4
  James M.                2
587-606
  James Conner           44      Va farmer
  Lavenia                40         (Hudson 1829cc)
  Armilda                18
  Lewis                  16         farmer
  Mary E.                10
  Abigail                 9
  Samantha                6
  John M.                 4
Pg 85
                                                    BALL'S GAP
588-607
  John Chapman           50      Va farmer
  Lucy                   45         (Hudson 1816cc)
  William                21         farmer
  Eli                    19         farmer
  Rhoda                  17
  Martha                 17
  Jameson                13
  Albert                  7
  Lucinda CHAPMAN        23         (OLDEST DAUGHTER ?)
589-608
  William Conner         82      Va farmer
  Susannah               67
  William                31         farmer
  Armintha CHAPMAN       34
  William JEFFERSON      18         farmer
  Martha A.JEFFERSON      6
```

```
590-609                                                        BALL'S GAP
  Ryland Keyton        43    Va farmer                         cem#S59
  Lucinda              41       (Conner  1828cc)               cem#S59
  William              21    farmer
  Mary                 19       (m Reason Wheeler 1850cc-cem#S59
  Susannah             17
  Calvary              13
  Preston              11                                      cem#S59
  Henry                 9                                      cem#S59
  Andrew                5
  John L.               7
  Amanda                3
591-610                                                        BALL'S GAP
  John S. Nicholas     48    Va farmer
  Lucinda              37
  Louisa               14
  John A.              12
  James B.              9
  Calahill              6
  Preston T.            3
  Ahaz H.               1                                      cem#S60
592-611
  John Nicholas        73    Va farmer
  Margaret             69
----612
  William Smith        44
  Margaret             45
  Mahala               25       (m Ralph Smith 1851cc)
  Albert               19    farmer
  Nancy                17
  Lucinda              10
  Clarinda ADKINS       4
p86
593-613                                                        BALL'S GAP
  William Wheeler      55    Va farmer
  Reason (m)           35       (m Mary Keaton 1850cc)cem#S59
  Mary                 14
  Joseph               22       teamster
  Zachariah            12                                      cem#S59
  Malvina              11
594-614                                      west of RIVER-SALT ROCK
  William Porter       44    Va farmer
  Sarah                22
  Sarah                18
  Susan                15
  John                 14
  Eliza                11
  Emily                 6
  William               4
  Martha                2
595-615
  Miriam Porter (f)    35    Va
596-616
  James Brown          69    Va farmer  (1st-Louisa M.Beuhring CCA)
  Mary                 72       (Hill 1819cc)
```

```
597-617
  Andrew Roberts          45    Va farmer
  Jane                    35
  Dicy                    14
  Richard                 12
  Warren                  10
  Nancy                    8
  John H.                  6
  Adele (f)                4
  Bradford                 2
598-618
  James Becket            39    Va farmer
  Sarah                   40
  William                 18       blacksmith
  Virginia                11
  America                  6
  Tabitha                  2
599-619
  David Porter            47    Va farmer
  Polly                   39
  John M.                 18       farmer
  Frances E. (f)          15
  James H.                13
  Martha J.               11
  David C.                 8
  Mary S.                  4
  Joseph A.             3/12
  John M.K. SMITH         25    Va laborer
p87
600-620
  Adolphus A.Newly        35    Va farmer
  Abigail H.              33
  John INGRAHAM           28       farmer
  Senate HUDLIN (m)       14
----621
  Nancy Pine              42    Va
  George M.               12
  William H.              10
  Victoria                 4
  John T.                  2
601-622
  Benj.Franklin Curry     37    Va farmer
  Sophia                  37
  Timothy                 14
  Mayberry (m)            12
  William H.               9
  Elizabeth                7
  Sarah A.                 5
  John C.                  2
602-623
  Benjamin B.Wilkinson    39    Va cabinetmaker ****ck-Dial
  Anna                    39
  Mary J.                 16
  Augustin F. (m)         13
  Martha M.               10
  William C.               8
```

```
603-624
  Squire Johnson          38    Va farmer
  Dempsey (f)             36          (Adkins 1838cc)
  Betsy                   12
  Cynthia                 10
  Susan                    8
  Polly                    6
  Sally                    4
  Sampson                  3
604-625
  Lewis Johnson           38    Va farmer (w/o Nancy Spears 1835cc)
  Jerremiah               13
  Vianna  (f)             12
  Sampson                  8
605-626
  Jane Person             30
  Nancy                    8
  William                  4
  Sarah                    2
p88
606-627
  Hiram Curry             36    Va farmer
  Barbara                 31          (Keyser SO)
  Benjamin F.             11          (m Emily Witcher 1860cc)
  Granville                9          (m Nancy Thompson SO)
  Martha A.                7
  Permelia                 4
  George E.                2
  Blackbourn            3/12          (m Lulu Samuels 1882 SO)
  Eli M.KEYSER            24    Va teacher
607-628
  James Johnson           24    Va farmer
  Druzilla                19          (Adkins 1848cc)
  Mary J.                  1
608-629
  Jessee King             37    Va farmer
  Judy                    41
  Nancy                   15
609-630                                                     SALT ROCK
  Creed Wysong            32    Va farmer
  Emeline                 27          (Funk SO)
  John                    12
  Eden                    10
  Calvin                   8
  Merrett(Wm)              4
  Mary                     2
610-631
  Catharine Wysong        60    Va
  Susan                   23
611-632
  Henry Ashworth          33    Va farmer
  Susan                   28
  Lewis M.                 9
  Lelia                    7
  Ellenor                  3
  Adeline                  2
612-638
  John Forth              47    Va farmer
  Nancy                   45
  Margaret                22
  Susan                   18
  Elizabeth               12
```

```
613-634
  Harrison Roberts      36        farmer
  Susan                 37
  Henry                 14
  John                  12
  Elizabeth              5
  Sarah                  4
  America                1
p89
614-635
  William Webb          46   Va farmer
  Jane                  42
  John B.               10
  Elizabeth L.          17
  Samuel                12
  Hannah A.              7
  Helen E.               3
615-636
  John Jordan           27   Va farmer
  Oney (f)              28
  Lucinda                6
  Malinda                4
  Emily                  3
  John JORDAN           75        farmer
  Sinah JORDAN          60
616-637
  Thomas Vickers        36   OH farmer
  Margaret              24
  Frances                7
  George                 4
  California             1
  Aaron MARTIN          14
617-638
  James Roberts         47   Va farmer
  Lucy A.               43
  Martha                17
  Mariane               10
  Daniel                 6
  Mary J.                3
  James BELL            16        farmer
  John BELL             14                              (cem #50)
618-639
  Jessee Harbour        46   Va farmer (1-Jane Newman 1828cc)
  Jane                  49          (2-Malcolm 1837cc)
  Elizabeth             17
  Montague              14
  Mary J.               13
  Joseph M.             10                              cem#S54
  David HARBOUR         85        minister (circuit rider)
                                  (w/o Mary Spurlock 1787 Mt)
619-640
  John Collins          54   Va farmer
  Abigail               53
  Mary WARNER           26
  Viletta WARNER         9
  Lewis CARPENTER       26   Va farmer
  Tabitha CARPENTER     27        (married daughters ???)
```

p90
620-641
  Thomas Harman   60   Va minister
  Jane   61
  Thomas   25   farmer
  Henrietta J.ELLISON 12
----642
  George P.Collins   19   Va laborer
  Elizabeth   18
621-643
  Ezekiel Reynolds   41   Va farmer
  Amy   43   (Jefferson 1829cc)
  John   20   laborer
  Minerva   16
  Henry   14
  Martha   12
  Thomas M.   10
  Josiah   8
  James V.   6
  Nathan E.   3
622-644
  George Brown   34   Va blacksmith
  Augheny (f)   39
  Thomas S.   11   (m Cynthia mcComas 1859cc)
  James   9
  John   8
  William   6
  Lucretia   11 ?(twin) (m Peyton McComas 1863cc)
  Morris   5/12
623-645
  Simon Reynolds   43   Va farmer
  Jane   36   (Brown 1830cc)
  William   19   farmer
  Celicia   17
  Jasper M.   13
  Mary M.   11
  James   8
  Dicy   4
  Joseph H.   2
624-646
  Morris Jordan   22   Va farmer
  Rebecca   15
  Mary A.   7/12
  Andrew H.JORDAN   19   laborer
625-647
  Peter Burns   31   Va farmer (s/o Peter & Jane SO)
  Ruth   23   (Burns 1845cc)
  Robertson   1
626-648
  Elkana Henkley(m)   30   Va farmer
  Rhoda   30
  Mary   9
  Jacob   4
p91
627-649
  Livingston Henkley 47   Va farmer
  Permelia   48
  Jacob   14
  Livenia   12

```
627-649 Henkley (con't)
  Hiram                  8
  Ruthie                 5
  Samuel ROSE           22        laborer
  Fleming ROSE          21
628-650
  Robertson Patton      35     Va farmer
  Harriett              27
  Margaret PATTON       59
  Jacob ADKINS          18        laborer
629-651
  James Burns           53     Va farmer (s/o Peter & Jane SO)?
  Nancy L.              53           (Alford 1818cc)
  Cynthia               13
  James                 10
  Mary ALFORD           76           (w/o George of Greenbrier Co. SO)
630-652
  Andrew Burns          25     Va farmer
  Mary                  17
631-653
  Isaiah Burns          28     Va farmer
  Lucy                  27
  Mary               11/12
  Jacob L.               7
  James ALFORD          24     Va constable (s/o George SO)
632-654
  Thomas L.Brown        43     Va farmer
  Mary                  43
  James H.              19        farmer
  John G.               14
  George P.             13
  Louisa                 9
  Mary                   7
633-655
  William Legg          25     Va farmer
  Almeda                23
  Nancy J.            8/12
634-656
  George W.Summers      38     Va          (1-Amazetta Laidley 1833cc)
  Sarah                 37                 (Black 1835cc)
  Sylvester A.S.        12
  Constantine R.         8
  Edgar L.               6
  Tyre C.             9/12
p92
635-657
  Wesley G.Wooton       25     Va farmer   (see 305)
  Frances               22
  Martha J.              2
  John H.                1
  Simon WOOTON          50        laborer
636-658
  George Gallaher       26     Va farmer   (s/o 943)
  Neoma                 19                            cem#S31A
  Ann SIMMONS           16
  Mary F.SIMMONS         6
```

```
637-659
  John Gwinn              21   Va farmer   (twin)
  Hetty F.                21        (Kilgore 1849cc)
                                                        MILTON
638-660
  Washington Gwinn        21   Va farmer (twin ?)     (cem# 49)
  Marietta                19
639-661
  Henry Johnson           24   Va farmer
  Ann                     18
  Henry                 6/12
  Agnes JOHNSON           50
640-662
  Lewis Fulterton         60   Va laborer   (black)
  Ann                     50               (mulatto)
  Charles McCOWN          60        cooper    (black)
641-663
  John J.Nash             41   Va millwright
  Sarah E.                33   Md
  Mary E.                 14   IN
  Jane E.                 14   IN
  Sarah                   12   OH
  Joseph A.                9   IN
  Rebecca E.               1   IN
642-664
  Benjamin Sandridge      25   Va corder
  Lucy                    24
  Frances (f)              1
643-665
  John Malcom             44   Va farmer   (s/o Joseph SO)
  Jemima A.               38
  William                  7
  Robert B.                5
  Charles E.               4    (cem #50)
  Mary                     3
  Nancy H.                 1
                                         TURNPIKE-BLUE SULPHUR
644-666
  Asa L.Wilson            33   OH farmer
  Mary                    33   Va    (d 1852-b Mud River Cem SO)
  Eliza A.                12
  Lemule (Samuel)         10
  Elizabeth J.             8
  Sarah F.                 6
  John T.                  5        m Amasetta Mahone FBL
  Emily                    3
  Nortimer WILSON         25        laborer
  William WILSON          21        laborer
  Isaac WILSON            17        laborer
  Peter WILSON            10
  Harvey WILSON            6
  Jestin Sanndge          65  farmer(Keeton w/o Reuben SandridgeCCA)
p93
645-667
  James Gibson            37   Va farmer
  Frances                 41
  William                 15
  Mary                    11        idiot
  Sally A.                13
  Amanda                   9
  Cynthia                  7
  Matilda                  5
```

```
646-668
  Beverly W.Maupin        41   Va farmer   (s/o Thos. see #1)
  Margaret                16
  Mary                    14
  William                 12        idiot
  Henry                   10
  John                     8
  Adaline                  5
647-669
  Edward Malcom           26   Va farmer   (s/o Joseph SO)
  Mary    MALCOM          69        (w/o Joseph SO)
  Margaret MALCOM         35
  Eliza MALCOM            31
  Robert MALCOM           23        farmer (m Juliet Yates 1852cc)
  Thomas GILISPIE         18        farmer
      (mother and unmarried children ?)
648-670                                         HOWELL'S MILL
  John Denison            35   Eng farmer
  Mary                    35   Eng                   cem#13
  John                     4   Eng
  Mary                  3/12 Va
649-671
  Alexander Newman        49   Va farmer
  Betsy                   44
  Winston                 22        farmer
  Emily                   19
  Eliza                   16
  America                 13
  Alexander                9
  Joseph                   5
  Morris NEWMAN           26   Va farmer
  Polly NEWMAN            69
650-672
  Peyton Newman           21   Va laborer
  Emily                   26        (Spears  1842 LCoh)
  John M.                  7
  Greenville               4
p94
651-673
  William Jones           28   Va tailor
  Mary                    26        (M.Jane John 1846cc)
  Henry C.                 3
652-674                                    MARTHA-BOOTEN CREEK
  Patrick Morrison        59   TN farmer
  Anna                    59   Va   (Scales 1830cc -d 1855 DD)
  Matilda                 25
  Milly                   17
  Henry                   19        farmer
  Anna                    16
  John SCALES             40        farmer
653-675                                  west of RIVER-MARTHA
  James Butcher           23   Va laborer
  Rachael                 23
  Emily                   27        (m Greenville Harrison 1850cc)
  Sarah                   24        (m Jim cowens 1855 DD)
  Ellen                   16           (m Charley Shipe 1855 DD)
  America                 12
  Andrew DICK             23   laborer(m Cynthia leonard 1851cc) Wright FBL
  Reuben DICK             20   laborer
  Layfayette DICK         18   laborer    (see 381 Dick family)
  America DICK             6
  John THOMAS             26   laborer
```

```
654-676                                    west of RIVER -MARTHA
   Charles K.Morris      31    Va farmer                 cem#S29
   Martha                30       (Kilgore-Saunders will 1848cc) #S29
   Mary                  11          (m Dr.V.R.Moss 1855cc DD)
   Ellen                  8          (m Arthur Williams SO)
   John A.                5          (m Emily Gwinn 1866cc) cem#S29
   James J.               3
   Edna E.            11/12          (m M.T.Heber Reece SO)
   William MORRIS        18       laborer
   Benjamin HARRIMAN     20       laborer
655-677
   William J.Harris      32    Va laborer
   Catharine H.          25
   Emeline MORRISON      22
656-678
   William Messsinger    35       laborer
   Nancy                 33
   David                 13                              cem#17
   Isaac                 10
   Emily                  6
   Francis M. (m)      2/12
p95
657-679                                               MARTHA
   Ralph Smith           58    Va farmer
   Viley                 58       (Morrison 1818cc)
   Ralph                 26       (m Mahala Smith 1858 SO)
   Joanna                21
   Viley                 19
   Ambrose (m)           17       farmer
   Wesley                15       farmer
   Lavenia               12
   William A.             7
658-680
   Hannah Jenkins        54
   John H.               18       laborer
   Thomas                16

659-681
   James Morrison        43    Va farmer
   Frances               42    NC    (Thacker 1829cc)
   Fredrick              19    Va
   Angeline              17          (m Evermont Adkins 1852cc)
   Nancy                 15
   Ellen                 13
   Rachael               11
   James                  9
   Mary                   7
   Henry                  5                         (cem #s33)
   Frances (f)            2
660-682
   Abram Childers        24    Va farmer
   Elizabeth O.          20
   Mary J.            10/12
661-683  (see 453)                        head of BOOTEN CREEK R#10
   John Hensley          38    Va farmer
   Malinda               35       (Keyser 1837 LCoh)
   Virginia              12
   Missouri (f)          10
   Bird (m)               9
   Elizabeth              7
```

```
661-683 Hensley (con't)
  Hiram              5
  David              4
  Ephraim            3
  Eveline            1
p96
662-684
  Samuel Hensley    46    Va farmer
  Parthena          46
  Andrew J.         18       farmer
  Samuel            16
  James A.          14
  Martha            12
  Mary              10
  Lucy               8
  Washington         5
663-685
  Matthew Knight    38    KY farmer
  Nancy             30    Va    (Morrison 1837cc)
  Wayne W.          12
  Mary J.           11
  James T.           9
  William W.         7
664-686
  Jacob Smith       26    Va farmer
  Elizabeth         26          (Barbour 1850cc)
  William A.         4
  Mary J.            3
  Sally              2
  Martha             1
665-687
  Henry Smith       48    Va farmer
  Rebecca           52
  Henry             18
  William           17
  David             12
666-688
  Peter Smith       20    Va
  Lenia             19
667-689
  Edward Elmore     50    Va farmer
  Rhoda             41
  William           17
  Arianna TOPPING    5    (see 865 & 944)
668-690
  Abram Lions       44    OH farmer
  Peggy             36    Ky
  John              12    Ky
  Wilson            10    OH
  Sally              6    Ky
  Eliza A.           4    Va
  Polly              2
669-691                           head of BOOTEN CREEK-R#10
  Martin Dillon     61    Va farmer
  Lucy              54
  Sarah             25
  Ellenor J.        22
  Amanda V.         14
  Bersheba (f)      12
  John L.           25       laborer( twin ?)
  Rhesa (m)         21       farmer
  Benjamin          17       farmer
```

p97
670-692

Eliza Davis	59	Va	
Allen M.	22		farmer
Lockardy (f)	25		
Martha C.	24		
Daniel W.	17		farmer
Angeline A.	8		
Christopher C.	6		

WEST PEA RIDGE

671-693

John Deboy	33	Va farmer		cem#S22A
Polly	33		(Cook 1835cc)	
Julia A.	13			cem#S22A
Elizabeth	10			
John A.	6			
Margaret	5			
Mahala	3			

672-694

William Jenkins	59	Va farmer

673-695

Paulina Hughes (f)	34	Va	(m William Davis 1852cc)
Margaret V.	15		
Jerutha A. (f)	12		
Mary E.	9		
Lorenzo D.	7		
Ralph	5		
Jemima F.	2		

674-696

Paul Davis	64	Va farmer	
Mary	60		(Gilkerson ?cc)
William	39		farmer (m Paulina Hughes 1852cc)
Elizabeth	23		
James F.	22		farmer
Adaline A.	16		

----697

John Cobourn	32		farmer
Sarah Louise	31		(Davis 1848cc)

675-698

John Dolen	45	Va farmer	
Judy	40		
John D.	21		
George W.	17		
James W.	12	twin	
Judy F.	12		
Sarah E.	8		
Luckey DOLEN (f)	83		

p98
676-699

EDENS BRANCH of DAVIS CK

Abner Cook	45	Va farmer	
Polly	34		
Mary	17		
Abner	10		
Nancy	7		cem#S24A
Catharine	6		
Eliza	4		
Jane	1		

```
677-700
   John Cook              37    Va farmer
   Sarah J.               30           (Smith 1840cc)
   Mary A.                 7
   John L.                 4
   Martha V.               2
   Elizabeth SMITH        19
678-701
   Alexander Roberts      43    Va farmer (d-1854 SO)
   Mary                   51
   Rebecca D.             19
   Mary E.                17
   Sarah J.               14
   Amanda R.              10
679-702
   John Ward              59    Va
   Susannah               46           (Smith 1850cc)
   David                  20
680-703
   Thomas Ward            29    Va farmer
   Cynthia                29           (Morrison 1843cc)
   Eliza A.                7
   John H.                 4
   Patrick                 1
681-704
   Thomas Scales          38    Va farmer
   Ruth                   30           (Martin 1837cc)
   Abigail A.             11
   Otis J.                 2
682-705
   Mathew Butcher         38    Va laborer
   Lucinda                38
   Elizabeth              18
   Thomas J.              17
   Adaline                14           (David Stanley 1853cc)cem#S43
   Sally                  12
   Lewis M.               10
   Julia                   8
   John F.                 7
683-706
   John Smith             22     Va laborer
   Mary A.                21
p99
684-707    (see 700)
   Sarah Cook             60    Va
   Peter                  35        laborer
   Abner                  16
   Eliza                  14
685-708
   Solomon Cook           22    Va farmer
   Elizabeth              21
686-709                                            WEST PEA RIDGE
   Thomas C.Cook          26    Va farmer
   Louisa                 24
   Benjamin                6
   Sarah A.             6/12                              cem#S22A
```

```
687-710
  Henry W.Shelton        31    Va farmer
  Sarah C.               27
  George W.               8
  Henrietta               6
  John W.                 5
  Henry W.                5    twin
  Sarah A.                1
  John POAGE             25
  Mary MANN              22    OH    (m Andrew Seamonds 1852cc)
688-711
  James Dodd             41    Va farmer
  John DODD              69       (Hus/wife and son
  Mary W.                43       (or hus/wife and father-in-law ???)
689-712
  Enrich Underwood       33    Va joiner
  Cynthia                30
  John M.                12
  Mary E.                10        m William Douthet FBL
690-713
  Albert Huffman         31       farmer
  Ellen                  32
  Mary A.                13
  Virginia C.             9
  Eliza J.                7
  Lewis T.                3
  Martha A. M.            1
691-714                            across river west of BARBOURSVILLE
  Solomon Thornburg      59    Va farmer              (cem #s23)
  Mary                   57       (Stanley   CCA       cem #S23)
  Mary                   21       (m James Everett     cem #S23)
  John W.                17    farmer (m Emily Handley 1852cc)
  James                  14       (m Virginia Handley SO)Putnam Co.
  Moses THORNBURG        49    farmer                (cem #s23)
p100
692-715
  Albrecht Becker        38    Germany    tanner
  Mildred W.             30    Va     (Maupin 1840cc)
  Joanna M.               6
  Fredrick                4
  Matilda C.              1
  Nancy HENRY            24
  Jacob WAGNER           22    Germany    tanner
  Julius SCHAMBART       23    Germany    tanner
  Arnold WESTHOFF        32    Germany
693-716                                        DAVIS CREEK
  John Mills             32    Va cooper       cem#S23
  Mary                   32       (Thornburg)   cem#S23
  William                10                    cem#S23
  Orsamus   (m)           6                    cem#S23
694-717
  Thomas Kyle            50    Va gunsmith
  Mary                   43       (Polly Pinnell 1825Gb)cem#S25
  Emily A.               19       (m Samuel Ward 1850cc)
  Phebe S.               15
  Melieta (f)            11
  Teresa                  9
  Martha T.               5                         cem#S25
  Henrietta               3
```

```
695-718
  John Baumgardner        25    Va painter
  Louisa                  22         (Baumgardner 1849cc)
  Francis A. (m)         6/12
696-719                                       ⸱⸱ BARBOURSVILLE
  Greenville Harrison     35    Va blacksmith(mEmily Butcher 1850 DD)
  Rachael HARRISON        50              (Greenville-cem#S51)
  Mary HARRISON           22
  John FOUNDLAND         6/12
          (?mother,son.daughter & grandson ?)
697-720                                               B'VILLE
  Irvin Lusher            39    Va lumberer
  Jane                    39         (Blake SO)
  Frances (f)             18         (m Lafayette Samuels 1850cc)
  Lewis W.                12
  Robert M.               10
  John                     8
  Charles                  6
  Henry W.                 4         (m Sarah Williams SO)
  Mary                     2
698-721                                               B'VILLE
  John Lacy               38    Va merchant
  Milly M.                19
  James W.                12
  Mary E.                 10
  Charles E.             7/12
p101
699-722                                               B'VILLE
  Thomas Hatfield         48    Va shoemaker
  Amanda                  37         (Pinnell 1829cc)
  John                    18         shoemaker
  Jane                    13
  David F.                11
  Joseph B.                9
  Martha E.                4
  George McDONALD         49    Ireland shoemaker
700-723                                       west of B'VILLE
  Thomas Thornburg        32    Va merchant   (s/o 714)      cem#S23
  Margaret C.             31         (Miller CCA)            cem#S23
  Mary J.                 12                                 cem#S23
  Sarah E.                10
  Ellen E.                 8         (m W.M.Hovey 1866cc)
  John S.                  6         (m Mary Long CCA) Mason Co.
  George E.                4         (m Nancy Wilson CCA)
701-724                                               B'VILLE
  Sanford Scott           45    Va innkeeper
  Sarah                   40
  Sarah A.                15         (m Andrew J.Keenan 1850cc)
  Algera (f)              14
  Sanford                 12
  Harvey                   6
  Eliza                    4
  Virginia                 2
  Tazwell B.SCOTT         21         blacksmith
  Francis SCOTT           26
```

```
---725    (hotel)                                        B'VILLE
  Orson Long              31   NY minister
  Ann E.                  21   Ky
  Laura                    2   Ky
  Thursday A.SHOEMAKER    16   Va
  Baptist EIBERNEISER     45   Germany  joiner
  Charles HERRENKOHL      24   Germany  cabinetmaker
  Adolphus LANDES         24   Germany  cabinetmaker
  Harrison DIRTON         26   Va       laborer
702-726                                                  B/VILLE
  Oscar W.Mather          28   Va tailor                 cem#H10
  Augusta J.              23
  Arianna L.               6
  Valcolon W. (m)          4
  Laura A.                 1
  Sidney ROBERTSON        12
703-727
  John Samuels            59   Va CLERK/CC  (w/o Emily Gardner CCA
  Lafayette               22      none  (m Frances Lusher 1850cc)
  Alexander               20                            cem#H10
  Mary                    17      (m Moses Thornburg 1857cc)
  John                    11      (m Mary Gardner of KY SO)
  America                  9      (m A.J. McMillan CCA)
  Sophia GARDNER          66   France
  Joseph GARDNER          76   Mass
---728
  Henry J.Samuels         25   Va lawyer                 cem#S23
  Rebecca                 21   OH     (Bartram SO)       cem#S23
  Sarah C.                 1      (m David Peters SO)
p102
704-729                                                  B'VILLE
  William C.Miller        40   Va merchant               cem#S25
  Eliza                   35      (Gardner CCA & DD)     cem#S25
  Eugenia                 13      (m B.H. Thackston CCA)
  Charles                 11
  Frank                    9
  William                  7
  Joseph                   2      (m Florence Tice CCA)
705-730
  Sidney Bowden           29   Va sadler
  Mary                    28      (Morris 1841cc)
  Charles                  5
  Alonzo                   4      (m Emma Midkiff SO)
  Rolanders A. (m)         2
  Sarah A. ADKINS         11
706-731                                                  B'VILLE
  John G.Miller           42   Germany  merchant
  Sarah A.                25   Va  (Chapman 1847cc-d 1855 DD)cem#H10
  Frances L. (f)           2
  Oltmar L.C.HEINERMAN    18   Germany  clerk
707-732                                                  BARBOURSVILLE
  Christopher S.Miller    44   Germany  merchant
  Mary F.                 33   Va   (Blake 1835 cc)
  Margaret BLAKE          73   Va   (w/o Isaac SO)
708-733
  Robert Allen            25   Scotland  Merchant
  Fran L. (f)             23   Va
  America G.               5   IN
  Jeannie E.               3   IN
```

709-734

John (Lewis)Keller	41	Germany blacksmith	
Hannah	37	Germany (Miller m Lewis Keller 1832cc)	
Eliza C.	16	Germany	
John F.	14	Va	
Junuis N. (m)	12		
Thomas J.	10		
Madison W.	8		
America C.	4		
Emma A.	1		
Frances HUMPHREY (f)	20		

p103

710-735

John Hibbins	27	Va wagonmaker	
Altemis (f)	24		
Sarah J.	2		
Susan E.	10/12		
Mary MATHERS	15		
John N. MATHERS	9		

711-736   B'VILLE

James Pinnell	73	Va sadler	cem#S25
Phebe	68		
Maletta RICHIE	41		

712-737

Arnold Kraus	59	Germany sadler	
Herodias (f)	54	South America	
Ann KRAUS	51	Germany	
Walter KRAUS	22	Germany merchant	cem#S25
Ellen HERRENKOHL	54	Germany	cem #17
Albert HERRNEKOHL	21	Germany tanner	
		(Louisa Fuller 1857 LCoh)cem #23A	
Adalaid SCHAAF	24	Germany	

713-738

Johnson Lusher	28	Va constable	
Lucy	22	(Dilley 1845 SO)	
Winfield S.	3		
Susan WILEY	28		

714-739   BARBOURSVILLE

Littleton Whitten	34	Va carpenter	
Emmerine	29		
Nancy E.	10		
Mary M.	8		
Hetty S.	6		
William M.	2		

715-740

William Agers	42	OH shoemaker	
Catharine	40	Ireland (Morrow/Morris 1837cc)	
Joseph	10	Va	
John MOORAN	14	Ky	

716-741

Susan J.Mather	45	Va (see 735)	
Ameretta	5		

717-742

James J.Mahone	32	Va teamster	
Mahala J.	26		
William	10		
Hellena	6		
Melitta V.	3		

```
718-743
  James Parish            33    Va  trader
  Julia                   33
  Nancy J.                10
  Harriet E.               8
  Mary C.                  6
  Frances M. (f)           4
  Martha A.                2
  Catharine CYRUS         20
  Barbary E.SMITH         30
p104
719-744
  Absalom Holderby        51    Va      (s/o Wm)
  America                 41          (Gardner CCA)
----745                           (s/o #1) (2nd w Lucinda Smith CCA)
  Henry B.Maupin          33    Va  physician              cem #50)
  Martha E.               21        insane (Holderby 1847 cc)div1855DD
  Mary E.                8/12       (d 1853)                   cem#50
720-746
  Elisha W.McComas        28    Va  lawyer
  Areanna                 27          (Holderby 1842cc)
  Alice                    7
  Henry F.                 3
  Walter                 8/12
721-747
  Edward Vertigans        35    Eng   school teacher
  Mariah                  36    Eng
  Edward G.               11    Eng
  George S.                9    Eng
  Walter F.                2    Va
722-748        (hotel)                                    B'VILLE
  Wilson B.Moore          32    Va  innkeeper   (s/o 81)      cem#S25
  Mary Jane               22          (McCallister 1844cc)  cem#S25
  John T.                  4
  Charles M.               2
  John HOLDROYD           22        laborer(Nancy Merritt 1866cc)cem #s35
  Peter HOLDROYD          20        laborer(Susan N.Mather 1855  (s/o 80)?
  Irains PRICE (m)        40          laborer
723-749
  Abner W.Wingo           30    Va  joiner
  Sarah L.                25
  Mary E.                  4
  Frances E.               2
  Eliza                  7/12
724-750                                                   B'VILLE
  Thomas A. Shelton       22    Va  joiner                cem#H10
  Eliza                   17                              cem#H10
725-751
  Benjamin McCune         24    Va  joiner
  Sarah                   20
  Julia                  6/12
  Elizabeth B.MATHER      12
726-752                                                   B'VILLE
  George F.Miller         33    Germany   butcher
  Mary                    24    Va        (Shelton 1843 CCA)
  Christian S.             6                              cem#S25
  Hannah C.                4        (m D.I.Smith CCA)
  George F.                2        (m Mary McConnell-Cattlesburg CCA)
```

```
727-753                                              BARBOURSVILLE
  George Proctor        34    Scotland   clothier
  Margaret              24       "
  Agnes                 12       "
  Margaret              10       "
  James                  8       "
  Ellen                  5       "
  John                   2       "
  Mary  ELDER           36    Scotland
p105
728-754
  George W.Fulweler     25    Va   joiner
  Matilda               21            (Shelton 1848cc)
  John R.        .     7/12
729-755                                      BARBOURSVILLE
  Anthony Shelton       55    Va   jailer                  cem#s25
  Margaret              41            (Moore SO)           cem#S25
  John W.               17
  James                 15
  David  HENSON         20         prisoner
730-756
  Elizabeth Derton      66    Va   insane
                              (E.Merritt m Peter Dartin 1802KCM)
731-757       (hotel)                        BARBOURSVILLE
  Robert McKendree      50    Va   innkeeper
  Mary                  43
  Everline (f)          17
  George                15
  Mary                   7
  Lucinda                5
  Evira                  2
  Notley DICK           25    Bar keeper(Catharine W.Cyrus 1853cc)
  Elijah C.SMITH        35    Shoemaker (Caroline McKendree 1848cc)
  Mary A.S.SMITH      10/12
732-758    (counted in B'ville had farm near Martha)(perhaps hotel)
  Cornwesley Simmons    26    Va   farmer               cem#S31A
  Elizabeth             28                               cem#S31A
  Malinda               12
  Sampson                8
  Charles SHOEMAKER     15    Va   farmer
  Oliver A. McGINNIS    25    Va   sheriff
  Helen S. McGINNIS     17    OH
  William WILLIAMS      19    Va   laborer
  James JONES           18    Va   laborer
  Melicia JONES         16    OH
733-759
  Edmond McGinnis       55    Va   farmer
  Polly                 55            (Hoagland SO)
  Fletcher              12
734-760                                      BARBOURSVILLE
  John Derton           32    Va   toll collector        (cem #17)
  Louisa Ann            29            (Seamonds 1840cc)
  Philip                 9
  Eliza A.               6
  William                3
  William DERTON        23         laborer
  Joseph CADENBACK      26    Germany   painter
```

p106
735-761
  Madison Thompson   31   Va
  Elizabeth   38
  Sarah McCARTHY   65
736-762
  Thorn Dusenberry   31   NY clerk(1/2 bro. to Father[Wm.C.])
  Louisa   23   Va (Moore 1849cc-d/oMartin&Mary #81)
736-763
  Cyrus M.Campbell   33   Va farmer
  Elizabeth   32
  John M.   10
  Sarah A.   6
  Robert W.   8
  Charles H.H.   4
  Mary V.   2
738-764
  Allen McGinnis   53   Va farmer
  Eliza   53   (Holderby 1822cc)
  Allen   22   Dr. Allen m Elizabeth Thornburg FBL
  Ira L.   18   Judge Ira m 1.Kate Hite 2.Beuhring FBL
  John   14
  Sarah P.   12   (m John Thornburg
  Henry H.   10
  Cinderella STAPLETON 16
739-765   OHIO RIVER
  Robert Holderby   57   Va farmer   s/o Wm.   cem#H10
  Susan A.   42   (Chapman   CCA)   cem#H10
  Dudly D.   21   physician d1862 CSA
  Fenton   18
  Robert   15   farmer   d1864 CSA
  Susan L.   14   (m Thomas Jenkins 1856cc)
  George W.   11   (m Adelaide Hite 1865cc)cem#H10
  Elizabeth   9   (m Samuel Cole 1859cc)
740-766
  Henry Clark   45   Va   school teacher
  Elizabeth   33
  Charles R.   17   farmer
  Rinaldo R.   16   farmer
  John T.R.   13
741-767
  William Partlow   40   Va farmer
  Mary   41   (?? 1829cc)
  James L.   15
  Henry L.   13
  William A.   11
  Benjamin P.   8
  George T.   5
p107
742-768   (see 306)   1 mile south of OHIO on GUYAN (east)
  John Everett   62   Va farmer   cem#H3
  Sarah   65   cem#H3
  Joseph H.WRIGHT   25   minister
743-769   GUYANDOTTE
  Isaac Ong   33   Va tailor
  Susan   28
  John W.   12
  Albina L. (f)   9
  Ernest M.   4
  Augusta V. (f)   1

```
744-770                                          GUYANDOTTE
   James Emmons          34   Va shoemaker
   Nancy                 28        (Dunkle 1833cc)
   Catherine             8
   James                 4
   William               2
745-771                                          GUYANDOTTE
   Edward Nixon          35   OH tailor
   Mary A.               35   Mass (Mary Ann Phelps 1840cc)
   Edward H.             8    Va
   Mary V.               6
   Edwin S.              1
   Caspar GEMENT         28   Germany
   Elizabeth COOK        30   Va
746-772                                          GUYANDOTTE
   Lewis Sexdinger       36   Pa shoemaker
   Rebecca               34   Pa
   James                 12   OH                       cem#H8
   Rachel                10   OH
   Margaret              3    OH
   John                  6/12 Va
747-773
   Jesse Dodson          25   Va boatman
   Lucretia              22
   Margaret              2
748-774                                          GUYANDOTTE
   Erastus Wellington    57   Conn   Joiner          cem#H6
   Charlotte             47   Conn      (Webb 1821cc)   cem#H6
   Erastus               19   Conn   carpenter    m 1.Hutchinson 2- 3- FBL
   James                 15   Conn
   Sarah                 12   Conn
   Lucinda               8    Conn
   Zachary T.            3    Conn        m Rebecca Smith d/D FBL
   Catharine MANN        25   Conn
749-775
   Noadiah Wellington    22   Conn   carpenter
   Elizabeth             17   Conn      McCarty   FBL
p108
750-776
   Jacob Hiltbruner      31   Pa    tinner
   Mary                  27   Pa
   Stephen               8    Pa
   William               6/12 Va
   William P.PREVINES    35   Pa    tinner
751-777
   William Hurd          33   NY    engineer
   Sarah                 24   TN
   Isreal                4    Ill
   Emetine   (f)         3    Va
   Cornella (f)          9/12 Va
   Moses RANSEL          21   Maine lawyer
   Charles WENTWORTH     24   Maine laborer
   James EDWARDS         34   Va    laborer
   Lawrence FORGEY       28   OH    lawyer
752-778                                          GUYANDOTTE
   Nathaniel Adams       39   Va lumberman
   Pauline               33        (McMahone 1838cc)
   Albert                7
   Fredrick              5
   Nancy McMAHONE        62
```

```
753-779                                         GUYANDOTTE
   Elizabeth Gardner      38    Va  (Brown-w/o Joseph 1829cc)
   Joseph                 14                        cem#H6
   Adaline                10
----780
   Lewis Peters           23
   Virginia               20
754-781
   Ezra Flowers           33    Ky lumberman
   Ellen                  35    OH       Chapdu   FBL
   Emily                  13    OH
   Eliza A.                7    OH
755-782                                         GUYANDOTTE
   Bushrod W.Kensolving   31    Va cabinetmaker
   Elizabeth J.           30
   Walter S.              10
   Alice L.                8
   Charles W.              6
   Louis W.                1
   John F.MURRAY          25    OH cabinetmaker
756-783
   Thomas Dunkle          37    Va cabinetmaker
   Charolotte M.          32
   Mary L.                14
   Harriett E.            12
   Miranda                 7
   Thomas J.               4
   Charles C.              3
   Romulus              3/12
   Eliza TARROW            7
p109
757-784                                         GUYANDOTTE
   Peter Clark            47    NH  lawyer
   Emeline A.             38    NY
   Philenum M.            19    NY   clerk
   George P.              18
   Mary E.                14
   John A.                 4
   Edgar B.                2    NY
   Silis M. CLARK         30    Maine-lawyer(Martha McCorkle 1851cc)
   Marie WHITE            30    Ireland
758-785
   Joseph Wheeler         35    OH minister
   Mary D.                35    OH
   Armand L. (m)           8    Ill
   Illinois M.(f)          5    Ill
   Joseph C.            3/12  VA
   John PAINE              8    Eng
759-786                                         GUYANDOTTE
   Sanders Arthur         33    Va boat builder
   Elizabeth              33          (Duncan 1836 LCoh)
   Mary                   12
   Elizabeth              10
   Sarah                   8
   George W.               6
   Emma                    3
   Thomas                  1
   William ARTHUR         21         lawyer
   Catharine ARTHUR       53
```

```
760-787                                              GUYANDOTTE
    Cyrus Andrews          39    Va  blacksmith
    Sarah                  37
    George F.              16
    Elizabeth              14
    David                  12
    James                   7
    Robert C.               4
    Polly ANDREWS          59
761-788                                              GUYANDOTTE
    Charles Chapdu         25    OH  confectioner
    Sarah J.               24    Va
    Olivia                  2    Va
    Peter CHAPDU           73    St.Dominge
    Eliza FINCH            19    OH
762-789
    Perceval Smith         53    OH  merchant                 cem#H10
    Mary D.                37    Va    (Chapman 1830cc)        cem#H10
    Edward A.              19        clerk   m Hite d/JW FBL
    Richard P.            17
    Percival S.            14         (m-Josephine Hite        cem#H10)
    James I.DOLIVER        30    NJ  minister
p110
763-790
    Gracey Stone (f)       53    Va
    Elizabeth              16
    Susan WEBB             23


----791                                              GUYANDOTTE
    James Vanderver        32    Va  Stage Agent
    Martha                 20         (Stone 1849cc)
764-792                                              GUYANDOTTE
    Henry H.Miller         36    Va  merchant                 cem#H10
    Eliza A.(Ann)          33         (Chapman 1837cc)        cem#H10
    Eliza F.               12
    Leonora (f)            10
    Chapman C.              3
    Arabella A.             1
    Edward BURKE           20        clerk
765-793  (see 832)
    John W.Hite            47    Va  merchant                 cem#H10
    Malinda                43         (McMahone 1825 LCoh)    cem#H10
    Salina C.              18            m Mason FBL
    Josephina              15         (Percival Smith Jr.     cem#H10)
    Victoria               12            m Romine FBL
    Adalaid C.              8         (m George Holderby 1865cc)
    Kate A.                 6            m  McGinnis FBL        cem#H10
766-794
    Thomas Christian       35    Va
    Mary A.                30
767-795                                              GUYANDOTTE
    Augustus S.Woolcott    41    OH  merchant
    Susan T.               31    OH
    Cordelia E. (f)         9    Va
    Bryan A.                7
    Robert B.               5
    Lois                    3
    William WALLACE         1         (is Wallace middle name ?)
    George BAYARD          16    OH  clerk
```

768-796	(3 wives)		(w/oHenrietta Wlotz Fincastle)cem#H6
A.M.McCorkle	42	Va physician (Alexander)	cem #15
Martha C.	19	Va (m Silas M.Clarke 1851cc)	
Phebe	17	OH	
Thomas C.	14	OH	cem#H6
Elizabeth KING	56	Va	
769-797	(see 455)	(1-Elenor Gueulle)	cem#H6
Victor Latulle	68	France merchant	cem#H10
Nancy	40	VA (2-Forgy 1838 LCoh)	cem#H10
Ellenor	12		
Victoria	10	(James S.Hayslip 1863 LCoh)	
Sarah J.	8		cem#H10
Louis Philippi	6		cem#H8
Josephine	4		cem#H10
James L.	2	(m Margaret	cem#H10)

p111

770-798			
James Elzey	44	Conn laborer	
Sarah	31	NJ	
Charles W.	7	NY	
Eliza M.	9	NY	
771-799			
Dudley D.Smith	47	OH farmer	
Ellenor C.	36	OH (Miller 1829 LCoh)	
Whitcomb	17	Va carpenter	
Sarah P.	15		
William P.	13		cem#H10
Mary P.	11		
Dudley J.	9		
Abraham M.	6		
Rebecca	5		
Georgia M.	3		

GUYANDOTTE

772-800			
James Todd	32	Scotland engineer	
Anna	28	Wales	
Mary	9	Wales	
Margaret	6	Wales	
Anna	4	Wales	
773-801			
W.Caspelman	45	Germany carpenter	
Caroline	39	Germany	
774-802	(Lucy Ann Hawthorn to Martin A.Emmons 1833cc)		
Lucy A. Emmons	32	Va	
Mary E.	16		
Frances S. (f)	12		
Serenas (m)	10		
775-803			
Kental Hezeltine	40	NH farmer	
Jane W.	50	Vt	
Sophia C.REED	24	Vt	

GUYANDOTTE

776-804			
Joseph S.Bradbury	40	NH printer	
Mary M.	39	Mass	
Charles W.	10	NY	
Octavia	8	NH	
Andrew J.	6	Mass	
Jenny Lind	8/12	Va	
Sarah BRADBURY	80	Mass	
777-805			
James Barnett	27	Va cooper	
Adelia	24	(Fuller or Fills 1845cc)	
Sylvester	3		
John C.	1		

p112
778-806   GUYANDOTTE
   Girard C.Ricketts   28   Md   physician
   Virginia   23   Va   (Everett 1844CCA)
   Albert C.   5
   Lucian C.(m)   3   (m Fannie Miller CCA)
   Girard C. (m)   1
---807
   E.Ricketts   56   Md   none
   Ellenor   50   Va   (Compton SO)
779-808
   Andrew S.Keenan   31   Va   (2-Sarah A.Scott 1850cc)
   Patrick H.   11
   Samuel N.   6
   Sarah KEENAN   60
780-809
   Fredrick Nichoof   50   Md
   Margaret   22   Va   (Ong 1845cc)
781-810
   Burgess Stewart   31   Ky   stonemason
   Mariah A.(Ann)   29   OH   (Ann Winger 1845cc)
   Hamilton W.   3   Va
                                                             PAT'S BRANCH
782-811   (1-Priscilla Wilson cem#H6-GUYANDOTTE
   John B.Hite   45   Va   tanner   cem#H6
   Elizabeth H.   32   Canada   (Johnson 1850cc) cem#H10
   Elizabeth A.   14   Va   cem#H6
   Sarah P.   12   cem#H6
  ·William HITE   71   none(Jane Hawkins 1820cc-bro-832)
   Eliza A.HITE   35
783-812
   Mary McMahone   36   Va   (Moore to Wayne McMahone 1841cc)
   John   16   clerk
   Emma   14
   Marcellus (m)   11
   Eliza   8
784-813
   Jacob Miller   35   OH   joiner
   Sarah   34   Va
   Abigail   10
   Heber   7
   George   5
785-814   GUYANDOTTE
   James Stewart   34   Va   stonemason   cem#H10
   Sarah J.   29   Ky   (Lakin ?)   cem#H10
   Jedediah F.   9   Ky
   Hansford H. (m)   7   Ky   cem#H10
   Joseph S.   5   Ky   cem#H10
   Columbia A.(f)   3   Va   (m Edward Holderby SO)
   Matilda BROWN   28   OH
786-815
   Henry Carter   28   Mass joiner   cem#H10
   Mary   24   Mass   cem#H10
   Mary   7   Mass
   Charles   4   Mass
   James   1   Va
   James THOMPSON   26   Mass laborer(Margaret Lattin 1851cc)

p113
787-816   PAT'S BRANCH
  Thomas I.Hayslip   42   Va   laborer   cem#H8
  Margey   42   cem#H8
  James   15   cem#H8
  Samuel   12   cem#H8
  Curry B. (m)   9
  Mary L.   6
  Thomas J.   3
788-817   PAT'S BRANCH
  Randolph Dietz   29   Germany carpenter
  Mariah   18   Mass
  Mary E.   7/12   OH
789-818   (see 788)
  Franklin Chapdu·   30   OH blacksmith
  Martha   29
  Francis   6
  Robert   4
  James   3
  Seymour   2
  Ellen EMMONS   18   OH
790-819   (see 809)
  John Ong   59   Va   butcher
  Margaret   47
791-820
  Sarah Windon   36
  Mary   16
  James   14
  Joseph H.   10
792-821
  Gilbert Stephenson   29   Va cooper
  America   26
793-822
  Enoch D.Blankenship   28   Ky laborer
  Louisa   24   Va   (Wellington 1844cc)
  Arabella F.   4
  Charlotte   3
  Leonara   1
                                          (west of river)?
794-823
  Francis Hite   30   Va tanner   cem#H9
  Mary   22   OH (Brammer 1844 LCoh) cem#H9
  Frances (f)   5   Va
  Isabel V.   1
795-824   PAT'S BRANCH
  Charles Dietz   32   Germany laborer
  Margaret DIETZ   64   "
  Hugo   26   "   laborer (m Minerva Clark 1855cc)
  Otto (m)   28   "   laborer   cem#H8
  Jeanet MANUS   47   "
  Barbry RANN   72   Germany
p114
796-825   PAT'S BRANCH
  George W.Grose(Grass) 45   Va sadler
  Elizabeth   38   cem#H4
  Alina   20
  Frances   8
  Mary L.   6
  Theodore W.   1

```
797-826
  George Chapman        72    Va farmer
  Elizabeth             63        (Parker CCA)
  Elizabeth             28
798-827                                              ˉGUYANDOTTE
  James Woods           30    OH plasterer
  Ann                   24    Va
  Jane                   3
  Carlos                1
799-828
  James W.Ward          36    Va lawyer
  Adaline               26
  Charles W.            4
  James W.              2
  Elizabeth          10/12
800-829     (hotel)                                  GUYANDOTTE
  Alfred Whitney        46    Maine   innkeeper
  Lucinda               46    NH
  Henry C.              19    Md
  Mary F.               17    Md
  Sarah J.              14    Md
  Anna SHAY             51    East Indies
  Richmond W.SHOEMAKER  22    Va    school teacher
  James MATHEWS         33    Pa    stage driver
----830
  A.JOGNEY              35    Mass artist
  Marietta Jogney       28    Mass
  Marietta              5    Mass
  John DUCEY            21    Ireland  laborer
  William McCOMAS       23    Va    physician (m Sarah French SO)
  Patience McHENRY      45    Va
801-831
  Nancy Walker          32    Va
  Elizabeth             19
802-832    (see 811 & 1011)
  Jacob Hite            74    Va   (grandson of Jost Heidt SO)cem#H10
  Sarah                 65    NC    (Scales CCA)            cem#H10
803-833
  Robert Stewart        46    Va farmer (1-Harriet McClung SO)
  Martha                31        (Wright SO) Hodges d/o Robt. FBL
  Druzilla              14        m John White FBL
  Ann E.                12        (m.Wm.Wallace SO) Bath Co.
  James A.              5
  Martha V.             1        (m Arthur Micthell SO)
  James H.              8
  William F.            6        (m Clara Barbour SO)
  Nancy E.              4
  Martha E.             2
  Sarah STEWART         50

                   (2 sets of step children ??)
p115
804-834                              OHIO RIVER -north
  Melcor Ansel (m)      69    Va farmer (d1853-SO          cem #23)
  Elizabeth             69
  Anne C.               18
805-835
  Jacob Ansel           40    Va
  Anna F.               39
  Sally J.              17
  Ellenor C.            15        deaf & dumb
```

```
805-835 Ansel (con't)
  Malakiah W.          13
  John J.              11
  Elizabeth F.          9
  Joseph H.             7
  Leonard F.            5
  Albert G.             3
  Anna C.               1
806-836
  Jacob Coffe          48    OH farmer
  Mary J.              36
  George               22       farmer
807-837
  Jacob Rake (Hoke ?)  43    OH farmer
  Lavicy               36
  John                 19       farmer
  Peyton               17       farmer
  Jasper               14
  Fredrick             12
  Susannah             10
  David M.              8
  Rebecca               6
  Claricy               3    Va
808-838
  Abram Pennel         24    Va farmer
  Elizabeth            21                      OHIO RIVER north 7 MILE
809-839
  Daniel Clark         35    Va farmer
  Jane                 35
  Evan                 16       farmer
  Rachael              14
  Harvey               12
  Lavenia              10
  David                 8                             ( Cem #23)
  Emily                 6
  William               4                             (cem #24A)
  Andrew T.             1
p116
810-840
  James Fife           38    Va farmer (Files ?)
  Elizabeth            37
  Eliza                15
  Margaret V.           8
  Mary E.               5
  Jacob A.              2
811-841                                        OHIO RIVER north 7 MILE
  George J.Grimes      38    Va farmer
  Harriet              28
  William H.            4                             (cem #23)
  James K.              2
  Presly WOODYARD      23       farmer  (m Eliza Syrus 1853cc)
812-842
  Epineter Wallet      27    Va farmer
  Phebe                21    OH
  Comodore P.           4    OH
  John                  3    OH
  Caroline E.           1    Va
```

```
813-843
   Benjamin Fifes         30    Va farmer    (Files ?)
   Martha A.              33    OH
814-844
   Michael Floyd          33    OH farmer
   Jane E.                20
   Patrick H.             1
815-845
   William McComas        56    Va minister    (s/o Elisha)
   Mildred                54         (Ward CCA)
   Hamilton C.            19         none
   Rufus                  17         farmer
   Benjamin J.            15         farmer
   Elizabeth SMITH        18
   Mathew McKENNON        50    Pa stonemason
                                        BARBOURSVILLE west
816-846                              (bro/o Solomon & Moses)
   Ephraim Thornburg      70    Va  farmer   w/o Rachael Simmons CCA
   John                   24    Md  farmer
   Moses                  21    Va  farmer(m Mary T.)        cem#s23
   Hezekiah               18
   Elizabeth HITCHKISS    33         (Thornburg dau.?
   William HITCHKISS      9
   Mary HITCHKISS         8
   Daniel GWINN           36    NY  Stage driver
   Margaret GWINN         33    Md      (Thornburg )           (cem #s23)
817-847
   William Smith          32    Va farmer          cem#H10
   Nancy                  32    OH    Payne 1840 LCoh
   Mary J,                7     Va
   Malissa A.             6
   James W.               4
   John M.                3
   Sarah E.              6/12
818-848
   Witfield G.Bryan       44    SC school teacher (1855 in Martha)
   Elizabeth              40    Va    (Carmack 1848cc)
p117
819-849
   Adam Kelly             51    Va laborer
   Elizabeth              51
   James                  18
   Samuel                 17
   Adam                   14
   Peter                  12
   Lucy J.                8
   Philip B.              8 twin
   Rolin ROGERS           19         laborer
820-850                         DAVID CREEK to WEST PEA RIDGE
   John W.Griffith        44    OH farmer              cem #s23
   Elizabeth              38    Va    (Thornburg 1832cc)   cem #s23
   Mary F.                10
   Eliza A.               7                          (cem #s23)
   Adalaide A.E.          5                          (cem #s23)
   Georgeanna T.          3                          (cem #s23)
   Solomon T.             1
   Joel K. SOLOMAN        21    NY farmer
   Benjamin NORRIS        21    Va farmer
   Mary J.ROBERTS         28    Va
```

```
821-851                                              WEST PEA RIDGE
   James C.Wilson          38   Va farmer              (cem #s22B)
   Sarah A.                31                           (cem #s22B)
   Charles M.               8                           (cem #s22B)
   Elizabeth F.
   Nancy A.                 3        (m George Thornburg SO)
   James MEADOWS           19   laborer   (Emily Keller 1853 LCoh)
   Harrison FORTNER        35   laborer
822-852
   Andrew Conner           43   Va farmer                    cem#S54
   Milly                   45        (Chapman 1829cc)         cem#S54
   William W.              20        farmer (Louisa Beckett)cem#S54
   John W.                 18        farmer
   America                 17                                 cem#S54
   Addison    (m)          15
   Amanda                  13
   Amicetta                11
   Permelia                10
   Cornwesley    (m)        8   (Pornnelsy on census but all others C)
   Joseph M.                5
                                                    WEST PEA RIDGE
823-853                         (s/o Syl.Sr. born 1793 RI SO)
   Sylvester Fuller        57   Pa farmer                (cem #s22A)
   Sarah L.                55   Va   (McGinnis 1812cc)    (cem #s22A)
   Edmund                  28        farmer              (cem #s22A)
   Adaline                 24
   Theodore                17        farmer
   Alphonse                16        farmer
   Mary                    11
   Jasper                   7
   Sylvester HATTON         6
----854
   Oliver W.Fuller         22   Va laborer            (cem #s22A)
   Louisa                  19
824-855                                          WEST PEA RIDGE
   Sylvester Fuller        32   Va lawyer
   Elizabeth A.            24        (Paine 1847cc)         cem#H12
   Cornelia                 2
   Oliver B.             2/12
825-856                                          WEST PEA RIDGE
   Achilles Fuller         36   Va lawyer             (cem #s22A)
   Elizabeth               39        (Ward 1834cc)
   John                    13
   Eliza                   10
   Albert                   8
826-857                                          8th STREET ROAD
   Edward Shy              63   Va farmer
   Elizabeth               55
   Mahala J.               25
   Rutha A.                24
   Benjamin C.             22        timberer (Mary Seamonds SO)
   Edward C.               19        farmer   (Lucinda A.Harrison 1854cc)
   Harvey                  17        farmer   (Josephine Plybon 1859cc)
                                (Harvey & Josephine SHY both cem#H10
827-858
   Layayette Stephenson 22      Va boatman
   Nancy                   19
   Sarah RIGGS             15
   James RIGGS             16        laborer
```

```
828-859                              1m W of Russel Ck-James River Turnpike
  Skelton Poteet        44    Va farmer
  Martha                41         (McGinnis 1831cc)
  Clementine J. (m)     16    farmer m 1.Am.Wentz,2.Sarah Dillon  FBL
  James                 13
  Susan                  8
  John                   2
  Eliza STEPHENSON (m)  21         laborer
p119
829-860                              1m W of Russel Ck on James River Turnpike
  William Wentz         42    Va farmer
  Matilda               42         (Riggs 1832cc)
  John                  15    farmer m Underwood FBL
  America               12            m Clem Poteet FBL
  Mary                  10            m R.C.Wright FBL
  Sarah A.               8            m John W.Fuller FBL
  Frances (f)            6            unmarried FBL
  Henry Clay             4            m Elizabeth Crump FBL
  Alexander              2            d at 21 FBL
830-861
  Adam Keller           45    Germany  shoemaker
  Nancy                 37    Va     (Arthur 1831cc)
  Emily                 18
  Albert                17
  Eliza                 15
  Lewis                 11
  Mary                   8
  Thomas                 7
  Rhoda L.               6
  Lucretia               5
  Edward                 2
831-862
  Hiram Carter          50    Va farmer
  Nancy                 50
  James J.L.            17         farmer
  Catharine M.          15
  Levi TOPPING          25         laborer
832-863
  Nancy Bates           56    Va
  Grisin L.             23    Ky  boatman
  Andrew J.             17    Va
  Eliza A.              16
  Susannah              12
  Ellen                 11
833-864
  Thomas Bates          28    Ky farmer
  Lydia                  3    OH
  Eliza E.               2    Va
834-865    (see 944)                       4 POLE about Green Valley
  William Topping       52    Eng farmer(1-Rebecca Stephenson 1819cc)
  Elizabeth             41    Va
  Sarah                 14
  William               10
  Elery M.               6
  Almeda                 2
  Greenville DAVIS      30    Va farmer
```

```
835-866
  Ira Blankenship        36    Va farmer
  Lockey                 35          (Shy 1837cc)
  Abigail                12
  Samatha O.              8
  George V.               3
  Orella (f)              1
p120        (s/o Benj.)                           4 POLE
836-867
  Isaiah Ray             42    Va farmer (1-Sarah Rece 1834cc)cem#S5
  Lucy                   25          (2-Barbour -CC Death Cert.)
  Joseph B.               7          (m Lucretia Keller FR)    cem#S13A
  Benjamin                5    (M.Imogene Cardwell 1866cc-FR--cem.#s13A
  Eveline                 3          (m William Spurlock FR)
  Caroline              6/12         (M James Dunkle 1865cc)
837-868
  William Dillon         30    Va farmer
  Julia A.               20    OH
  George P.               5    Va
  Lucy                    2
838-869                                           4 POLE
  John Topping           25    OH farmer
  Chloe                  22    Va    (Dillon 1847cc)
  Henry                   1
839-870
  William M.Stephenson   52    Va farmer
  Mary C.                49          (Paine           cem#H12
  Daniel                 21    farmer
  William                19    farmer
  Lucretia               18
  James                  14
  Calvary                11
  Samuel                  9
840-871
  William Ray            34    Va farmer                cem #s6
  Emily                  35          (Hatton 1838cc)
  Elizabeth              17    (m James Wilson 1851 SO)
  William                15                             cem #s6
  Isaiah                 13                             cem #s5
  Lemuel                 10                             cem #s6
  Victoria                8                             cem #s6
  Albert                  6
  America                 4                             cem #s6
  Virginia                2
841-872
  Samuel Blankenship     53    Va farmer
  Lelia C.               35
  Martin T.               6
  John T.                 5
  Samuel J.               4
  George L.               2
  William J.           4/12
P 121
842-873
  Dennis Obrien          34    Va shoemaker
  Malinda J.             25
  Jane                    5
  Frances M.              4
  Alice M.                2
  Thomas H.            9/12
```

843-874

Adam Seamonds	46	Va farmer
Delila	44	
Greenville	21	OH farmer
Catharine	19	
Lucinda	16	
Joseph	15	farmer
Robert	13	Va
Henry	10	
Nathaniel	6	
Joel	4	
Selena Kay	3	

844-875

John Thompson	37	Va farmer
Matilda	36	
Sarah	12	
Mary A.	10	OH
Andrew G.	7	
Martha J.	5	

845-876

Effy Owens	44	OH farmer
Saluda	45	(Irby 1825 SO) Pittslyvania Co.
Mary A.	23	
William	18	farmer
Henry	15	farmer
Jordan	14	
Monroe	12	
Elizabeth	10	
Edward	6	(m Emma Arthur 1871 SO)
Eliza	2	OH

846-877   4 POLE - BOWEN RIDGE

David Sulivan	65	NC farmer
Ellenor	55	Va
Mary A.	22	
Malinda	16	
Jacob	21	
Lewis	18	

p122

847-878   4 POLE - BOWEN RIDGE

John Plybourn	37	Va farmer	cem #s6
Elizabeth	32	(Beckner FR)	cem #s6
James C.	15	farmer(Emily Topping 1859 FR)cem#s6)
Jacob	12	(1Dunkle-2 Blankenship FR)cem#s13)
Louisa	9	(m John Bailey 1857 FR)
Lewis	7	cem #s6
John C.(Calvin)	5	(Eliza E.Flowers 1865cc FR)cem#s6
Henry W.	2	cem #s6

----879   (possible Polly Parker to John Beckner 1815Gpky

Mary Beckner	57	Va
Lydia	22 twin	
Irene	22	(2w/oJohn Plybon#878-1855cc)cem#s6
John C.	20	farmer
Stephen	18	farmer

848-880   8th STREET ROAD

John Roberts	32	Va wheelwright
Louisa	25	
James P.	4	
John W.	2	

849-881
```
John Adams              58      Va farmer
Jane                    50
James                   17              (Martha J.Andrews 1843 LCoh ?)
Julia A.                14
Jordan A.ADAMS          33              laborer
Jeremiah ADAMS          24              laborer (Elizabeth Antice 1851 SO)
```
850-882
```
George Hagen            62      Va farmer
Eliza A.                18
Mary E.                 17
George                  16
Louisa                  14
Frances                 12
```
851-883
```
Melville McGinnis       26      Va farmer
Elizabeth               20      OH
```
852-884
```
William Burks           40      Ky farmer
Mary A.                 40      Ky
Mahala                  18      IN
Thomas                  14      Ky
Jessee                  12
Isaac                   10
Elizabeth                8
Julia A.                 2              m Edward Douthet  FBL
```
853-885
```
James W.Hanly           38 Va farmer
Elizabeth               31
Mary E.                 15
Frances                 11
Virginia                 8
Matilda                  6
Margaret                 1
```
p123
854-886
```
James Sullivan          31      Ky farmer
Elizabeth               30              (Hollenback ?)
Celia                    7
Mary                     4      Va
Rebecca BURKS           80      NC
```
855-887
```
Ellen Hollenback        58 Va(Hampton w/oMartin Hollenback 1811cc)FR
Mary A.                 23              (m Wm.J.Thompson 1858cc)
Eliza C.                17
```
---888
```
Henry Sulivan           25      Va laborer                      cem #s6
Catharine                       (Hollenback ?)                  cem #s6
```
856-889   4 POLE
```
Manoah(Nathan)Cardwell 27      Va farmer
Sarah A.(Ann)           27              (Hollenback 1843cc)FR
Olivia                   7
Mary E.(Imogene)         5              (m Benjamin Ray 1866cc)
Amanda                   3              (m Alexander McComas 1866cc)
Edwenia (f)           8/12
```

857-890
```
   John R.Flowers       32    Va farmer                    cem #s4
   Mildred              30        (Roberts FR)             cem #s4
   Mary                 11        (1 Jarrell-2 Hatten FR)
   George W.             9        (m Julia Irby 1864  FR)cem #s4
   Fredrick             7        (Martha Wilks 1867 FR)    cem #s4
   Eliza E. (Ellen)     4        (J.Calvin Plybon 1865cc FR)cem#s6
   Louisa               2        (George Newcomb 1869 FR)
   Alice A.          3/12        ( 1 Irby-2 Hodge FR)
```
858-891
```
   Patterson Roberts    29    Va teamster
   Janetta              19
   Elizabeth         10/12
```
859-892
```
   John Houghland       48    OH farmer (Howland)?
   Mary R.              42
   Mariah               24
   Mary                 23         (Thomas Ball 1851cc)
   David                17
   John                 10
   Phebe H.              7
   Charles C.            2
```
860-893
```
   Joseph Neubacher     40    Germany   farmer
   Anna                 32    Ger
   Ludwig                9    Ger
   Frances               7    Ger
   Victor                5    Ger
```
861-894
```
   Henry Medlin         40    Germany   farmer
   Dosia (f)            45    Ger
   John                 12    Ger
   Bruno                10    Ger
   Hermma (f)            5    Ger
   Julius WEISSACKER    23    Ger    farmer
```
p124
862-895
```
   Ann Arnet            45    Va
   Hesekiah PORTER      25    OH
   Alonze PORTER         2    Va
   Sarah EDWARDS        23    OH
   Catharine EDWARDS    12    OH
   Joseph EDWARDS        8    OH
                                    (families of 2 dau.?)
```
863-896
```
   William Casey        21    Va farmer
   Jemima               15
   Eliza J.HULL          6
```
864-897
```
   Stephen Kelly        49    Ky farmer
   Esther               43    Ky
   Henry J.             16    Ky
   John                 13    Va
   Elizabeth            10
   Charles               8
   Doliver               5
```

```
865-898
   James Fortune          31    Va farmer
   Mary                   28    Ky
   Sarah J.                8
   Cynthia                 6
   Charles                 4
   Nancy                   2
866-899
   James Piatt            32    Ky farmer
   Tabitha A.             28    Ky
   Robert                 12    Oh
   Andrew J.              11    Va
   Emily J.                8
   James M.                3
                                                      CENTRAL CITY
867-900
   Martin Hull            73    NJ (1-Susanna Buffington CCA) cem#H15
   Anna                   41    Va    (Susanna A.Johnson 1822cc)
   Martin                 21
   John                   18
   Sarah A.               15
   Mary                   12
   Elizabeth              10
   Eliza                   7
   Harriet                 5
   Matilda                 2
p125
868-901
   Ann Poage              50    Va   (McCormick w/o William 1822cc)
   Amelia                 28
   James Harvey           25       farmer(Sarah Gallaher cc) cem#H10
   Jemima                 21
   Mary J.                14
   Lucretia               12
   Fredrick W.            10
                                                      CENTRAL CITY
869-902
   Sarah Hull             40    Va   Burket w/o Hiram Hull 1828 LCoh
   Heil B. (m)            18    OH       farmer
   Susan E.               16    Va
   Sarah J.                7
   Lewis                   4
   Ella                    1
----903
   John McCormack         23    Va farmer
   Nancy                  20
   Harvey HULL            47    NH
870-904       see 902
   William Burkett        38    Ky farmer
   Martha                 34    Va    McCormack 1836 LCoh
   Harriet A.             11
   Lucretia               10
   Martha                  5
   Walstein (m)            3
   George RUSSELL         18
871-905
   Gilbert Stephenson     37    Va   Cooper
   Nancy                  25    OH
   Melissia                1    OH
```

```
872-906
  Rebecca Kelly           32    Va
  Jessee Kelly (m)        41
  James M.                18
  Margaret                15
  Jane                     9
  Polly                    2
873-907                                      CENTRAL CITY
  John Morgan             31    OH wheelwright
  Martha                  31    IN    Peters 1844cc
  Orpheus R. (m)           5    Va
  Perry A.                 3
  Helen M.             10/12
  William GRANVILLE       38    Germany  blacksmith
p126
874-908
  John Belaney            38         farmer    (William ??)
  Ellenor                 35
  Charles H.              16
  Eliza A.                13
  Nancy E.                11
  Phebe F.                 9
  Samuel T.                6
  Malissa                  4
  Micena A. (f)            2
  Armstead T.M.         5/12
875-909
  Absalom Yates           41    Va laborer
  Barbry A.               35
  Alexander PINE          52         farmer(PINE home with son-in-law??)
  Julia      PINE         47
  Overton    PINE         21         farmer
  Bryon H.   PINE         16         laborer
  James E.   PINE         13
  Mary       PINE          8
  Clary      PINE          7
  Rufus      PINE          6
----910
  Floyd Pine              23    Va farmer
  Virginia                20
  Hester A.                1
876-911                                      7th STREET WEST
  William Johnson         30    Va farmer
  Mary (H.)               24         (McGinnis 1848cc)      cem#22A
  Fredrick M.              1
  John BOILING             9
877-912                                      7th STREET WEST
  James Johnson           63    Ireland   farmer
  Martha                  57    Ireland      (Logan 1817 m Ireland)
  Sarah                   24    Va
  John                    21
  Marcel    (m)           18
  Martha                  15
  Eliza KYLE               5
  William KYLE             4
878-913
  James Hawkins           35    Va carpenter
  Kesiah                  26
  Samuel                  12
  Josephine             8/12
  Rosanah BURNS           25
```

116

879-914   (owned 1st to 5th Street west from Ohio to 4 Pole)
  Samuel W.Johnson   38   Pa farmer(1-Rebecca Martin cc)cem#H10
  Eliza   25   Va (Kilgore CCA)   cem#H10
  Mary   13   James Gallaher CCA
  Ann   11
  Napeleon   9   Sarah Dundas CCA   cem#H10
  Frances (f)   6
  Martha   4
  Emily   2
  Sarah JOHNSON   35
p127
880-915
  Henry W. Hollenback 37 Va farmer
  Margaret A.   35   Md   (Ricketts 1833cc)
  Frances A.   15   Va
  Mary E.   13
  Leonidas   10
  William F.   8
  John M.   4
  Alvin   1
881-916
  Ansel A.Adams   28   Va farmer
  Malinda   25
  Jane   5
  Robert   2
  James EPES   28   Ky farmer
882-917
  John W.Allen   53   Ky farmer
  Nancy   48   Va
  John   18
  Samuel   15
  Runels (m)   13
  Henry C.   8
883-918
  Nancy Large   52
  Edford L.   29   farmer
  Joseph   19   farmer
  Henry   17   farmer
884-919   (see 1011)
  Albert Laidley   26   Va merchant   cem#H10
  Vesta   26   (Brown 1845 at Pt.Pleasant)cem#H10
  Alberta   3
  Benjamin   2   cem#H10
  John   5/12   cem#H10
  Matilda BROWN   53   NC   (Scales w/o Benjamin Brown SO)
  Cyrus BROWN   (f) 28   Va
  Levi WILSON   15   farmer
  Edmund PARKER   50 (black)
  Lillie PARKER   46 (black)
885-920
  Noah Fuller   44   Vt shoemaker
  Margaret   31   Va
  Marcellus   4
  Leonidas   3
  Juliet   1
  Francis M.(m)   3/12

p128
886-921

John B.Farrel	58	Pa wheelwright
Mary C.	55	Germany
Mary A.	5	Ky
Emily	3	Ky
Matilda	1	Ky

887-922   BLUE SULPHUR

William R.Seamonds	41	Va farmer (s/o Elijah SO) cem#S51
Nancy	40	(Harshbarger 1829cc) cem#S51
Andrew J.	20	lumberer(Mary Mann 1852cc)cem#S51
David A.	18	farmer
Charles	15	
Mary	16	(m Benjamin Shy CCA)
Elizabeth	13	(M McCain CCA
Lucy	12	(m Noah Coffman 1859cc)
William H.	11	(m Sarah Lusher) both cem#H10
Eliza	9	(m James Dundas 1860cc)
Peyton H.	7	cem#H10
America S.	5	(m George Crump CCA)
Nancy	3	(m V.B.Davis CCA)
John P.	5/12	

888-923

Philip Bumgardner	67	Pa. Farmer
Mary	38	Va.
Hetty CONNER	36	(Bumgarner w/o Lorenzo D 1840cc)
James W. CONNER	1	Ohio

----924

John Ward	26	Va. Labourer
Joanna	23	

889-925

James H. Walker	27	Farmer (2 Mrs. Ardelia Burnett 1852SO)
Eliza J.	21	
William (M)	3	Va.
Adolphus (M)	1	
Hannah WALKER	46	Va.
James STEEL	8	

890-926   WEST PEA RIDGE

Daniel Dunkle	45	Va. Farmer (Samuel?) cem#S22A
Eliza	46	(Catlett 1831cc cem#sS22A
Emma	17	cem#S22A
Arianna	15	cem#S22A
James	13	cem#S22A
Theodore	8	
Lucy	5	(m F.M.Tucker cem#S22A)
Alexander	1	cem#S22A

p129
891-927

Overton H.White	45	Va schoolteacher
Matilda C.	39	(Hite 1829cc)
Albert G.	20	laborer
John H.	18	
Mary E.	16	
Ezra	14	
Jacob E.	12	
George W.	10	
Alice J.	8	
William	6	
Artemicia	3	

```
892-928
  Edward Wright          39    Va farmer
  Elizabeth              34        (McGinnis 1836cc)
  William                13
  Richard                11        m Mary Wentz FBL
  Drucilla                8       (m John B.Gallaher 1860cc)
  Sarah                   5
  James                   9
  Mary                    3
  Lucy                    1
  Virginia McGINNIS      23
  William McGINNIS       28    Va      (in-laws)
893-929
  Isaac Crump            27    OH farmer              cem#H10
  Nancy A.               19    Va   (Miller 1849 SO)  cem#H10
  Elizabeth CRUMP        56    Va
  George CRUMP           13    Ky                     cem#S51
894-930
  William Harrison       46    Va farmer
  Linia                  41        Cynthia    Dillon (Andy Earl)
  Otis                   21
  Celia                  18      m David Earl s/o Jessie & Mary
  Abigail                17
  Catharine              15
  William R.             13
  John H.                11
  Mary V.                 9
  James R.                5
  Columbia J.             4
  Salena                  1
  Rebecca F.PLYBON       14
895-931
  Lewis Arthur           54    Va. Farmer
  Lucy                   50
  Susan L.               20
  William G.             19        farmer
  Eliza E.               16
  Tempy P.       (f)     14
  Leonora        (f)     12
p130
----932
  Absalom Roberts        30        laborer(1-Jane Arthur 1844 LCoh)
  Pernetta G.            24
  John L.                 4
  Lucy F.              6/12
896-933
  George W.Stephenson    26    Ga   farmer
  Rebecca                29    Va
  Jeremiah                4
  Reuben                  2
  George W.            3/12
897-934
  Frances Chapman        60    Ga
  Evelene                18    Va
  Alexander              15        farmer
898-935
  Morgan Mays            55        farmer
  Nancy                  50
  Dianna                 17
  William                15
  Mary R.                12
  Martha A.              10
```

```
899-936
  Andrew J.Stephenson    21          farmer
  Martha                 23
  Rutha                  23
900-937
  Henry Miller           48      OH farmer
  Susanah                34          (Chapman SO)
  Abigail                16
  Josephine              14
  Martha H.              11
  Margaret A.             8
  Georgia                 4
901-938
  Robert Denton          53      Eng  brushmaker
  Jane                   58      Eng
  William DENTON         25      Eng  school teacher
  Elizabeth DENTON       18      Eng
902-939
  James McCorkle         25      OH farmer
  Sarah                  25      Ky
  George W.              10
  Mary J.                 9
  Catherine               7
  Lafayette               4
  Sarah                   2
  Sarah McCORKLE         30      Ky
p131
903-940                                    16th Street Road
  Hannah Stephenson      80      Va
  Elizabeth              40          blind
  Henry                  20          laborer
  Joseph                 16          laborer
904-941                                    16th Street Road
  Calvary Stephenson     34      Va farmer              cem#H12
  Mary                   28          (d/o William Paine)   CCA
  Georgia                 4
  Charles V.              2
  William             10/12                              cem#H12
905-942                                    16th Street Roadd
  Mark Stephenson        54      Va farmer (b Franklin Co.Va)cem#H12
  Mary                   56                              cem#H12
906-943      (see 658)
  James Gallaher         66      Pa farmer              cem#H10
  Sarah                  56      Va   Crouch   (WSL)    cem#H10
  Eliza                  30      . (Thomas Jordan 1855 d1856 SO)
  James                  22        (m Mary Johnson 1854/5cc)cem#H10
  Thomas                 18
  Sarah                  20        (m J.Harvey Poage 1851cc)
  John                   14        (m Drusilla Wright CCA)
907-944                           (1- Frances Ellenor Dannenberg SO)
  F.G.L. Beuhring        59      Germany farmer          cem#H10
  Melcina M.             21      OH      (McGinnis 1847cc)
  Nora C.              3/12      Va
  Corenora E.          3/12      Va twin
  Andrew TOPPING         25      OH  (see 689 & 865)
908-945
  Aaron Sullivan         34      Ky laborer
  Polly                  65      N.C.
```

```
909-946
  David McAlavy        34   Pa.  Joiner
  Mary                 24   Pa.     (M.E.Layman 1844 LCoh)
  Minerva               3
  Nacy                  2   Va.
910-947
  Burwell Wilkes       32   Va. Labourer
  Barbary              33          (sheff 1837)
  James                12
  George                9
  Mary                  7
  Sarah                 4
  Alexander             1
911-948
  George Chadison      38   Eng  Farmer
  Mary                 35
  Olivia                8
  Henry                 2
p132
912-949
  Alexander Johnson    44   Pa. Farmer
  Nancy                37
  Samuel               17
  Louisa J.            15
  Alexander            12
  Anna M.              10
  Josephine             8
  Nancy                 6   Va.
  Rachael               5
  Armstead              3
  Henry C.              2
  John               6/12
  David NEFF           26   Pa. Laborer
  William BURKS        15   Ky. Laborer
913-950
  Rufus P. Balser      26   Va. Cabinetmaker
  Elizabeth PETERS     22   Ind
  Louvicy T.PETERS      3   Va.
  Rufus    PETERS       2
  Albert D.PETERS     4/12
914-951
  William Peters       49   Va. Farmer
  Amicetta             39   Va.
  Hannah               19   Ind
  Lavenia              17
  William              16   Ind Farmer
  Andrew J.            13
  James M.             12
  Amicetta             10
915-952  (s/o 943)
  William Gallaher     24   Va. Farmer
  Mary                 19   Oh
  James F.           10/12  Va.
916-953
  Thomas Bradshaw      24   Va farmer
  Cynthia A.           27
  William F.            4
  Allen M.              2
```

```
917-954
  David A.Lovejoy        39   Md farmer
  John T.                34
  Jenetta                36                        ↲
  James YANKEE           24   Pa laborer
918-955
  Michael Shultz         44   Pa joiner
  Sarah                  30   Va   (Wright 1837cc)
  George E.              12
  Senie A. (f)           10
  Eugenia L. (f)          9
  James H.                7   Maine
  Lucy K.                 5   Maine
  William W.              3   Va
  Susan J.SCHULTZ        20   OH   (oldest daug)
p133
919-956
  Jesse Crump            23   OH farmer
  Ellen                  29   Va
920-957                      (must be 2nd)
  Malinda Stephenson     47   (Hunter m Thomas Stephenson 1845cc)
  William                19      laborer
  Ruben                  17
  Elizabeth              14
  Willy (m)              12
  Mary                   10
921-958
  James J.Mays           74   Va farmer
  Winifred               54
  Henry J.               23      laborer
  Adaline                21   |
  Joseph                 16      laborer
  Beverley J. (m)        16      laborer twin
  Julius H. (m)          15      laborer
  John T.                11
922-959
  Real Ferguson          45   Va cooper
  Mary A.                40   OH
  Syrena                 13   Va
  Lucinda                13      twin
  Anderson L.             5      laborer
  Andrew L.BLAKE         18      laborer
  James M.BLAKE          16
  George W.BLAKE         14
  Almarina V.SUMMERS      9 (f)
923-960
  John Kelly             23   Va farmer
  Sarah J.               25   !
  Nancy A.                7
  William A.              5
  Joseph V.               2
  Sabrienthey KELLY      40 (f)
  Darly A. KELLY(m)      13
  Mourning C.KELLY(f)     9
  Wm. P. Byrington       16
p134
```

```
924-961   (see 977)                          OHIO RIVER west of GUYANDOTTE
  Peter C. Buffington   35   Va farmer                        cem#H10
  Eliza                 35   Md.   (Standard)CCA
  Willie A.   (f)        7   Va.
  Eugenia     (f)        5
  Standard    (m)        3                                    cem#H10
  Columbia    (f)       19
  Georgenna NICHOLS     17
  Rebecca STANDARD      57        (w/o Edward)                cem#H10
925-962   (s/o WM.)      (James cem#H10-Arianna #H6)     OHIO RIVER
  James Holderby        68   Va. farmer  (1-Arianna Lane 1821 GAoh)
  Lucy                  46   NY           (Wright CCA)
  James                 16   Va.
  Emma                  13        (Dr.James A.Rodgers SO)Kanawha
  Hannah                10
  William                8        (m/Hallie Valentine SO)
  Edward                 6        (m Columbia Stewart SO)cem#H10
  Henry                  4
  Sarah R.               2
926-963
  Janes Ayslis (f)      38   Va
  Christopher C.        24   Ky laborer
  James W.              18
  Adalaide              16
  Minerva A.            13
927-964
  Christopher Peters    25   IN farmer
  Cynthia               25   Va
  Eliza V.               8
928-965
  Samuel Hunter         49   Va laborer
  Martha                40
  Thomas J.             18        laborer
  Emily R.              16
  Sarah E.              14
  Samuel T.             12
  Joseph M,              6
  Martha E.              4
  Peter E.               1
  Margaret HUNTER       20
929-966
  Michael Staly         45   Va farmer
  Jacob                 30
  Elizabeth             26
  Elizabeth M.           2
  Charles L.             1
  Joseph              3/12
p135
930-967
  Joseph Staly          48   Va farmer
  Margaret              33        (Highsey 1832cc)
  Susannah              15
  Mary B.               13
  Eliza M.              10
  Henrietta              8
  George A.              6
  Michael C.             1
  Elizabeth HISEY       55
```

```
931-968
  Henry B.Paine          25   Va carpenter (1-McGinnis CCA)
  Virginia A.            18        (McCormick 1848cc)
  Emma                    1
932-969                             across RIVER from PAT'S BRANCH
  Beverly B.Burks        39   Va boat pilot          cem#H8
  Martha                 28                           cem#H8
  Lewis                  10
  Charles W.              8
  Beverly B.              6
  Martha E.               3
  Emma                    2
  William CLARK          18        engineer
933-970
  John Harden            32   Va steamboat pilot
  Phebe                  28
  Thomas J.               9
  Charles N.              5
  Creed M. (m)            3
  Fenton A. (f)        10/12
934-971
  Charles Burks          56   Va farmer
  Nancy                  43
  James                  26        laborer
  George                 28        laborer
935-972                                             16st ROAD
  William Paine          65   Va physician          cem#H12
  Elizabeth B.           59        (Russell CCA)
  Sarah                  20        (Albert Russell CCA)
  Charles                19
  Frances (f)            16        (Alfred Seamonds CCA) cem#H12
  Ann                    14
936-973
  James Graham           44   Vt farmer
  Mary                   44   OH
  William                18        farmer
  Julia A.               15
  Amanda M.              13
  Jefferson              10        twin
  Marion (m)             10
  Virginia                3
  Margaret DENISON       13   MO
p136
937-974
  John Duke              37   Va farmer
  Eliza S.               31
  James W.               13
  John H.                11        (Mariah H.Thompson 1862SO)Boyd CoKy
  Cynthia E.              9
  Eugenia                 7
  Adaline                 5
  Eliza F.                2

938-975
  Park Wynn              57   Va farmer
  Judy                   44
  Enos                   20
  George W.              19        laborer
  Horatio                17        farmer
```

```
938-975  Wynn (con't)
    Robert                  12    Ky
    James                   11    OH
    Ellenor                  7    OH
    Elizabeth                4    OH
939-976
    William Wynn            24    Va  farmer
    Mary                    24    OH
    Leonara (f)              1    OH
    Surdena HARLEY    (f)  18    OH
940-977          (s/o Thos)        OHIO RIVER west of GUYANDOTTE
    William Buffington      62    Va  surveyor(b Hampshire Co.CCA)cem#H10
    Nancy                   55    NC   (Scales SO)CCA          cem#H10
    John N.                 18    Va   (1-Thompson/2-Julia Garland)SO
    William N. HAGEN        27         merchant                cem#H10
    Mary J.    HAGEN        25         (Buffington 1849cc)     cem#H10
941-978         (s/o Mark)                         1st WEST
    St.Mark Russel          47    Va  ferry man
    Dolly                   48          (McMillian 2nd CCA)
    Albert G.               23          boatman (m Sarah Paine CCA) cem#H10
    William M.              20          stage driver
    Theodore                18          horsler
    St.Mark                 15          (m Esther Dean 1851cc)
    Melvina (f)             20        twin or wife ??
    Mary A.                  4
942-979                                            PATS BRANCH
    William Douthet         41    Va  farmer              cem#H4
    Charlotte               30          Arthur d/o Sanders FBL
    William                  9          m Jennie Underwood d/Enric FBL
    John                     7          m Liza Moore d/Martin FBL
    Alice                    4
    Edward                   2          m Julia Burks d/Wm. FBL
943-980
    Jacob Plybon            54    Va  farmer
    Mary (Polly)            44          (Polly Derton 1840cc)2nd
    Josephine               13
    Eliza A.                10
    Elizabeth                4
    William                 18        farmer    twin
    John                    18        farmer
    Frances (f)             15        m Robert Reynolds 1855 GH
                                (children just out of order ?)
p137
944-981          (s/o 768)                         PAT'S BRANCH
    John S. Everett         27    Va  farmer (2-Emily Flowers 1853 LCoh)
    Amicetta                21          (Moore SO)d/o #81       cem#H3
    Mary                     3
    Louisa                   1
945-982
    Thomas Turner           30    Va  farmer
    Susannah                30          (Susan Varnum 1841cc)
    Sophia A.                8
    Albert                   6
    Victor                   3
    Thomas               10/12
946-983
    Joseph Turner           65    Va  farmer
    Lucy                    65
```

```
----984
   Nathaniel Turner      28         farmer
   Zerrelda              23
   Leonard               27         farmer
----985
   Andrew J.Dunkle       27         laborer
   Mary                  25
947-986
   Samuel A.Walker       36      Va joiner
   Jane E.               28
   Mathew                11
   Nancy H.               9
   John W.                7
   Mary M.                2
948-987                          GUYAN RIVER east half way B'VILLE & GUY
   James Shelton         57      Va farmer              cem#17AA
   Susan(Susannah)       55         Hannon(d/oThomas) KCMG1810
   Washington            36
   Nancy                 33
   Miriam (f)            22
   Charles               21         farmer
   Almeda (f)            19            (m Wm.R.Macconi 1851 Kanawha SO)
   Margaret              18
   Emiretta (f)          14
   James W.              12
949-988
   David W.Thornburg     36      Va farmer
   Joanna                23          (Bowen 1849cc)
950-989                                               B'VILLE
   John Merritt          61      Va farmer               (cem #17
   Jane                  45
   Mary DICK             13
p138
----990
   Elizabeth Turner      33
   Octavia               12
   Susan                  9
   David                  5
   Eliza                  1
                                                      B'VILLE
951-991
   Melchor Merritt       40      Va farmer   (s/o Wm)SO    cem #S35
   Mary                  43          (Rece SO)            cem #s35
   Mahala A.             18
   Mary M.               16
   Joseph A.             14          (m Edna Blake)       cem #s35
   Harriet F.            12
   Nancy J.              11          (mJohn Holroyd 1866cc) cem#s35
   Thomas H.              8
   Emily E.               4
   Martha J.             1
952-992
   Joseph Webb           45      Va farmer
   Christina             30
   Nancy                 15
   Dicy                   3
   Betsy               4/12
953-993
   William L.Maupin      25      Va school teacher(Dr.)(s/o 1)cem#S10
   America               25          (McGinnis)               cem#S10
   Margaret E.            3
   Robert M.              1
```

```
954-994         (s/o 768)
   John A. Merritt      29      farmer
   Susan E.             27
   Eugenia               3
   Fanny                 2
   Octavia           10/12
955-995                                              B'VILLE
   James Newman         45      Va blacksmith(1-Elizabeth Blake 1829cc)
   Virginia             26          (2-McGinnis 1849cc)
   Ann E.               10
   Frances (f)           8
   Henry A.              6
   James L.              4
   Mary J.            4/12
956-996
   William Black        30      blacksmith            (cem #50)
   Virginia             28                            (cem #50)
   Isabel H.             6
   Rufus T.              3
957-997
   Adam Black           71      Va farmer
   Elizabeth            63
   John                 41      farmer
   Melitta (f)          23
   William THOMAS       22      wheelwright
p139
958-998
   Gerhard Henri        35      Switzerland   farmer
   Bolomy VALENTIN      25      Switz.        farmer
   Bernard TAGUS        40      Switz.        farmer
959-999
   Prospire Deliniere   35      France    farmer
   Hulda                35      Eng
960-1000
   Francis Dupin        38      France    farmer
961-1001
   John L.Chapman       75      Va
   Polly                34
   Cassy A.  (f)        13
962-1002
   William Chapman      38      Va farmer
   Elizabeth A.         30      Ky    (Fancy 1841cc)
   Henry G.              6      Va
   John A.               4
   Elijah                3
   Sally              6/12
963-1003                         (Monroe Co. SO)
   Daniel Lake          56      Va farmer (s/o Christopher Leake)
   Sally                40
   Christopher          24      school teacher(Lavinia Miller SO)Boone Co.
964-1004        (s/o Wm)
   Thomas Merritt       38      Va farmer
   Margaret L.          35          (Hite 1843cc)
   John                 15      farmer
   William              13
   Thomas                8
   Margaret              6
   Sarah              4/12
```

```
965-1005
   John Turley          65    Va farmer
   Sarah                50
   Jonathan             25    lawyer                        cem#S51
   Isaiah               20    farmer
   Joseph S.            11
   Rachael              30
   Eliza                24
   Sarah                17
   Martha               15
966-1006
   Harrison Defore      35    Va farmer
   Polly                34
   John                 14
   Martha J.             8
   James                 4
   William H.         8/12
   Eliza MERRITT        10
967-1007
   Stephen Davis        45    Va farmer
   Cecelia              28
968-1008                                        east of BLUE SULPHUR
   David Harshbarger    38    Va farmer  (1-Betsy Carroll 1834cc)
   Mary                 30          (Cremeans 1845cc)
   John                 13
   Peter                 9
   Henry                 4
   Elizabeth E.          3
   Georgia            6/12
   Malinda CREMEANS      8    step children ?
   Julia A.CREMEANS      6
----1009
   Elizabeth Harshbarger 63
   Margaret A.          23
969-1010
   Winston Wotten       27    Va farmer
   Louisa A.            26
   Nancy J.              8
   Susan M.              5
   Louisa E.             2
                                                            B'VILLE
967-1011     (father/o 919)(s/o Thos.) Pro.Atty. 1817-1838)
   John Laidley         60    Va lawyer(1-Rachael Pettit 1808 GpKy)#H10
   Mary J.              50    (Hite d/o Josh&Mary Scales Hite)1816CCA#H10
   Thomas M.            23    physician
   John M.              18    farmer
   Eliza M.             15                                  cem#H10
   James H.             13
   William S.           11    (m Virginia Brown)CCA 1869
   George S.             9    (m Mary V.Walton 1865cc)
   Heber M.              6
   Isabella HITE        26    (m W.T.Moore 1884 SO) d/o#832
971-1012     (s/o Charles & Susan Childs -cem #s13)-POOR's HILL
   Daniel Love          52    Va farmer 1797-1876)(Bro/o#22)  cem#16A
   Cynthia A.           49    (Chadwick 1800-1892) 1818GpKy
   Fanny                16    (m Charles W.Handley 1857cc)cem#16A
   William              14
   Shelby               11    (m Katherine McClary)CCA
   John E.               9    (m Irene Kimbrough)CCA
   Leonidas   (m)        7
   Alphonse              4    (m Mary Sweetland)CCA
```

p141

972-1013

Edmund H.Hill	43	Va	farmer
Elizabeth	35		
William D.	16		farmer
Robert L.	15		farmer
Virginia	13		
Charles T.	12		
Littleton W.	10		
Walker G.	8		
Sarah A.	5		
Margaret E.	3		
Paulus P.	8/12		

973-1014

John Wotten	54	Va	farmer
Jane	43		(2Chapman 1841cc)
Elizabeth	14		
John	24		farmer (son of !st marriage ?)
Caroline	12		
Susana	13		
Sarah	8		
Lucy V.	7		
Anna E.	2		
Nancy L.SHOEMAKER	87		pauper

974-1015

William Irby	43		farmer insane
Irene McCOMAS	9		
George DISMAR	25	Germany	miller
Isaiah FILES	27	Va	laborer
Jonas ADKINS	14	Va	
John B.McGINNIS	53	Va	school teacher(w/o Marcy E.)cem#S22A
Anderson JENKINS	65	Va	farmer
Ivan BLOOM	26	OH	sadler

975-1016

Isaac Johnson	26	Ky	wagonmaker
Hulda	20	OH	
Isham WARD	55	Va	(black)
Celeia A.STEEL (f)	75		

976-1017

John Tinchen	45	Eng	minister

5710 Free Inhabitants
141 pages

2775 White males
2929 White females
   5 colored males
   1 colored female

Slaves were counted on a separate schedule

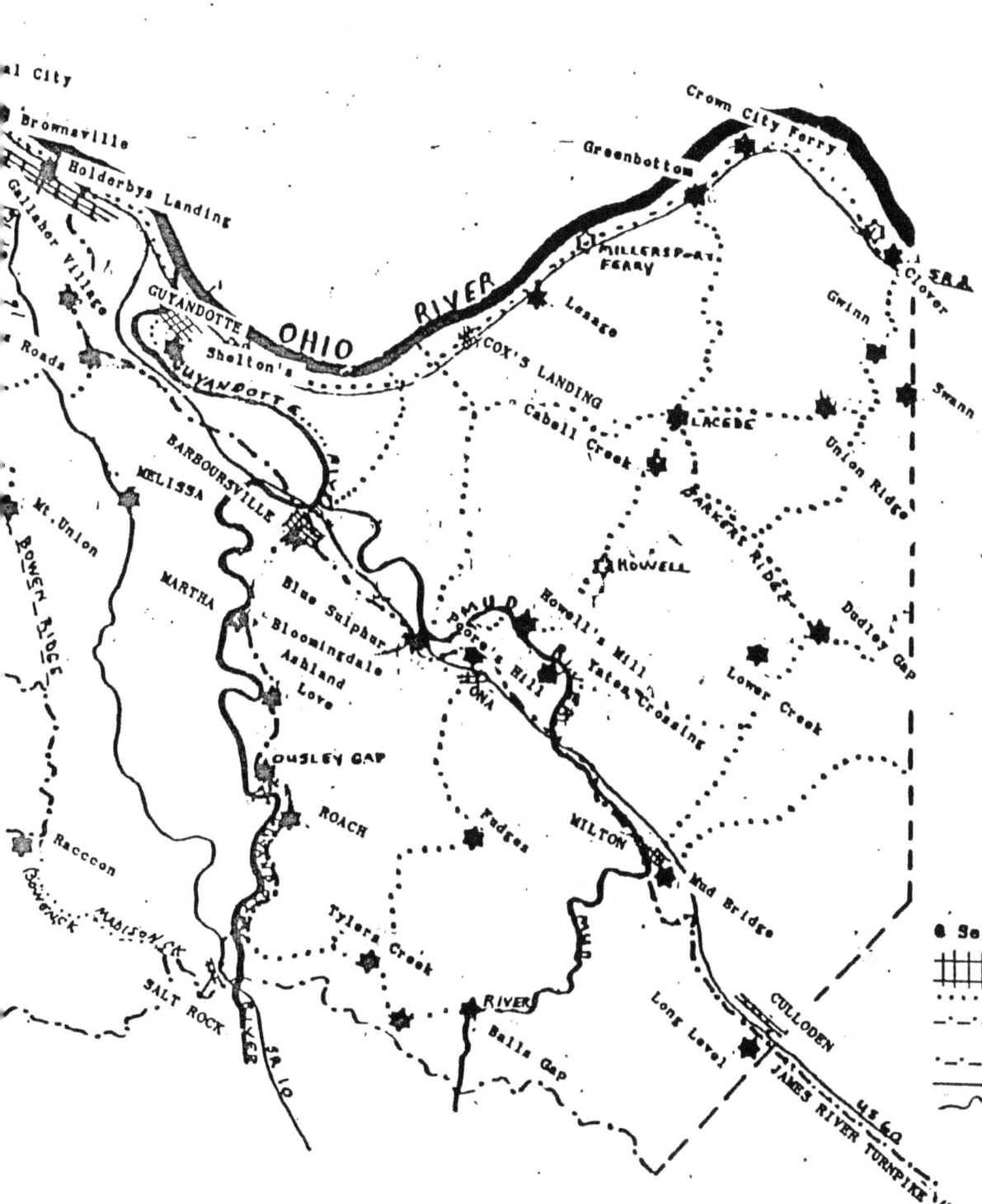

(WEST) VIRGINIA

1850

Crown City Ferry
Greenbottom
MILLERSPORT FERRY
Lesage
COX'S LANDING
Cabell Creek
Gwinn
Clover
S&A
Swann
Union Ridge
LACEDE
BARKERS Ridge
HOWELL
Howell's Mill
Yates Crossing
Dudley Gap
Lower Creek

al City
Brownsville
Holderbys Landing
Gallaher Village
GUYANDOTTE
Shelton's
GUYANDOTTE
OHIO RIVER
Roads
BARBOURSVILLE
MELISSA
Mt. Union
MARTHA
BOWEN RIDGE
Blue Sulphur
Bloomingdale
Ashland
Love
BERMUDA
Forks Hill
ONA
Racoon
Owerick
OUSLEY GAP
ROACH
MADISON CK
SALT ROCK
SR 10
Tylers Creek
Fudges
RIVER
Balls Gap
MILTON
Mud Bridge

Long Level
CULLODEN
JAMES RIVER TURNPIKE
US 60

@ Settlement site
|||||PRESENT town
.... County Road
-.-.- James River
       Turnpike
-..-..- McComas Road
_____ Modern highway
~~~~ River

1990
CWS

OCCUPATIONS LISTED IN THE 1850 CENSUS

```
                         5        10       15
BLACKSMITH     XXXXXXXXXXXXXXXXXXX
BOATMAN        XXXXXXX
BUTCHER        XX
CABINETMAKER   XXXXXXX
CARPENTER      XXXXXXXXXXXXXXXXXX
CLERK          XXXXXXXXX
CONSTABLE      XXXX
COOPER         XXXXXXX
CORDER         XX
DOCTOR         XXXXXXXXXXXXX
ENGINEER       XXXX
GUNSMITH       XX
INKEEPER       XXXX
JOINER         XXXXXXXXXXXXXXXXX
LAWYER         XXXXXXXXXXXXX
LUMBERER       XXXXXXXXXXX
MANAGER        XX
MANUFACTURER   XX
MERCHANT       XXXXXXXXXXXXXXXXXXXXXXXXXX
MILLER         XXXXXX
MINISTER       XXXXXXXXXXXX
PAINTER        XX
PILOT          XX
SADLER         XXXX
SAWYER         XX
SHOEMAKER      XXXXXXXXXXXXX
STAGE DRIVER   XX
STONEMASON     XXXXX
SURVEYOR       XX
TAILOR         XXXXXX
TANNER         XXXXXXXX
TEACHER        XXXXXXXXXXXXXXXXXX
TEMASTER       XXX
TINNER         XX
TRADER         XX
WAGON MAKER    XX
WHEELWRIGHT    XXXXX
```

OCCUPATIONS WITH A SINGLE LISTING

Artist	Clothier	Horsler	State Agent
Barkeeper	Coal Digger	Jailer	Superindent PW
Boat Builder	Confectioner	Judge	Tinker
Brushmaker	County Clerk	Plaster	Toll Collector
Brickmason	Dentist	Printer	Wood Dealer
	Ferryman	Sheriff	

and 549 household heads listed as farmer

OCCUPATIONS LISTED ON 1850 CENSUS

The listed occupations help to determine the location of doubtful households. Barboursville, the county seat, and Guyandotte, a riverport, are the only communities that offer a complete range of needed materials and services.

ARTIST
A.Jogney-----------Guy

BAR KEEPER
Noltey Dick--------B'ville

BLACKSMITH
Cyrus Andrews------Guy
William Becket-----Salt Rock
Andrew Billups-----Mud Bridge
William Black------B'ville
George Brown-------Salt Rock
Franklin Chapder---Guy
Watson S.Davis-----Martha
William Granville--Central City
Greenville Harrison-B'ville
Sampson Hanly------Poore's Hill
George A.Holton----Salt Rock or south
Hezekiah Hudson----Mud Bridge(Fudge)
John S.Keller------B'ville
Thomas McComas-----Tyler Creek
James Newman-------B'ville(E)
Edwin Pillow-------Clover
Jerome Shelton-----Salt Rock or s
Tazewell B.Smith---B'ville

BOAT BUILDER
Sanders Arthur-----Guy

BOATMAN
Grisin L.Bates-----4 Pole
Ezekiel Bowen------Clover
James Cowens-------Martha/Roach
Jesse Dodson-------Guy
Albert Russell-----Guy
George Sheff-------Howell's Mill
Lafayette Stephenson-Russell Ck

BRUSHMAKER
Robert Denton------4 Pole

BRICKMASON
David B.Lacy-------Clover

BUTCHER
George F.Miller----B'ville
John Ong-----------Guy

CABINETMAKER
Rufus P.Balser-----Guy(W)
Thomas Dunkle------Guy
Charles Herrenkohl-B'ville
Bushrod W.Kensolving-Guy
Adolphus Landes----B'ville
John F.Murray------Guy
Benjamin B.Wilkinson-Salt Rock

CARPENTER
Nathaniel F.Burrel-Salt Rock
Madison Collins----Little 7 Mile
W.Caspelman--------Guy
Randolph Dietz-----Guy
Thomas Dunkle------Guy
James Hawkins------Guy
Charles Latton-----Dudley Gap
Henry B.Paine------Guy
Stephen Poor-------Poore's Hill
Whitcomb Smith-----Guy
Samuel Wade--------Mud Bridge
Erastus Wellington-Guy
Noahiah Wellington--Guy
Littleton Whitten--B'ville
George W.Zircle----Long Br
SHIP CARPENTER
Samuel Kelly-------Salt Rock
A.M.Kennison-------Salt Rock

CLERK
George Bayard------Guy
Edward Burke-------Guy
Philemon M.Clark---Guy
Thorn Dusenberry---Guy
Lawrence Letulle---Salt Rock
John McMahone------Guy
Oltmer L.C.Heinerman-B'ville
Conred Rued--------Union Ridge
Edward Smith-------Guy

CLOTHIER
George Proctor-----B'ville

COAL DIGGER
William Pully------7 mile

CONFECTIONER
Charles Chapder----Guy

CONSTABLE
James Alford-------?B'ville
John Alford--------?B'ville
John Chapman-------Salt Rock
Johnson Lusher-----B'ville

COOPER
James Barnett------Guy
Real Ferguson------Guy w
John H. Kleningen--Greenbottom
Charles McCown(black)-Mud Bridge
John Mills---------B'ville
Griffin Reynolds---Fudge
Gilbert Stephenson-Central City

CORDER
Benjamin S.Davis---?
Benjamin Sandridge-Mud Bridge

COUNTY CLERK
John Samuels-------B'ville

DENTIST
Willaim F.Dusenberry-Martha

DOCTOR
Howard Clark-------Dudley Gap
Dudley D.Holderby--Guy
William A.Jenkins--Greenbottom
Thomas M.Laidley---B'ville
Henry B.Maupin-----B'ville
William McComas----Guy
A.M.McCorkle-------Guy
Milton McCoy-------Clover
Allen McGinnis-----Guy
William Paine------Guy
John W.Peyton------?Salt Rock
Girard C.Ricketts--Guy
Joseph Sidebottom--Tyler Ck.

ENGINEER
William Clark------Guy
Joseph Gill--------Union Ridge
William Hurd-------Guy
James Todd---------Guy

FARMER
549 households of 1017-%

FERRYMAN
St. Mark Russell---Central City

GUNSMITH
Henry Jefferson----7 Mile
Thomas Kyle--------B'ville

LORSLER
THeodore Russell---Guy

INN KEEPER
Robert McKendree---B'ville
Wilson B.Moore-----B'ville
Sanford Scott------B'Ville
Alfred Whitney-----Guy

JAILER
Anthony Shelton----B'ville

JOINER
Henry Carter-------Guy
Samuel Childers----Martha
Baptist Eiberneiser-?
George W.Fulweler--B'ville
Elia A.Jenkins-----B'ville e
David McAloy-------4 Pole
Benjamin McCune----B'ville
Jacob Miller-------Guy
Edmund C.Rece------Mud Bridge
Michael Schultz----Guy w
Thomas A.Shelton---B'ville
Enrich Underwood---B'ville
Samuel A.Walker----Guy e
Erastus Wellington-Guy
Robert Wiley-------Clover
Abner Wingo--------B'ville

JUDGE
David McComas------?Salt Rock

LAWYER
William Arthur-----Guy
Peter Clark--------Guy
Silas M.Clark------Guy
Lawrence Forgy-----Guy
Achilles FUller----Russel Ck.
Sylvester Fuller---Russel Ck.
John Laidley-------B'ville
Elisha W.McComas---B'ville
Moses Ransel-------Guy
Henry J.Samuels----B'ville
Elijah Turley------B'ville
Jonathan Turley----?
James M.Ward-------Guy

LUMBERER
Nathaniel Adam------Guy
John McCrumm-------?
Everett Feasle-----Roach/Martha
Ezra Flowers-------Guy
John H.F.Hannan----Clover
Irvin Lusher-------B'ville
Abel Rock----------Salt Rock
Albert Moore-------Martha
Orson Moore--------Martha
James White--------
Willalm Turner-----Falls of Guyan

MANAGER(overseer)
Joseph B.Scott-----Greenbottom
Abraham Coobs------Salt Rock

MANUFACTURER
Ambrose L.Doolittle-Howell's Mill
George W.Merritt---B'ville

MERCHANT
Robert Allen-------B'ville
William C.Dusenberry-Martha
William N.Hagen----Guy
John W.Hite--------Guy
Walter Kraus-------B'ville
John Lacy----------B'ville
Albert Laidley-----Guy
Victor Latulle-----Guy
Patrick H.McCullough-B'ville
Christopher S.Miller-B'ville
Henry H.Miller-----Guy
John G.Miller------B'ville
William C.Miller---B'ville
James A.Poteet-----Howell's Mill
John Lacy----------B'ville
John M.Rece--------Mud Bridge
Charles L.Roffe----Marhta
Godfried Scheiltine-Union Ridge
Perceval Smith-----Guy
Thomas Thornburg---B'ville
Eli Whalton--------Salt Rock
August Woolcott----Guy

MILLER
Benjamin Bowman----Miller
George Dismar------?Guy
Charles Holton-----Long Br.
Armstead Howell----Salt Rock
John Merritt-------B'ville
Nicholas Messinger-Long Br or South

MINISTER
William Adkins-----Madison Ck.
James I.Doliner----Guy
David Harbour------Salt Rock
Thomas Harman------Salt Rock
Orson Long---------B'ville
William McComas----B'Ville
Benjamin L.Perry---Tyler Ck.
John Pinchen-------?
Josiah B.Poage-----Mud Bridge
Andrew Warren------B'ville
Joseph C.Wheeler---Guy
Joseph H.Wright----Guy

PAINTER
John Baumgardner---B'ville
Joseph Codenbach---B'ville

PILOT
Beverly Burks (boat pilot)-Guy
John Harden(steam boat pilot)-Guy

PLASTER
James Woods--------Guy

PRINTER
Joseph S.Bradbury--Guy

SADLER
Sidney Benden------B'ville
George W.Grose-----Guy
James Pinnell------B'ville
Arnold Kraus-------B'ville

SAWYER
Martin L.Doolittle-Howell's Mill
Thomas W.Reece-----Clover

SHERIFF
Oliver A.McGinnis--B'ville

SHOEMAKER
William Agers------B'ville
Peter Edey---------Salt Rock
James Emons--------Guy
Noah Fuller--------Guy
Thomas Hatfield----B'ville
William Howard-----Poore's Hill
Chapman Jordan-----Mud Bridge
William Jordan-----Mud Bridge
Moses McCoy--------Clover
George McDonald----B'ville
Dennis Obrien------4 Pole
Lewis Sexdinger----Guy
Elijah C.Smith-----B'ville

STAGE DRIVER
Daniel Gwinn-------B'ville
James Mathews------Guy

STATE AGENT
James Vanderer----Guy

STONEMASON
John McClasky------Fudge
Mathew McKennon----B'ville
James Newman-------B'ville
Burgess Stewart----Guy
James Stewart------Guy

SUPERINTENDENT/PUBLIC WORKS
Cyrus Moore--------Martha

SURVEYOR
William Buffington-Guy
James Felix--------Union Ridge

TAILOR
Gasper Gement------Guy
William Jones------Martha or Howell's
Oscar W.Mather-----B'ville
Edward Nixon-------Guy
Isaac Ong----------Guy
Jessee Wade--------Mud Bridge

TANNER
Albrecht Becker----B'ville
John L. Franklin---s/o B'ville
Jesse W.Hannon-----Clover
Albert Harrenkohl--B'ville
Francis Hite-------Guy
John B.Hite--------Guy
Julius Schembart---B'ville
Jacob Wagner-------B'ville

TEACHER
William C.Bramlette-about Heath Ck.
Witfield G.Bryan---B'ville
Henry Clark--------Guy
William Denton-----4 Pole
Francis J.Duffin---Mud Bridge
Eli Keyser---------Salt Rock
Benjamin Hughes----Long Br.
Christopher Lake---B'ville
William S.Maupin---B'ville
Richmond W.Shoemaker-Guy
Benjamin Suttle----Poore's Hill
Edward Vertigans---B'ville
Porter Wallace-----Poore Hill
Richard Walsh------Fudge
Chapman M.White----Greenbottom
Overton H.White----Russel Ck.

TEAMSTER
James J.Mahone-----B'ville
Patterson Roberts--4 Pole
Joseph Wheeler-----Ball's Gap

TINKER
Thomas Sherman-----Salt Rock

TINNER
Jacob Hiltbruner--Guy
William P.Provines-guy

TOLL COLLECTOR
John Derton--------B'ville

TRADER
Benjamin F.Hannan--Clover
James Parish-------B'ville

WAGON MAKER
John Hibbins-------B'ville
Isaac Johnson------Guy ?

WHEELRIGHT
Burton Cremeans----Long Branch
John B.Farrel------Guy
John Morgan--------Central City
John Roberts-------4 Pole
William Thomas-----B'ville

WOOD DEALER
Jacob Brandon------Clover

INDEX-EXTRA PERSON PER HOUSEHOLD 1850
This index is for those persons that were extra
members of the household. Although not children(usually),
they can be brothers or sisters, parents other relatives,
hired help or servants, boarders

ADAMS		**BIAS**		**CARTER**	
Henry	x210	Mary	x497	Silas	x 36
Jeremiah	x881	Thomas	x 53	**CHAPDER**	
Jordan A.	x887	**BLAKE**		Peter	x788
Sarah F.	x472	Andrew L.	x959	**CHAPMAN**	
ADKINS		George W.	x959	Armintha	x608
Anderson	x 30	James M.	x959	**CLARK**	
Barlett	x353	Margaret	x732	Nancy	x514
Caroline	x532	**BLANKENSHIP**		Silas M.	x784
Clarinda	x612	Elizabeth	x354	William	x969
Elina	x566	Ralph	x354	**CONNER**	
Henry	x565	**BLOOM**		Hetty	x923
Ida	x353	Ivan	x1015	James W.	x923
Jacob	x650	**BOILING**		**COOK**	
James	x330	John	x911	Elizabeth	x771
Jessie	x566	**BOOTH**		**CRUMP**	
Jonas	x1015	Nathaniel	x482	Elizabeth	x929
Lucinda	x565	**BOWEN**		George	x929
Lucretia	x567	Rebecca	x 34	**CURTIS**	
Mabala	x532	**BRADBURY**		Jane	x322
Milton	x532	Sarah	x804	**CYRUS(Cyres)**	
Sarah A.	x730	**BRIANT(Bryant)**		Catherine	x743
William A.	x569	Catherine	x225	Joseph	x385
ALFORD		**BROWN**		**DAVIS**	
James	x653	Cyrus	x919	Albert G.	x158
John	x567	Matilda	x814	Greenville	x865
Mary	x651	Matilda	x919	**DENISON**	
ANDREWS		**BRUCKS**		Margaret	x973
Polly	x787	Willis	x108	**DENTON**	
ARTHUR		**BURKE**		Elizabeth	x938
Catherine	x786	Edward	x792	William	x938
William	x786	**BURKS**		**DERTON(Dirton)**	
ASHWORTH		Rebecca	x886	Harrison	x725
Jackson	x546	William	x949	William	x760
James	x280	**BURNS**		**DIAL**	
James	x592	Rosiah	x913	John A.	x465
Virginia	x592	**BUTCHER**		Mary	x465
William	x592	James	x433	**DICK**	
BALL		Mary A.	x552	America	x675
Nancy	x262	**BRYINGTON**		Andrew	x675
BAYARD		William P.	x960	Joseph	x381
George	x795	**CADENBACK**		Lafayette	x675
BECKET(t)		Joseph	x760	Mary	x989
Andrew L.	x429	**CARPENTER**		**DICK**	
Emily	x429	Lewis	x640	Noltey	x757
BELL		Tabitha	x640	Polly	x472
James	x638			Reuben	x675
John	x638			**DIETZ**	
				Margaret	824

DISMAR			**FORTH**			**HARSHBARGER**	
George	x1015		William J.	x264		Mary	x 31
DODD			**FORTNER**			William	x 31
John	x711		Harrison	x851		**HATTEN**	
DOLEN			**FOUNDLAND**			Sylvester	x853
Luckey	x698		John	x719		**HEINMERAN**	
DOLIVER			**GARDNER**			Oltmer L.C.	x731
James I.	x789		Joseph	x727		**HENSON**	
DORMAN			Sophia	x72?		David	x755
Serena	x382		**GEMENT**			**HENWOOD**	
DOUGLAS			Casper	x771		Isabella	x 62
Elizabeth	x477		**GILISBIE**			**HENRY**	
DRAKE			Thomas	x669		Nancy	x715
Elizabeth	x347		**GILLENWATERS**			**HERRENKOHL**	
Francis	x344		James	x434		Albert	x737
DUCEY			**GRANVILLE**			Ellen	x737
John	x830		William	x907		Charles	x725
DUFFEN			**GRAVNER**			**HISEY**	
Nancy	x280		Thomas H.	x205		Elizabeth	x967
DUNDAS			**GRIFFITH**			**HITCHKISS**	
Eliza	X383		Julia	x555		Elizabeth	x846
EDBEY			**GULDIN(Golden)**			Mary	x846
Peter	x438		Gustav	x214		William	x846
EDWARDS			**GUTHRIE**			**HITE**	
Catherine	x895		James	x174		Elizabeth	x811
Elisha	x373		John	x174		Isabella	x1011
James	x373		**GWINN**			Priscillia G.	x 54
James	x777		Daniel	x846		William	x811
Joseph	x895		Margaret	x846		**HODGE**	
Sarah	x895		**HAGEN**			Elizabeth	x37
EIBERNEISER			Mary J.	x977		(Holdryed)**HOLDWRIDE**	
Baptist	X725		William N.	x977		James W.	x 80
ELDER			**HAGLEY**			John	x748
Mary	x753		Adriadre	x 68		Peter	x748
ELKINS			Harrison	x 68		**HOLLY**	
Amanda	x464		Henry	x 68		Andrew S.	x529
ELLINGTON			Joseph	x 68		Woodward	x537
William	x464		Julian	x 68		**HOLTON**	
ELLISON			Minirva	x 22		Sharon	x518
Henrietta J.	x641		**HANLY**			**HUDLIN**	
EMMONS			Andrew	x 13		Senate	x620
Ellen	x818		Napeleon	x 13		**HUGHES**	
EPES			Polly	X292		Benjamin	x540
James	x916		**HARBOUR**			**HULL**	
FERRELL(Furel)			David	x639		Eliza	x895
Jane	x198		**HARLESS**			Harvey	x903
Sarah J.	x253		Elizabeth	x477		**HUMPHREY**	
FILES(Fife)			**HARLEY**			Frances	x346
Isaiah	x1015		Surdena	X976		Frances	x743
FINCH			**HARRIMAN**			**HUNTER(s)**	
Eliza	x788		Benjamin	x676		Margaret	x965
FORGEY			**HARRISON**			Pecky	x157
Lawrence	x777		Mary	x719		**INGRAHAM**	
			Rachel	x719		John	x620

INDEX-EXTRA PERSON 1850

1850 HOUSEHOLDER INDEX

ESTES
    James H.   239
EVERETT
    John   768
    John A.   994
    John S.   981
    Sarah   306
FARLEY
    Thomas   52
FARREL
    John B.   921
FARY
    John   515
FEASLE
    Everett   319
FELIX
    James   214
FERGUSON(Fur)
    James   76
    Jesse   70
    Joseph   73
    Real   959
    Sarah   71
FIELDER
    Jonathan   96
FILES(Fife)
    Benjamin   843
    James   840
    Joseph   207
FIZER
    Peter   589
FLOWERS
    Ezra   781
    John R.   890
FLOYD
    Michael   844
FORD
    James M.   437
    Morris L.   436
FORTH
    John   63
FORTUNE
    James   898
FRANCE
    Anna   363
FRANKLIN
    Edward   327
    John L.   370
FULLER
    Achillies   856
    Noah   920
    Oliver W.   854
    Sylvester   855
    Sylvester Sr 853
FULLERTON
    Lewis   662

FULWELER
    George W.   754
GALLAHER
    George   658
    James   943
GANNE(O)
    Ralph   585
    William   952
GARDNER
    Elizabeth   779
GARRETT
    James   590
    William T. 552
GIBSON
    James   667
    Thomas   265
GILL
    Joseph   208
GOFF
    Leonard   194
    Lisbon   195
    Ludwill   196
GRASS (GROSE)
    George W.   825
GRAHAM
    James   973
GRIFFITH
    Alexander   555
    John W.   850
GRIMES
    George J.   841
GUE
    Linsey   102
GUTHRIE
    Preston   174
    Robert   175
    William   176
GWINN
    Andrew   11
    John   659
    Washington 660
HAGEN
    George   882
HAGER
    George   360
HAGLEY
    Joseph   69
    Mary A.   60
    Peter   59
HAMRICK
    David   232
    John   233

HANLEY
    Erastmus   286
HANLY
    W.   885
    Sampson   302
HANNAN
    John   186
HARBOUR
    Jessee   639
HARDEN
    John   970
HARLESS
    William H. 477
HARMAN
    Thomas   641
HARRELL
    William   153
HARRIS
    Samuel   470
    William J. 677
HARRISON
    Greenville 719
    William   830
HARSHBARGER
    David   1008
    Elizabeth   1009
    Jacob   35
HARVEY
    Calvery   79
HATFIELD
    Adam   429
    Andrew J.   428
    Fernandez   356
    George   311
    Glouchester 318
    Henry   310
    Isaac   317
    James   349
    Moses   430
    Thomas   722
HAWKINS
    Elijah   501
    Henry S.   500
    James   913
HAYSLIP
    Thomas I.   816
HENKLEY
    Elkana   648
    Livingston 649
HENRI
    Gerhard   998

HENSLEY
    Bird   493
    John   683
    Jonathan   297
    Samuel   684
HERNDON
    James J.   304
HETH
    Nelson B.   149
HEZELTINE
    Kental   803
HIBBINS
    John   735
HILL
    Edmund   1013
HILTBURNER
    Jacob   776
HINCHMAN
    William   106
HITE
    Francis   823
    Jacob   832
    John B.   811
    John W.   793
HODGE
    Preston   37
HOLDERBY
    Absalom   744
    James   962
    Robert   765
HOLDRYED
    John W.   80
HOLLENBACK
    Ellen   887
    Henry W.   915
HOLLY
    Andrew   543
    James A.   531
    William   528
HOLSTEIN
    Allan J.   530
    William   540
HOLTON
    Charles   529
    George   584
    George A.   537

HOUCHING
    Henry A.   17
HOUGHLAND
    John   892
HOWARD
    William   303

McALAVY
  David   946
McCALLISTER
  Andrew   235
  Alexander 502
  Isaac   486
  James   292
  John   492
  Joseph   289
  Malcom   291
  Preston   493
  Richard   490
McCLASKY
  James   259
  John   247
McCOMAS
  Alexander 315
  Andrew   454
  David   324
  David   334
  Elisha W. 746
  Harrison 373
  Isaac   372
  James   141
  James   145
  James   489
  Jessee W. 371
  John   478
  John   594
  Thomas   142
  Thomas J. 143
  Thomas   491
  William   335
  William   845
McCORKLE
  A.M.   796
  James   939
McCORMACK
  John   903
McCULLOUGH
  Patrick H. 393
McCUNE
  Benjamin 751
McGINNIS
  Allen   764
  Edmond   759
  Melville 883
McKEAND
  John   421
McKENDREE
  Aaron F. 330
  Robert   757
McMAHONE
  Mary A.   812
McMILION
  Daniel   374
McVICKERS
  Archibald 394
McWHARTER
  Frances   294

HOUSEHOLDER INDEX 1850

TRY YOUR HAND AT TRANSLATION

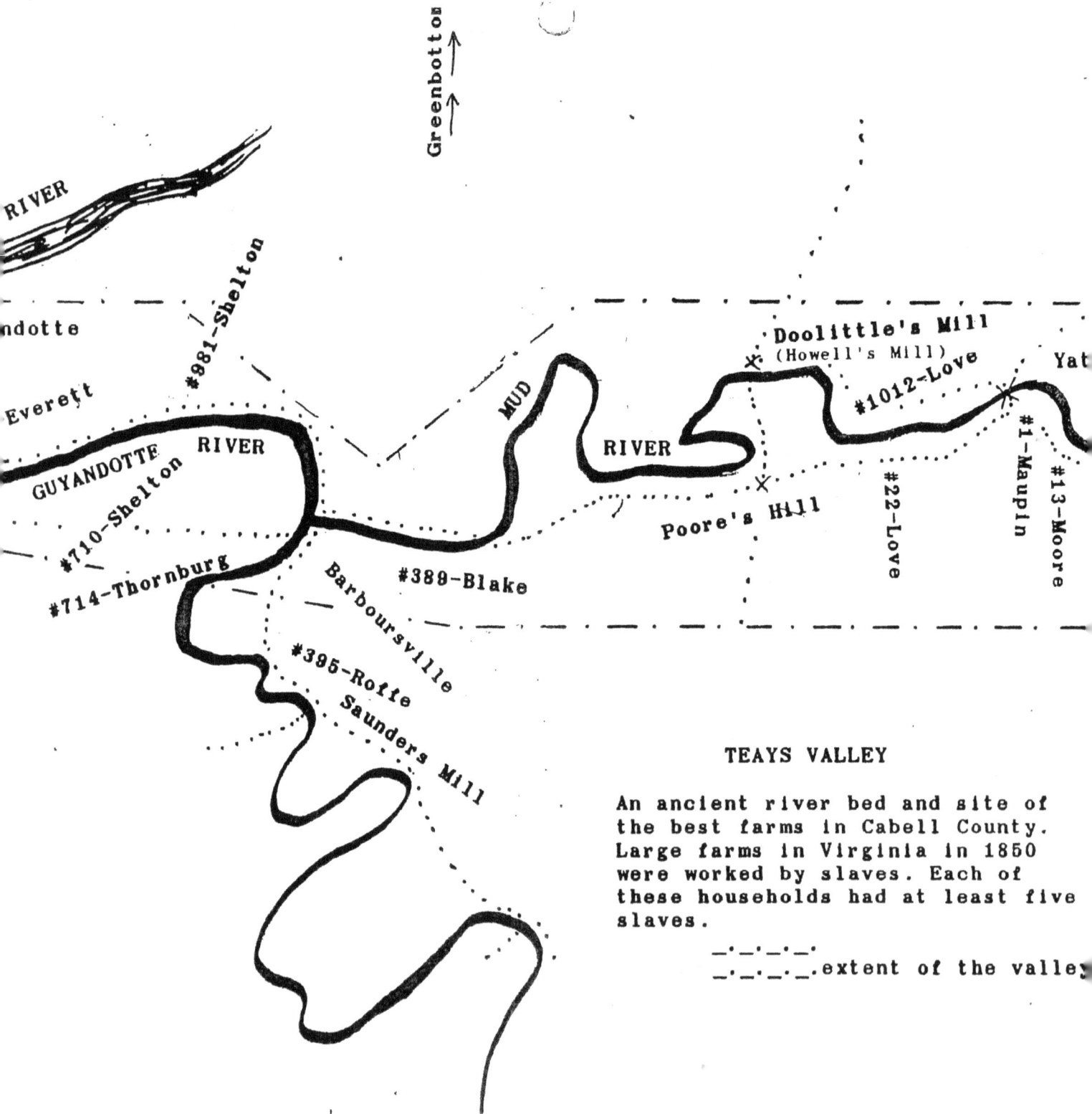

Greenbottom ↑

RIVER

ndotte

Everett

#981-Shelton

GUYANDOTTE RIVER

#710-Shelton

#714-Thornburg

Barboursville

#395-Rolle

Saunders Mill

#389-Blake

MUD

RIVER

Poore's Hill

Doolittle's Mill
(Howell's Mill)

#1012-Love

#22-Love

#1-Maupin

#13-Moore

Yat

TEAYS VALLEY

An ancient river bed and site of
the best farms in Cabell County.
Large farms in Virginia in 1850
were worked by slaves. Each of
these households had at least five
slaves.

_._._._.
_._._._.extent of the valley

1850 Cabell County, VA - Census Slave Schedule
Only owner's name given - slave identified by sex & age

# Census household/ owner	#178 - Thomas Jenkins	ᴗ #179 (con't)
	4f	8/12m
#1 - Margaret Maupin	21m	40f
30m *1824 Will*	#179 - William Jenkins	65m
42f *Fontain*	(Greenbottom)	55f
40m *William*	28f	6m
38m *Charles*	26f	3f
36m *Butain*	9f	#182 - Thomas Brandon
33m *MARY*	7f	17f
#11 - Andrew Gwinn *Harriet*	5m	1f
35f	5m	#186 - John Hannon
20m	3f	50f
18f	1f	21m
16f	20f	18f
13m	18m	8f
11m	5m	6m
#13 - Martin Moore (d 1850)	3m	3m
60m *1855 Dusenberry*	1m	#188 - David P. Lacey
47f *Judy*	28m	22f
43f *Martha*	35f	5f
31f	23f	5/12f
30m	5m	#202 - Daniel Spurlock
28m	6f	65f
14m	9/12m	37m
9m	40f	#242 - James Duncan
9m	19f	1f
10m	17f	#263 - Henry Ball
8m	13f	29m
7m	6f	10m
#21 - John M. Miller	3m	#270 - John M. Rece
14f	11/12f	17m
#22 - William Love	55f	9m
37f *1824 store*	25m	#272 - Abia Rece
16m *Betty*	16f	49f
12m *Polly*	14m	22m
11f *Lida*	1f	18f
10m *Alexander*	35f	15m
9m *ELIZA*	25m	11m
6f	7m	7f
3f	4f	5m
2f	2m	#278 - Thomas Kilgore Jr.
#36 - William P. Yates *Cem*	40f	15m
Henry 1831-1851	5f	34f
11f *Nelson 1789-1854*	3m	12m
#38 - William C. Chapman	50m	4f
12m	40f	2m
#110 - John Morrison	18f	#279 - George Kilgore
9f	15f	37m
#113 - John Porter	13f	25m
36f	7f	
19f	4f	
	2f	

Cabell County Slaves
 # Census household/ owner

#282 - John Morris
85f *1825 will Thos. Morris*
59m *Reuben*
31m *Catts / Gabe*
40f *Jarrett*
25f *Clara*
22f *Lucinda*
25f *Reuben Jr.*
19m
12f
11f
9m
7m
20f
#287 - Josiah B. Poage
13f
#291 - Malcolm McCalister
21f
7m
#292 - James McCalister
26m
16m
#302 - Sampson Hanly
23m
#332- Joseph Atkins
36f
#334 - David McComas
19f
17m
#378 - William Derton
6f
4m
3f
#383 - Sophia Peyton
30f
6m
#383 - Eliza Dundas (sisters) *decd*
60f *Ann*
17f
11f
8m
#389 - Sarah Blake
19m
18m
16f
1m
#395 - Charles L. Roffe
54f *Dusenberry Diary*
36m *Ike + family / Ben*
28f *"Fred Lambert" Hester Henry*
15m *Louise Will*
#421 - John McKeand
19f

#424 - James Morris
21m *Dingess*
21f
#446 - Smoot Johnson
94m
#455 - Eli H. Walton
18f
#461 - Sarah Witcher *1840 will*
58m *Daniel Tom Wesley Mary*
45f *Marshall Stephen*
#546 - Nancy Roberts
4f
21f
#558 - James King
20m
#590 - James Garret
80m
35m
35m
18m
12f
10f
14m
12m
6/12m
#656 - George W. Summers
21f
20m
$658 - George Gallaher
9f
#676 - Charles H. Morris
30m
25f
10m
6f
2f
#710 - Henry W. Shelton
38m *1845 Murray*
18f
15m
23f
14m
12m
3f
#714 - Solomon Thornburg
55f
24m
22m
20f
17m
14m
#724 - Sandford Scott
10f
#727 - John Samuels
48f
22f

#729 - William C. Miller
22m
#731- John G. Miller
15m
#744 - Absolum Holderby
54m *w*
19m
#746 - Elisha W. McComas
13f
#748 - Wilson B. Moore
8f
#749 - Abner Wingo
10m
#758 - Cornwesley Simmons
16f
#762 - Thorn Dusenberry *Dusenberry 1856 Martha*
11f
#764 - Allen McGinnis
24m
#768 - John Everett *Dusenberry Uncle Tom - Preacher*
50f
50m
40m
22m
19m
12m
#778 - Nathaniel Adam
19f
1f
#789 - Percival Smith
37f
18m
16m
14f
12f
9m
#790 - Gracey Stone
30f
#792 - Henry H. Miller
23f
4f
1f
#797 - Victor Letulle
4f
#806 - J.C. Ricketts
49m
36f
13f
9m
4f
1f
#826 - George Chapman
18f
16m
6/12m

Cabell County Slaves
Census household/ owner

#829 - A. M. Whitney
   26m
   21m
   20m
#833 - Robert Stewart
   25m
   16f
   12m
   10f
#845 - William McComas
   15m
#851 - James C. Wilson
   16f
   12m
   8m
#908 - William Bellany
   20m
   14f
#914 - Samuel Johnson
   9m
#919 - Albert Laidley
   55f
   42f
  (manumitted by B. Brown)
  Edmund Parker 50
  Lillian Parker 46
#934 - Francis Chapman
   48m
   35f
   17m
   12m
   10m
   6m
   4m
   2f
#944 - F. G. L. Beuhring
   30m
   28m
   19m
   7f
   3m
   1m
   30m
#949 - Alexander Johnson
   16f
   6/12f
#961- Peter C. Buffington
   35m
   32f
   17f
   17f
   2f
   6/12f

#962 - James Holderby
   50m
   47f
   46m
   23f
   17m
   2m
   15m
   9f
   7f
   7m
   6f
   3m
#972 - William Paine
   38m
   19f
#977 - William Buffington
   52m
   54f
   26f
   22m
   20m
   18m
   16f
   14f
   12f
   11m
   7f
   4m
#981 - John Everett
   14f
#987 - James Shelton
   33m
   30m
   35f
   23f
   20m
   18m
   10m
   9m
   9f
   5f
   5f
   1f
#993 - William L. Maupin
   12f
#995 - James Newman
   14f
#996 - William Black
   15f

#997 - Adam Black
   45f
   45f
   30f
   24m
   19m
   14m
   10m
   8m
   10m
   8f
#1008 - David Harshbarger
   55f
#1011 - John Laidley
   40f
   16m
   13m
   10f
   7f
#1012 - Daniel Love
   65f   will
   40m alexander
   15m
   12f
   10f
#1013 - Edmund Hill
   10f

Male Slaves - 191
  (53 -10y or under)
Female Slaves - 198
  (59 - 10y or under)

Total slaves - 389

NOT EMUNERATED
Hetty Kilgore (w/Thomas)
Martha Morris(w/Charles)

INDEX
SLAVE HOLDERS

90 households - 389 slaves
112 children 10 & under
28 children 11-13
1 - 94 years old

Households - 90
3 had infants under 6
29 had 1 slave
23 had 2 slaves
6 had 3 slaves

Jenkins family/Lacy - 58
Shelton family - 19
Buffington family - 18
Love family - 17
Kilgore family/Ball/
Simmons/Morris - 15
Holderby family - 14
Moore (decd 1850) - 12
Black family - 11

NOTE: Slavery was concentrated along the Ohio River, up the Guyandotte River, and in Teays Valley.

1819 Cabell County Deed Book
Greenbottom Slaves (Jenkins)

1819	1820
Ben	same -plus
Moses	Milly's ch.
Jack	Nelson
Kit	Maria
Davey	Nathan
Charles	infant
Bob	Isabel's ch.
John	Solomon
Joe	Winney
Jim	infant
Armstead	
Cimon	Moses is runaway
Peter	
Washington	
Phillip	
Dolly	
Daphney	
Isabell	
Milly	
& all Children	

Greenbottom was plantation of 4444a
first patented by Joshua Fry.
Fry and partner Peyton Short sold to
Wilson Cary Nicholas(Virginia Governor)
1805 who then sold to William H.Cabell
(Governor of Virginia) by default at
public sale in 1820. Greenbottom was
then purchased by William Jenkins of
Rockbridge Co. in 1825.
David Lacy -Jenkins son-in-law

1824 Cabell County Will Book I
  will of Charles Love
    Betty
    Polly
    Lidda
    Alexander
    Eliza

Dusenberry Diary 1855

  #13 Moore
    Judy

  #395-Roffe
    Ike & family
    Ben

  #768-Everett
    Uncle Tom

Sanders slaves manumented

will/Martha 1834	Love inventory'45
Bristoe	James
Robin	Solomon
Charles	Calvary
Charlotte	Daniel
Jenny	Charles
Mary	
Lorry	

CABELL COUNTY

	MALES	FEMALES	TOTAL
0-5	562	540	1102
5-10	412	437	849
10-15	362	341	703
15-20	310	310	620
20-30	465	383	848
30-40	251	237	488
40-50	177	149	326
50-60	92	81	173
60-70	62	65	127
70-80	21	15	36
80-90	3	4	7
90-100	1	1	2
100+	1		1

TOTAL FOR COUNTY 5,884

SLAVES	MALE	FEMALE
	191	198

TOTAL SLAVES 389

TOTAL INHABITANTS 6,283

TOWN OF BARBOURSVILLE

MALE	FEMALE
10	10
6	5
4	10
4	9
16	11
9	4
2	5
3	1
	1

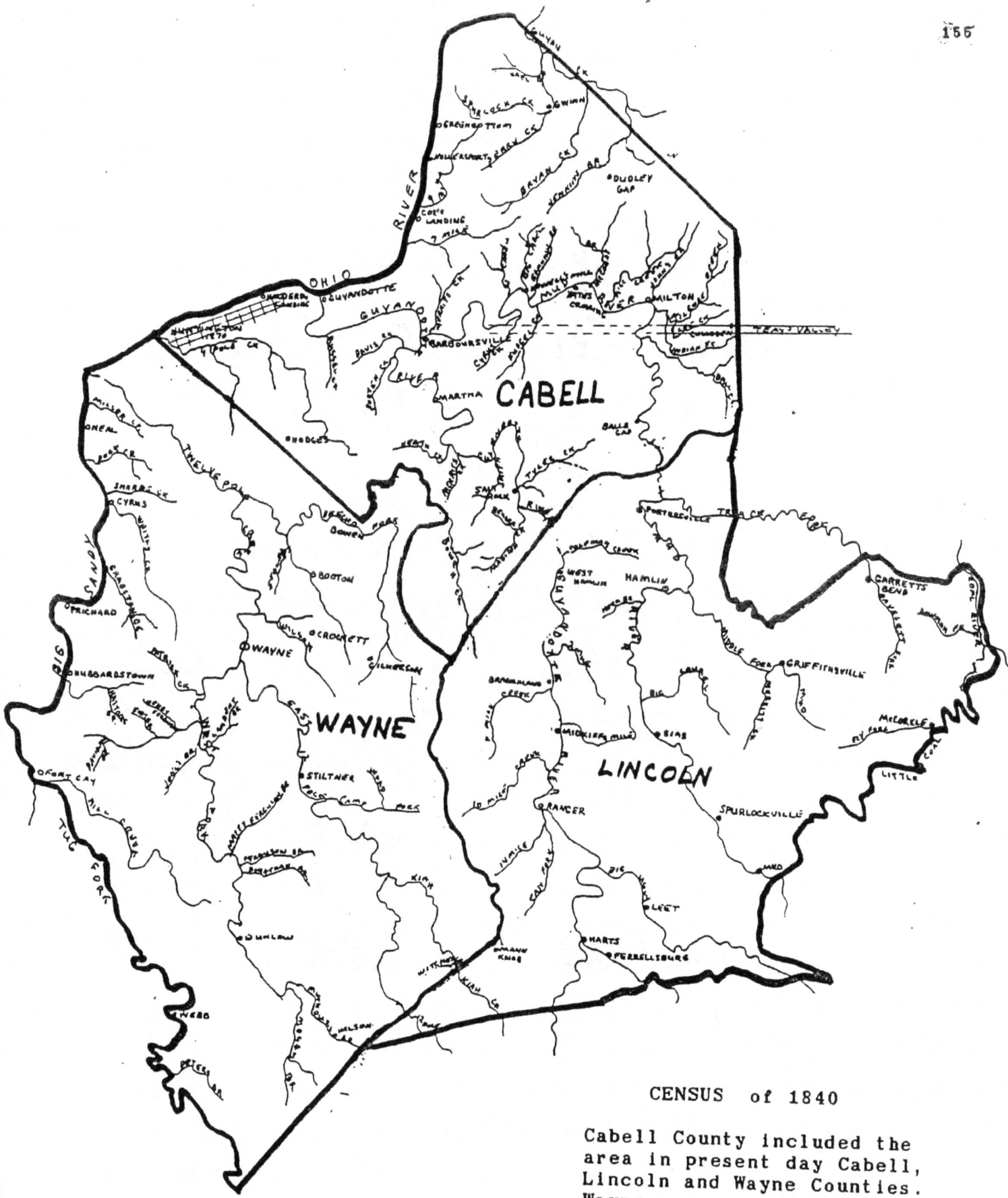

CENSUS of 1840

Cabell County included the area in present day Cabell, Lincoln and Wayne Counties. Wayne was created in 1842. Lincoln was created in 1867.

The pleasure of
Miss Elizabeth Herefords
company is solicited to a
Ball
at Mr. Gardners
in Barboursville
on the 4th day of July

John Laidley

F.G.L. Beuring

John Shanuels

June 1823

1840 CENSUS

The 1840 census was returned to the Census Bureau with house to house listing instead of the alphabetical listing that characterized the 1820 and 1830 census. For the first time it is possible to locate households and their relationship to one another. Knowledge from the several sources used to identify the 1850 households have been used with the 1840. There is a large section unidentfied that will be found in the 1850 Wayne County Census.

Marriages have been added and cannot be definite.

c or cc=Cabell County   CCA=Cabell County Annals
Gpky=Greenup,Ky   KCM=Kanawha   LCoh=Lawrence,OH
Gb=Greenbrier   MM=Mason   Mt=Montgomery

GUYANDOTTE
(total 312 souls)-(46 households)

p1
Gardner,Joseph P.M.
  m1-Rebecca Gilkerson 1828c
  m2-Elizabeth Brown 1829c
Adam,Nathaniel L.
Varnum,Moses
Hite,John W. J.P.
Latule,Lewis
Latule,Peter
Wellington,Erastus
  m-Charlote Webb 1821c
Latule,Victor
Dodridge,Enoch
Walker,Cyrus
Morgan,Elijah
  m-Mabel E.Russell 1835c
Nixon,Edward
Dunkle,Thomas
Sharpe,John W.
  m-Anna Dotson 1839LCoh
Emmons,James
Chittenden,James
Ong,John
Judd,John
  m-Dotlethy Spangler 1834c
Holderby,Robert
Wright,John G.
Douthat,William
Turner,William
  m-Rebecca Hall 1830
Walker,David
Miller,John

McCorkle,Dr.Alexander
Hite,John B.
Smith,Perscival
  m-Mary D.Chapman 1830c
Wolcott,Augustus
Dodson,Mrs.Nancy
Perrill,Henry K. (Penill ?)
p2
Stone,Mrs.Gracie
Hite,William
  m-Jane Hawkin 1820c
Emmons,Martin H.
  m-Lucy Ann Hawthorn 1833c
Cash,William
Wigner,Abraham
Field,Rev.Elijah H.
Deatz,Christian
Andrews,Cyrus

Dunkle,Henry
Davis,James M.
  m-Mary E.Smith 1839c
Smith,Dudley
Miller,Jacob
Hazletine,Kenton
Gillet,Lawrence
  m-Amelia McClure 1833LCoh
Arthur,Sanders
  m-Elizabeth Duncan 1836LCoh
Turner,Walker

End Guyandotte

p2   (Cabell County)
Cazy, Jonathan(Casey)
    m-Polly Kerby 1811cc
Ansel, Malcolm
Ansel, Jacob
    m-Nancy Joy 1832cc
Cazy, Mary
Hagley, Peter
Lutel, John(Latule)
Pannell, William
Files, Joseph
Blake, Pannel
Brian, William
Cox, William
    m-Sally White 1813cc
Cox, Andrew Jackson
    m-Mary Ann Hite 1839cc
McComas, James M.
Thompson, Michael-Anna Becket
p3   (1828LCoh)
Dunkle, William
Hunter, Samuel
Kyle, Samuel Jr.
    m-Hannah Hagely 1831cc
Kyle, Samuel Sr.
Hagly, George
    m-Emily A.Kyle 1832cc
Ferguson, Sarah
Ferguson, Joseph
    m-Sally Turley 1833cc
Knight, Henry
    m-Mary Bryant 1831cc
Crom, James
Joy, William F.
Poteet, John
Stephenson, Mark
Holderby, James
Beuhring, Fredrick G.L.
Everett, John Jr.
Laidley, John
Buffington, William
    m-Mary Ann Russell 1828LCoh
Adam, Peter
Scales, Peter
Buffington, Peter
Stephenson, Edward
    m-Cynthia Shy 1837cc
Burke, Charles
Stephenson, Jeremiah
Barber, Henry
    m-Susan Barnhart 1838cc
Wright, William Sr.
Galigher, James

Brown, Benjamin
    m-Nancy Bartram 1827cc
Adams, John
Johnson, James
Hatten, William Sr.
p4
Pine, Alexander
    m-Patsey Barbour 1834cc
Miller, Henry
Morgan, John
Morgan, Robert-Emily Casey 1839LCoh
Hull, Martin
    m-Susannah Johnson 1822cc
Poage, William
    m1-Eliza Vanhorn 1822cc
    m2-Ann McCormick 1822cc
Poage, James
    m-Jemima McCormick 1821cc
Naglee, Joseph
Brown, Richard
McGraw, Archibald-Mahala Brown1830 LCoh
McCormick, Mosses
Peters, William
Walker, Urban
McCormick, Levi
McCormick, Mrs.Mary Ann
McCormick, George
Hanly, Isaac E.
    m-Eliza mcCormick 1839cc
Roberts, John H.
Bellamy, Ezekial
Roberts, Elisha-Rebecca Cartmill 1817LC
Williams, William
    m-Nancy Cornell 1836cc
Bellamy, Mathew Jr.
Kelly, Mrs.Mary
Bellamy, John W.
Brown, John
Eves, Thomas
Ansel, Martin
    m-Nancy Defore 1853LCoh
Staley, Joseph
    m-Margaret Highsey 1832cc
Duncan, William
McComas, William
p5
Chapman, George
Bellamy, Bennett
Bellamy, Mathew H.
Jones, Daniel-Elizabeth Edwards 1845LC
Bellamy, John Sr.
Hensley, John

Russell, John
    m-Buffington, Rebecca 1820cc
Harris, Lowell F.
Barber, Elisha NO
    m-Let, Lucinda 1816cc
Green, Enoch
Ray, Elias
Perdue, Isaiah ←
Elkins, William
Clark, Henry
Owens, Eppypodatus
Ray, Isaiah
Seamonds, William R.
    m-Nancy Harshbarger 1829cc
Floyd, Morris
Hager, George
    m-Borrows, Jemima 1833cc
Clark, Samuel F.
Hatten, Solomon
    m-Affa Ferguson 1834cc
Boggs, Joseph
McKeand, William M.
Bowan, John B.
Burket, William
    m-Martha McCormack 1836 LCoh
Baily, Hugh
    m-Sarah Johnson 1838cc
Davis, Marshall
Wilson, Stephen
    m-Agnes Witcher 1810cc
Childress, Samuel
    m-Catherine Wintz 1840cc
Lucus, Vincent
    m-Rebecca Epling 1838cc
Thacker, Harrison
    m-Louise Merrix 1836cc
Perdue, Lewis
McGinness, James-
    m-Eliza Fields 1836LCoh
Welman, Jeremiah
    m-Zarilda Bowen 1836cc
Morris, William
    m1-Mecky Brown 1819c
    m2-Ann Shelton 1820c
Fuller, Sylvester
    m-Sally McGinnis 1812c
Anderson, John
Woods, Nancy
Cornell, Benjamin
Winters, Jacob
Kyle, Robert
Perry, Robert

Knight, George
Knight, Abner
Neff, Jacob
Clonenger, John B.
Maupin, Thomas
Clark, Thomas A.
Barringer, Joseph
Oliver, John
Chase, Seth
Burtin, Nathaniel
Meadows, Enoch
Jenkins, William
Sherrin, Alexander L.
Duncan, John
Wilcox, Erasmus D.
Goff, Leonard
Spurlock, Daniel
Perry, John
    m-Lucy Toney 1826cc

p7
Lacy, David
    m-Eustacy Jenkins 1834cc
White, James
Wiley, Robert
Defoe James
    m-Nancy Cox 1813cc
Hannon, John
Bowen, Abner
Hambrick, David
    m-Levisa Cremeans 1838cc
Blake, Isaac
Perry, William
    m-Nancy Toney-1838cc
Perry, James
    m-Polly Russell 1826cc
Perry, William Sr.
Ray, Creed T.

Rigg, Thomas
Brian, John
Jenkins, Cazy
Jenkins, Anson
Cremeans, Sarah
McCallister, Andrew
    m-Minny Cremeans 1838c
Conrod, Lewis
Smith, David
    m-Asena Jarrett 1829c
Collins, William
Yates, William P.
Duke, John

Arthur, James
Kellar, Adam
Cornell, Daniel
Ferguson, James H.
Ferguson, Charles
Becket, James Sr.
  m-Hannah Lee 1814cc
Stock, James
p8
Wilson, Asia N.
Sires, William
  m-Rebecca Boulton 1813cc
Moore, Martin
Thornburg, Solomon
Seamones, Elijah G.
Miller, William C.-PM
  m-Mary Crocket 1829cc
Pore, Ferdenand
Roffe, Ingram
Hinchman, William
Thompson, Patterson W.
Derton, Philip
Newman, Alexander
Bias, Daniel
Adkins, John
Keller, John L.
Turley, John
Hatfield, Thomas
  m-Amanda Pinnell 1829cc
Richey, Luther
  m-Matilda Pinell 1830cc
Love, William
  m-Eliza E.Morris 1832cc
Smith, Eldridge
Turner, Dr.David
Pinell, James
Thornburg, Thomas
Stewart, Robert
Miller, John G.
McMahon, Wayne
  m-Mary Moore 1832cc
Pore, Mrs.Elizabeth
Thorn, Rev.Adi E.
Knight, William
  m-Ansel,Mary Elizabeth 1836cc
Ross, James
p9
Doolittle, Ambrose L.
  m-Sarah Brown 1821 cc
Cook, Adam
Childress, Thomas
Reynolds, James

Eggers, William
Johnson, Epps-Ann Durton 1833LCoh
Swan, Josiah
Merritt, Thomas J.
   2-Margaret L.Hite 1843
Epling, Jacob
Henderson, John
Arthur, Thomas
Dundass, Thomas
Newman, Harvie
   Mary Ann Jefferson 1828cc
Sires, James
Newman, Joseph
Jefferson, Henry
Carter, George W.
Washington, Samuel T.
Davis, Thomas
  m-Rebecca Gilkerson 1839cc
Noble, Mrs.Martha(Newman)w/o Wm.1819cc
Brown, George
Handley, Sampson
Cammeron, John D.
Dundass, John
Mitchell, John H.
Wootten, Simon
Reese, Thomas
Shoemaker, William
Chapman, John M.
Holwright, John D.
p10
Walker, John
Defoe, Harrison
Chapman, John
  m-Lucy Hudson 1816cc
Ellis, Ebbenezar M.
Partlow, Henry
Yates, Richard M.
Herndon, William
Herndon, Valentine
Herndon.James
  m-Mary Yates
Swan, Benjamin
Everett, Mrs,Sarah
Beach, Walden
  m-Polly Steel 1831cc
Cox, Mrs.Elizabeth
Sandridge, Reuben-Justin Keeton CCA
Cook, John
Deboy, John
  m-Polly Cook 1835cc
Wilson, Samuell
Stevens, Abraham

Saxton,John-Sarah Pinkerman '29LC
Saxton,Abraham
Carrol,James T.
Baumgardner,Jacob
Sprouce,Lewis
  m-Cynthia Doolittle 1822LCoh
Davis,Benjamin Jr.
Harshbarger,David
    m-Betsey Carroll 1834
Harshbarger,Jacob
Arthur,Thomas
Blake,Jeremiah
Adams,Mrs.---
Bryant,Jacob
Pore,Elisha
    m-Lucy Conner 1832cc
Malcom,John
Carroll,Charles
    m-Mary Briant 1836cc
Gwinn,Andrew 1827cc
    m-Rachael Harshbarger
Newman,Vincent
    m-Sarah Elmore 1826cc
Reynolds,Griffin
Newman,Leroy
Newman,Russell
    m-Sarah Harbour 1828cc
Morris,Charles
    m-Martha Kilgore CCA
Simmons,William
    m-Polly Kilgore 1823cc
Legg,Mrs.Susan
Chapman,James
Legg,James
Hamrick,John
Chapman,Jerman   1838
    m-Catharin Hambrick
Cremeans,Elizabeth
Deal,Henry
Smith,Jesse
Smith,Thomas
    m-Mary Deal 1819
Smith,Uriah
    m-Susan Carpenter 1836
Chapman,William
Rece,Abia
    m-Elizabeth Harmon 1808K
Jourdon,Andrew
Summers,George W.
    m-Sally Black 1835cc
Wallace,Peter
Ball,Zachariah
Jourdon,William
    m-Ester Trippet 1836cc

Jourdon,Thomas L.
Wallace Benjamin
p12
Fullerton,Lewis
Miller,James
    m-Elizabeth Stowers 1821
Black,Adam
Keaton,George
McGinnis,Edmund
Lovejoy,John-Sarah Wilson 1821LCoh
Davis,Paul
Shy,Edward
Knight,James
Lane,Mrs.Penellopy
Wright,Edward
Mays,James M.
    m-Jane Garrett 1812cc
Chapman.Mrs.Frances
Arthur,Lewis
Summers,Fredenand F.
    m-Caroline Everett 1835cc
Dunkle,Daniel
Poteet,Skelton
    m-Martha McGinnis 1831cc
Fuller,Achilles
    m-Elizabeth Ward 1835cc
Davis,Achilles
Booth,Samuel
    m-Monroe Suprlock 1831cc
Blankenship,Levi
Jarrol,William
Pippins,William
Booton,Asia Sr.
    m- Frances Spurlock 1813cc
Stevens,John
Jackson,Thomas W.
Clark,William Jr.-Mary Lewis 1811LCoh
Spurlock,Jesse
Bowen,Alderson
    m-Ann Shelton 1830
p13
Spurlock,Cassender
Laughorn,Daniel
Booton,Reuben Sr.
Dunkle,John
    m-Matilda Dick
Blankenship,Mrs.Margaret
Blankenship,William
Vaughan,Daniel
    m-Clarinda Plyman 1838LCoh
Crocket,Andrew
Adkins,Enoch
    m-Margaret Stokes 1827cc

Booton, Asia Jr.
   m-Roxanna Spurlock 1834cc
Stafford, James
   m-Hulda Blankenship 1832cc
Crocket, Asher
Davis, Thomas
Spurlock, Burwell
Smith, John N.
Booth, Thomas
Davis, Samuel
   m-Lucretia Stephenson 1812cc
Booth, Jameson
   m-Cynthia Garrett 1838cc
Booth, Mrs. Elizabeth
Smith, Henry
Trout, Abraham Sr.
Trout, Abraham Jr.
   m-Rebecca Garrett 1834cc
Blose, Isaac
   m-Prudence Ferguson 1828cc
Stephenson, William
Ferguson, Mrs. Mary
   Truit m-Edmund 1838cc
Dovenor, Robert
Booton, Reuben Jr.
Ferguson, Washington
   m-Malinda Ferguson 1840cc
Booton, Sampson
   m-Joan Bowen 1827cc
Ferguson, James
p14
Davis, Mrs. Elizabeth
   Stephenson m William 1812cc
Hensley, Alexander
Davis, Daniel
   m- Mary Douthat 1817cc
Davis, Benjamin
Hensley, Solomon
Kizer, Christopher
Bartrum, Charles
   m-Cynthia Dean 1840
Ferguson, John
Polly, Hiram
   m-Elizabeth Ferguson 1827
Lackens, Morris(Lickens)
   m-Mary Ann Dean
Ferguson, Milton
Ferguson, Westly
   m-Betsey P. Brown 1829cc
Ferguson, Lewis
Booth, Mrs. Jonathan
   (Celia Walker) 1828cc

Watts, Ambrose
   m-Jane Swearingen 1818cc
Ross, Granville
Stephenson, Benjamin
   m-Mourning Low 1827cc
Stephenson, John
Johnson, David
   m-Emily Syrus 1839cc
Murphy, Alexander
Ferguson, Kelly
   m-Amoss 1821/Damron 1838cc
Ball, James
   m-Virginia Walker 1840cc
Stephenson, John Jr.
   m-Betsey Jackson 1831cc
Stephenson, Gilbert
   m-Dorice Peyton 1827cc
Jackson, Miles
   m-Nancy Ann Tell 1832cc
Ross, James K.
Blose, Hiram
   m-Mariah Ferguson
Osbourne, Edmund
   m-Sarah Walker 1838cc
Merritt, William
Ferguson, John Jr.
p15
Lycan, Goodden
   m-Martha Vaughan 1817cc
Dean, Joseph
   m-Russell 1816/Ferguson 1821cc
Mathews, Forrester
Fry, James
Spurlock, Stephen
Sharpe, James
Christian, Thomas
Yonker, Abraham
Yelly, George
Kelly, Joseph
Cooly, Edmond
Rutherford, Alexander
Adkins, John
Hensley, Samuel
Fuller, James-Eliza Short 1839LCoh
Daniel, William
   m-Martha Ward 1838cc
Thacker, Charles
   m-Elizabeth Amos 1836cc
Price, Neely
Lett, Joseph
Rutherford, Thomas

Johnson, Andrew
   m-Alcey Rutherford 1835
Hazlet, Alexander
Newman, Joseph
Balenger, Absalom
   m-Thinia Hazlet 1829cc
Smith, William J.
Shadwick, Hiram
Newman, Peyton
Hatten, Philip
Canterberry, John
   m-Nancy Newman 1829cc
Gilkenson, John
   m-Delilah Drown 1825cc
Poler, Squire
Vaughn, James
Luther, Henry
Maupin, Mrs. Margaret
Newman, James
Kilgore, Thomas
Kilgore, Jeremiah
Kilgore, George
Simpson, Charles
   m-Catharine Sites 1836cc
Morris, John
   m-Everett 1814/Conard 1818cc
Hudson, Lewis
Hudson, Hezekiah
Wallace, William
Conner, James
   m-Levina Hudson 1829cc
Chapman, Greenberry   p18
Conner, Andrew
   m-Milla Chapman 1829cc
Smallridge, John
   m-Mary Bell 1820cc
Wilson, Mrs. Mary
Brown, Thomas
Brown, Samuel
Meadows. Daniel B.
Roberts, Roda
McCallister, Miss Olive
McCallister, Malcolm
Duke, James
Webb, Edwards
Webb, William
Kertley, Joseph
Kertley, Jeremiah
Wilson, John
   m-Sarah Humphreys 1840cc

p17
Hamner, Isaac N.
   m-Mary Miles 1835cc
Thompson, Robert B.N.
   m-Julia Ann Morris 1833cc
Syries, Mailand
Billups, William
Canterberry, John
Carpenter, Thomas-Nancy Estis 1818LCoh
Giles, Samuel
Hill, Nelson
Billups, Thomas
Ford, Chesley
Smith, Mrs. Hannah
Olliver, James
Kertley, Thomas
Mayse, George
Mayse, Lewis
Billups, Richard
Harbour, David
Ford, Jesse
Roberts, Harrison
Billups, Peter
McKenny, James
McCallister, Thomas
Hanley, Thomas
Mathews, William
Roberts, Howell
Newman, Herman
Handley, Mary
McQurter, James
Becket, Moses
   m-Rebecca Wilson 1831cc
Dundass, Henry
Wintz, Joseph
   m-Polly Merritt 1820cc
Stroupe, William
   m-Peggy Merritt 1817cc
Merritt, Margaret
Holderby, Absalom
Adkins, Price
   m-Elizabeth Cremeans 1832cc
Cummins, William
Samuels, John
Merritt, John
Mather, William
Shelton, Anthony
Emmerson, James
Lusher, Irven
Rigg, Joseph
   m-Ann Wintz 1829cc

Hazlett,Peter
  m-Sarah Rutherford 1827cc
Durton,William
  m-Sarah Wintz 1832cc
Bates,James
White,Overton
Collens,Charles
Nelson,Joseph
Payne,Dr.William
Chapman,John
Conner,William
Keaton,Rayland
  m-Lucinda Conner
Grass,Jacob
  m-Elizabeth Bias 1842cc
Rose,Joseph
Dilley,John A.M.
Porter,William
Porter,David
p19
Macolm,Joseph
Maupin,Beverly
Wilson,Samuel E.O.
Chapman,John
Martin,Joshua
Brown,Thomas S.
Brown,James
Lakeman,John W.
  m-Elizabeth Roberts 1836cc
Patton,David
Burns,James
  m-Nancy Alford
Roberts,William
King,Jesse
Ashworth,Isaac
Flint,James
Ashworth,John
Ashworth,Jonathan
Roberts,Gabriel
Webb,James Jr.
  m-Margaret Alford 1837LCoh
Becket,Thomas
Mines,Isaac
Carpenter,Elias
  Rebecca Laynell 1834 cc
McClaske,John
Hicks,Ahiz
Smith,James
  m-Martha Snodgrass
Roberts,Pleasant
Roberts,James
Becket,William
Wheeler,John

Obaugh,Michael
Paul,James
p20
Carpenter,John F.
Paul,Daniel
Wheeler,Joseph
Carpenter,William-Nellie Paul 1838cc
Carpenter,Alexander
Buzard,Mrs.Nancy
    m-Lee Pall 1836cc
Johnson,Benjamin
McCallister,James
Johnson,David
  m-Emily Syrus 1839cc
Hazlett,Mrs.Mahaly
Holly,Francis
McCallister,Richard
Smith,Peter
  m-Asentha Alford 1828cc
Smith,William M.K.
  m-Elizabeth Ellmore 1831cc
Nicholas,John
Wheeler,James
Wheeler,Edward
  m-Mary Fleshman 1832cc
Ballard,James
Chandlis,Richard
Wheeler,Eli
Carpenter,Joseph
Roberts,Alexander B.
Alford,Mrs.Mary
Alford,Robert
Burns,Andrew
Holstine,Allen G.
Holstine,Peter
Fox,Gilbert N.
Alford,William
Spurlock,Richard H.
  m-Elizabeth Roberts 1838LCoh

p21
Holton,George
Payne,Harrison
Burrell,Andrew
  m-Dicy McComas
Roach,William-Martha Smith 1827LCOh
Smith,John M.
Burns,Peter
Holten,Joseph
Pinell,Philip
Harman,Rev.Thomas
Reynolds,Simon
  m-Jane Brown 1830cc

-Harman, James H.
Ellison, Ames
Harbour, Jesse
Roberts, James
    Louisa Adams 1845LCoh
Forth, John
Jourdan, John
Comer, Michiel (Conner)
Reynolds, Zekiel
McComas, Andrew Jr.
  m-Cinderella McComas 1832cc
Pine, John
  m-Beckett, Polly 1814cc
Roberts, Anderson
Burns, Francis M.
McComas, George
Burns, David
Burns, Mrs. Jane
Burns, Thomas
Burns, Job
Sanford, Walker
  m-Sarah Brumfield 1818cc
Cremeans, Moses
Garrott, James
  m-Nancy Ray 1816cc
Roberts, Thomas
Williams, William
  m-Nancy Cornell 1836cc
Stanley, John
  m-Elizabeth Mays 1841cc
Wintz, William
  m-Matilda Rigg 1832cc
Wilks, Burwell
  m-Barbara Sheff 1837cc
McComas, Gen. Elisha
  m-Areana Holderby 1842cc
McComas, James
McComas, Burk
Shelton, John
Shelton, Elisha
Sites, Christopher
McComas, Thomas
McComas, Thomas J.
McComas, Andrew
  m-Cinderella McComas 1832cc
McComas, Moses
McComas, Sanders
Midkiff, Spencer
  m-Vituria McComas 1839cc
Midkiff, Lewis
  m-Elizabeth Condon 1832cc
McComas, Jesse
  m-Arminda Drake 1833LCoh
McComas, John M. (Burns 1813/Johnson 1822cc)

-Hatfield, Henry
  m-Catherine Dial 1832cc
Payne, Simon
Franklin, Edward
McComas, David
Spurlock, Charles
McComas, Hiram
Douglass, Jacob
McComas, Elisha M. Jr.
Dial, John
Dial, Thomas
p23
Pine, Abbot
Lucus, Parker
  m-Chloe Dial 1834cc
Adkins, Littleberry Jr.
Adkins, Randolph
  m-Polly Johnson 1833cc
McGinnis, Col. John
Lucus, Calvin
Epling, Henry
  m-Jane Adkins 1823cccc
Epling, John
  m-Julian Parsons 1834cc
Parsons, John
  m-Amesetta Eplin 1841cc
Smith, John
Stephenson, George
  m-Nancy Moore 1824cc
Adkins, John
Baker, John L.
  m-Amanda McComas 1839cc
Stephenson, Benjamin
  m-Mourning Low 1827cc
Smith, Ballard
Parsons, Samuel
Adkins, Gordon
  m-?Cynthia Lovejoy 1837cc
Smith, Harvey
Smith, James
  m-Martha Snodgrass 1823cc
Hatfield, James
  m-Bias-1817/Brown 19/Dunlap 22cc
Drake, Henderson
McComas, Wiliam Sr.
Adkins, Richard
  m-Mrs. Lucinda Hunter 1828cc
McComas, Harrson
Hatfield, Isaac
  m-Rachael Drake 1827cc
Chapman, Andrew J.
  m-Julia McComas 1820cc
McComas, Isaac

Johnson, Nancy
   m-Lewis/Spears 1835cc
Wilkes, James
Messinger, William
p24
Miller, Henry
Messinger, Nicholas
Merritt, Malcolm
Wheeler, William
Latten, Charles
Love, Lewis L.
Johnson, Lewis
   m-Spears, Nancy 1835cc
Johnson, Sugar
Johnson, Perry
Johnson, Squire
   m-Serena Adkins 1833cc
Johnson, Benjamin
   m-Mandana Green 1830LCoh
Porter, Jarrel
Gibson, Burwell
Johnson, George
Ray, William
   m-Emily Holton 1838cc
Swan, Reason
Heath, Nelson
   m-Sarah Porter 1838cc
Bias, James
   m-Betsey Adkins 1837cc
Bias, John
Bias, Absalom
   m-Elizabeth Butcher 1838cc
McCallister, Richard
Morrison, Washington
Williams, Mrs.Mourning
Williams, William M.
Pate, Sterman
Conway, William-Johnson 1831LCoh
Midkiff, Solomon
Hatfield, George
   m-Jane Swan 1821cc
p25
Black, James
Bumgardner, John
   m-Malinda Lusher 1835cc
McCarty, John
McComas, James
Sheff, William
Sheff, Andrew
Sheff, John
Porter, Alexander
Johnson, Samuel
   m-Rebecca Martin 1833cc

Knight, Mathew
   m-Nancy Morrison 1837
Gillingwaters, John J.
Gibson, James
Witcher, Jeremiah
Smith, Ralph
   m-Viley Morrsion 1818
Morrison, James
   m-Frances Thacker 1829
Childress, Royal
Swan, Thomas R.
Swan, John K.
   m-Nancy B.Adkins 1830cc
Jenkins, Bennett
Tooly, John
Noel, Winston
Swan, Josiah
   m-Edith Maab 1819cc

Cornell, Parkerson
   m-Jane Russell 1841cc
Wintz, Philip
Severn, Mrs.Osia
Nicely, Jonas
Bias, Larkin
   m-Porter 1826/Childers 1830cc
Johnson, Mrs.Margarett
Marrs, Andrew
Cremeans, Burton
   m-Polly Adkinson 1811cc
p26
Cremeans, Sanders
   m-Sally Curtis 1837cccc
Cremeans, Hiram
   m-Catherine Cook 1834cc
Collins, John
   m-Nancy Curtis 1823cc
Porter, John
Sites, John
   m-Susannah Porter 1839cc
Rogers, William
   m-Clarinda Bias 1838cc
Swan, Hezekiah
   m-Catherine Hatfield 1819cc
Henderson, Dinges
   m-Margaret Hatfield 1819cc
Roffe, Joseph W.
Bias, Anderson
Roffe, James H.
Morrison, William
Morrsion, Thompson
Hatfield, Adam

Dial, Ransom
Hatfield, Andrew L.
    m-Dennison 22/Pinell 36cc
Bias, Andrew Jackson
Turley, Floyd
Cowen, James J.
Fielder, William
Turley, Anderson
Morrison, John
Peyton, Charles
Peyton, Margarett
Butcher, Mathew-Lucinda Tacket'32LC
Peyton, Henry Sr.   p28
Peyton, Henry Jr.
Peyton, John-Julia Marcum 37LCoh
Spearse, William
   m-Lucretia Boothe 1824LCoh
Howell, Armstead
p27
Dick, Joseph
    m-Eleanor Butcher 1822cc
Blake, Peter
Thompson, Mathew
Thompson, John
    m-Elender Hutchinson 1820cc
Walters, Joseph
Mays, Charles
Scales, Lyman
    m-Ruth Martin 1837cc
Spearse, Mrs. Elizabeth
   Miller to George 1818cc
Russell, James
    m-Rhoda Poteet
Drown, Benjamin
Orr, Charles
Oback, John
Donathan, Catherine
Keazer, Henry
    m-Abigail Clark 1822cc
Bailey, John
    m-Sally Pyles 1824cc
Carter, Aneus
    m-Kessiah Ray 1829cc
Napper, Thomas F.
Newman, Green-Eliza Garret 35LCoh
    m-Sarah Hazelett 1822cc
Newman, John
Pile, George
    m-Sally Chandler 1829cc
Pile, Jacob
Booth, Jefferson
    m-Margaret Garret 1836cc

Garret, Benjamin
Thacker, Reuben
Adkins, Agnes
Adkins, Henry
    m-Polly Ferguson 1836cc
Vaughn, John
    m-Luddie Crabtree 1812cc
Vaughn, Benjamin
    m-Emaline Clark 1838cc
Blose, John
    m-Martha Ferguson 1834cc
Blose, Ezekiel
Brumfield, Mrs. Ellenor
Brumfield, Bostick   .
Plymale, Anthony
    m-Polly Ferguson 1827cc
Plymale, John
    m-Ferguson 1819/Shelton 1833cc
Haney, William
    m-Rebecca Williams 1845LCoh
Christian, Allen
Burket, Fredrick-Susannah Hull 1844LCoh
Crump, Elizabeth
Price, Cornelius
Harman, Thomas
Brumfield, Mrs. Ellinor   (twice)
Brumfield, George
Foster, Nathan
Newton, Isaac
    m-Susannah Christian 1831cc
Hollenback, Martin
    m-Elinor Hampton 1811cc
Hollenback, Henry
    m-Margaret Ricketts 1833cc
Hizey, Philip
    m-Nancy Pine 1831cc
Irby, William
Barber, James D.
Harris, William
Russell, Saint Mark
Clark, John
Staley, Michael
Burke, Beverly
Adkins, Izaiah
    m-Nancy Bowen 1822cc
Bowen, Hugh
Stevens, John
Adkins, William
Childress, Benjamin
    m-Elizabeth Adkins
Adkins, Ezekiah

p29
Adkins,Hezekiah Jr.
    m-Spears 1819/Childers 1821cc
Pooly,Charles
Toppins,Rebecca
Eastep,Shaderick
Adkins,Sherrod
    m-Abigail Johnson 1832cc
Eapling,Lidia
Massie,Bazel D.
Adkins,Parker Sr.-Jane Holt'20cc
Adkins,Sherrod
Adkins,John
Adkins,Harrison,
    m-Eleanor Collins 1850LCoh
Witcher,Daniel
Adkins,Sherrod Jr.
Gilkerson,Thomas
Adkins,Lewis
Fry,David
    Christina Adkins 1820cc
Adkins,Jacob
    m-Adkins 1822/Fernatt 1827cc
Gilkerson,Morris
    m-Lucinda Adkins 1839cc
Stith,Mrs.Hannah
Ross,Covington
    m-Henrietta Nappier 1835cc
Ross,Robert
    m-Elizabeth Adkins 1840cc
Defoe,William
Adkins,Hiram
    m-Rachael Ross 1832cc
Elkins,Rease
    m-Mary Blankenship 1839cc
Adkins,Jacob
Elkins,Darby K.
    m-Linda Adkins 1829cc
Parsons,George
Adkins,Parker
Johnson,Merritt
    m-Rhoda Adkins 1834cc
Hunter,Samuel
p30
Johnson,John
Parsons,William
Mayse,James
    m-Jane Garrett 1812cc
Shelton,Henry
McCormick,John
Hite,William Sr.
    m-Jane Hawkins 1820cc

Bartrum,David
Ferguson,William
    m-Lucinda Vaughn 1827cc
Ferguson,Jamason
Napper,Edmund
Osbourne,John
    m-Cynthia Ferguson 1817cc
Eastep,Corben
Eastep,John
Stephenson,William
Napper,Patrick
Napper,William-Nancy Queen 1835cc
Sellards,Cornelius
Bartrum,Stephen

Watts,Daniel J.
Bartrum,Thomas
Napper,Moses
Adkins,Littleberry
Adkins,Ezekiel
Moore,Mrs.Elizabeth
    m-Stephenson/Moore 1817cc
Defoe,James
    m-Crisa Moore 1838cc
Stafford,Ralph
Smith,Robert G.
Wilkerson,William F.
Adkins,Jesse
Belcher,All
p31
Stephenson,Daniel
Adkins,George
    m-Margaret Adkins 1829cc
Nelson,Isaac
Cole,James
    m-Jane Adkins 1836cc
Watts,Hawkins
Queen,Walters
Nelson,William-Jane Russell 1837LCoh
Maner,James
Queen,Absalom
Queen,James
Maner,James
Smith,Sarah
Dammeron,Samuel
Dammeron,Samuel Jr.
Spence,Job
Dammeron,Moses
Dammeron,Richard
Wells,Moses
Roman,James
Maner,George

Dammeron, George
Smith, Henry
Maner, James
Maner, Sampson
McConn, Richard W.
Ratliff, Jeremiah
Ratliff, Fredrick
Preston, Thomas
Dean, John
  m-Julia Spurlock 1828cc
Lowe, Carr
  m-Sarah Withrow 1829cc
p32
Lowe, William
Wheeler, Stephenson
  m-Polly Love 1838cc
Penson, John
Cox, John
Lowe, Jacob
Bartrum, John
  m-Mary Pinson 1832cc
Lambert, Elijah
  m-Elizabeth Wilson 1827cc
Wilson, Anderson
  m-Joannah Isaaks 1837LCoh
Wilson, Jackson
  m-Nancy Lycan 1835cc
Lambert, Isaac
  m-Nappier 1827/Wilson 1832cc
Wilson, Allen
  m-Jane Rutherford 1839cc
Stratton, Milton
Isaacks, Samuel
Isaacks, Fielding-Wilson'53LCoh
Ball, Westley
Lambert, Philip
  m-Margaret Jones 1822cc
Stephenson, Workman
Bench, Lewis
Osbourne, Edmond
Reed, Thomas
  m-Merisa Osburn 1839cc
Osburne, Charles
Osburne, Thomas
Dean, Amos
Dean, Jonathan
Workman, Pleasant
  m-Sarah Ferguson
Workman, Joseph
  m-Elkins 1813/Oburn 1822cc
Bias, Rolin
  m-Dicy Brumfield 1813cc
Merritt, William

Doolittle, Luther
Stith, John
p33
Partlow, William
Piles, John
  m-Nancy Bloss
Bartram, Lewis
Ferguson, Joel
Ferguson, Edmond
Acres, Robert
Willman, Robert
  m-Mahala Short 1829cc
Moore, Fredrick
Mitchell, David
  m-Levina Webb 1839cc
Hardy, Berry
Welman, John
Parks, James S.
Frazier, John
Sullivan, Eli
Frazier, Lewis
Thompson, John
  m-Ellendor Hutchinson 1820cc
Miller, George R.

Frazier, George R.
Adams, William
  m-Elizabeth Arter 1836cc
Artrip, William
Sellers, Anthony
Sperry, Benjamin
Adkins, Enoch
  m-Margaret Stokes 1827cc
Donathan, Rachael
Stone, Zekiel
Stone, James
Welman, Madison W.
Ratliff, Wm.-Susannah Hatcher 1832LCoh
Copley, James
Indacot, Benjamin
p34
Indacot, Joshua
Copley, Thomas-Mary Burk 1828LCoh
Copley, Thomas Sr.
Workman, Jesse
Chafin, Stanley
Chafin, Mrs, Mary
Roberts, Isaac
Horn, Henry
Hagerman, William
Hall, Ison
Dinges, William
Crom, Jesse

Crom, William   Robertson, Richard
Crom, William Jr.   McHenry John
Harden, John   p36
Lowe, Jarrett   Frazier, Hasting
Eidens, Elijah   Thompson, Findley
Kirk, John   m-Nancy Wilson 1839cc
Goodwin, Theophelis   Thompson, Flemming
Step, James   m-Zella Ferguson 1838cc
Step, John   Welman, James
Collins, William   m-Nancy Wilson 1822cc
   m-Zelphia Conner 1837cc   Bartrum, William
Spaulding, Flemming   Selbee, Charles
Spaulding, William   Roberts, Ezekiel
Markum, Joseph   Short, William
   m-Elkins 1813/Oburn/1822cc   Brown, Mary
Patterson, William
   m-Elizabeth Rhodes 1834LCoh   Fulkerson, Joseph
Crom, Adam   m-Susannah Lane 1817cc
Crom, Frerdrick   Lour, Mrs.Elizabeth (Love)?
Markum, William   Lour, Andrew (Love)?
Copley, James   Burke, , Michael
p35   Loar, Mrs.Mary Ann (Love)?
Johnson, Eli   White, James
Kirk, Thomas   m-Lucy Elkins 1814cc
Vinson, Mrs.Rudo(Rhonda Sperry)   Billops, Samuel
Thompson, John   Walker, John
Belcher, James-Sarah Evens'36LCoh Parks, Robert
Thompson, Stephen   Ally, Samuel
Faris, William   Hoozier, Peter
Hampton, Henry   Hoozier, Rudolph
Baker, Nathaniel   Peery, Martin
Jarrol, Harrison   Strother, Stephen
Chaney, Abraham   Peery, David
Thompson, Ali   m-Jane Perry 1830cc
Watts, Ali L.   Buskirk, Thomas
Robertson, Joseph   Bellamy, William L.
Robertson, John   Lour, Michael(Love ?)
Robertson, George   Peery, William
   m-Susanna Adams 1823LCoh   Bellamy, Mathew S.
Ratliff, Thomas   Tomlinson, Isom
Bromley, William   Tomlinson, John
Wilson, Charles   Tomlinson, Alexander
   m-Garrard, Hannah 1822cc   Scisson, Charles
Jarrol, John   Dean, Jacob
Holt, Nathan   m-Elizabeth Burks 1827cc
Welman, David   Dean, John
Wilson, James   m-Julia Spurlock 1828cc
Robertson, Jesse   Hatten, Johnson
Webb, David   Hatten, Samuel
Webb, Samuel   Burges, George
Wilson, Alexander   Stith, James
   m-Sally Ball 1822cc   Smith, John
Welman, Samuel   Blakenship, Clabourn

Hatten,Samuel Jr.

Workman,James

Hatten,Elijah
    m-Elizabeth McGinnis 1818cc

Harrison,Edmond

Massie,Mahala

Vaughn,Thomas

Ferguson,William
   m-Lucinda Vaughn 1827cc

Christian,Alexander

Ferguson,Abraham
   m-Nancy Vaughn 1821cc

Riggs,Jarrett

Hutchinson,Thomas
   m-Agnes Newman 1831cc

Rutherford,William
   m-Rutha Hazlett 1835cc

Hutchinson,William

Christian,Allen

Smith,Samuel
   m-Polly Eastridge 1830LCoh

Smith,Harrison,A.C.
   m-Frances Hayslette 1840cc

Ward,Robert-Judy Harrison'40LCoh

Ward,Harrison

Sires,Smith

p38

Huggens,John

Johnson,John

Staley,Stephen

Hines,Elias

Sires,Abraham

Burkheart,Daniel

Sires,John

Johnson,Shockly
   m-Cinthia Hazlett 1833cc

Lockhart,William

Hampton,Dr.Anthony

Holt,George

Fipps,George

Hutchison,John

Tally,Elizabeth

Thacker,Joseph
   m-Jane Rutherford 1834cc

Thacker,Daniel
   m-Elizabeth Syrus 1835cc

Sperry,William
   m-Mahala Syrus

Harman,Eli
   m-Margaret Brumfield 1837LCoh

Kizer,William

Kizer,John

Becklehimer,Isaac

Shy,Jeremiah

Hatten,Wily

Hatten,William Jr.

Dishman,Churchwell

Bellamy,William W.

Stuart,William
   m-Ellanor Acker 1817cc

Walker,Harrison
   m-Armilda Rodgers 1837LCoh

Holly,Thomas

Dillon,Martin

Ray,Luke
   m-Marietta Drown 1839cc

Holton,Charles
   m-Fanny Holly 1822cc

Johnson,Franklin

Adkins,Thomas T.

Adkins,William

Adkins,Wayne
   m-Betsey Holton 1837cc

Adkins,Hambleton
   m-Jane Lovejoy 1826cc

Adkins,Parker
   m-Jane Holt 1820cc

McCallister,Piler

Cummins,John
   m-Susan Adkins 1839cc

Rice,James H.

Snodgrass,James

Lovejoy,William

Adkins,John M.

Adkins,Luke
   m-Sinthia Smith 1838cc

Plumley,Mathew

Webb,James Sr.

Adkins,Goolsberry (Goulder)
   m-Cynthia Lovejoy 1837cc

Cooper,Levi

Holton,Harrison W.

Cooper,William
   m- Elizabeth Smith 1835

Holton,James

Smith,Henry-Harriet Briant 1838LCoh

Adkins,Mark
   m-Caty Lovejoy 1820

Lovejoy,Anderson

Mosby,David

Stanley,Joseph
   m-Polly Lovejoy 1838cc

Smith,William

Lovejoy,Richard

Gano,William

p40
Adkins, Alexander
    m-Sally Bragg 1828cc
Adkins, John
Thompson, Sally
Brooks, Richard
Adkins, Samuel
    m-Susanna Sims
Cooper, Thomas
Cooper, Silus
Holten, Allen
Snodgrass, James
Merritt, Jacob
Sires, Daniel (?)
Lusher, Margaret
    (Blake)-Mathew 1841
Kyle, Thomas
Kinsolving, James
Lookadoo, Jourdan
Richards, Ludwell
Huggard, William G.
White, Samuel L.
Ward, John
 m-Elizabeth Pusey 1837
Cook, Solomon
Hughs, Spotswood H.
Jenkins, William
Plybon, Jacob
    m-Polly Derton 1840cc
Blankenship, Ira
    m-Lockey Shy 1837cc
Turner, Joseph
Cambell, John
Hensle, Samuel
Roberts, Alexander
Morrison, Patrick-Ann Scales 1819cc
Arthur, Isaac
p41
Smith, Mrs. Susan
    (Carpenter)Smith 1836cc
Pemberton, James
Carson, William
McKindry, Robert
Carter, Hiram
Rigg, Charles B.
Seamonds, Adam
Ray, Mrs. Levina
Stephenson, Mrs. Hannah
Stephenson, William
Sullivan, Aaron
Chandler, Thomas
Sires, Thomas
Toney, John

Wilcox, Moses
McCroskey, William
Harmon, Solomon
Lett, Vance-Mary Roberts 1843LCoh
Perdue, James
    m-Sarah Lett 1819cc
Cazy, Hiram
Kelly, Stephen
Shelton, James
King, John
Cannon, Mathew
Dodd, Lewis
    m-Lassa Aten 1839cc
Saunders, Sampson
    m-Ann Guin 1821cc
McGinnis, Allen
    m-Eliza Holderby 1822cc
Wall, James
Bumgardner, James
    m-Elizabeth Wilson 1836cc
Hite, Jacob

p42
Payse, James Jr.
Beard, Calvin
Doct.---
Stith, John
Guthrie, Robert
Jefferson, Thomas
Ward, Shadrick
    m-Eveline Boothe 1837LCoh
Blankenship, Mrs. Ann

Total 1840   5,954

ACRES	**ANSEL(1)**	**BELLAMY**	**BOOTON(en)**
Robert 169	Jacob 158	Bennett 158	w Asia Jr. 162
ADAM(S)	Malcolm 158	Ezekial 158	Asia Sr(Asa) 161
John 158	Martin 158	w John Sr. 158	w Reuben Jr. 162
Mrs.-- 161	**ARTHUR**	John W. 158	w Reuben Sr. 161
-Nathaniel 157	Isaac 172	w Mathew H. 158	w Sampson 162
-Peter 158	James 160	Mathew Jr. 158	**BOWEN**
w William 169	Lewis 161	u Mathew S. 170	Abner 159
ADKINS	Sanders 157	w William L. 170	w Alderson 161
w Agnes 167	Thomas 160	William W. 171	w Hugh 167
Alexander 172	Thomas 160	**BENCH**	w John B. 159
Enoch 161	**ARTRIP**	w Lewis 169	**BRIAN(Bryan)(t)**
Enoch 169	w William 169	**BEUHRING**	Jacob(t) 161
Ezekiah 167	**ASHWORTH**	Fredrick G.L. 158	John 159
Ezekiel 168	Isaac 164	**BIAS**	William 158
w George 168	John 164	Absalom 166	**BROMLEY**
Goolsberry 171	Jonathan 164	Anderson 166	William 170
Gordon 165	**BAILEY**	Andrew Jkson 167	**BROOKS**
Hambleton 171	w Hugh 159	Daniel 160	Richard 172
w Harrison 168	w John 167	James 166	**BROWN**
u Henry 167	**BAKER**	John 166	Benjamin 158
w Hezekiah Jr. 168	John L. 165	Larkin 166	George 160
w Hiram 168	Nathaniel 170	Rolin 169	James 164
Izaiah 167	**BALENGER**	**BILLUPS**	John 158
w Jacob 168	Absalom 163	Peter 163	Mary 170
w Jacob 168	**BALL**	w Richard 163	w Richard 158
w Jesse 168	w James 162	w Samuel 170	Samuel 163
w John 168	w Westley 169	Thomas 163	Thomas 163
w John 172	Zachariah 161	William 163	Thomas S. 164
John 160	**BALLARD**	**BLACK**	**BRUMFIELD**
John 160	James 164	Adam 161	w Bostick 167
John 165	**BARBER**	w James 166	George 167
John 171	w Elisha 159	**BLAKE**	w Mrs.Ellenor(2) 167
John M. 168	w Henry 158	Isaac 159	**BUFFINGTON**
Lewis 168	James D. 167	Jeremiah 161	Peter 158
w Littleberry 168	**BARRINGER**	Pannel 158	William 158
L'berry Jr. 165	Joseph 159	Peter 167	**BUMGARDNER (au)**
Luke 171	**BARTRUM**	**BLANKENSHIP**	Jacob (a) 161
Mark 171	w Charles 162	Clarbourne 170	James 172
w Parker 171	David 168	Ira 172	John 166
Parker 168	w John 169	w Levi 161	**BURGES**
w Parker Sr. 163	w Lewis 169	Mrs. Ann 172	George 170
Price 165	w Stephen 168	Mrs.Margaret 161	**BURKE**
Randolph 165	w Thomas 168	William 161	Beverly 167
Richard 172	w William 170	**BLOSS(Blose)**	Charles 158
Samuel 168	**BATES**	w Ezekiel 167	Michael 170
w Sherrod 168	James 164	w Hiram 162	**BURKET**
w Sherrod 168	**BEACH**	w Isaac 162	Fredrick 166
w Sherrod Jr. 168	Walden 160	w John 167	William 159
Thomas T. 171	**BEARD**	**BOGGS**	**BURKHEART**
Wayne 171	Calvin 172	w Joseph 159	Daniel 171
w William 167	**BECKET**	**BOOTH**	**BURTIN**
William 171	James Sr. 160	w Jameson 162	Nathaniel 159
ALFORD	Moses 163	w Jefferson 167	**BURNS**
Mrs.Mary 164	Thomas 164	Mrs.El'beth 162	Andrew 164
Robert 164	William 164	Mrs.J'athan 162	David 165
William 164	**BECKLEHIMER**	w Samuel 161	Francis M. 165
ALLY	Isaac 171	Thomas 162	James 164
Samuel 170	**BELCHER**		Job 165
ANDERSON	w All 168		Mrs.Jane 165
John 159	w James 170		Peter 164
ANDREWS			Thomas 165
Cyrus 157			

PINELL
Henry K. 157
James 160
Philip 164
w Wm(Pannel) 158
PLUMLEY
Mathew 171
PLYBON
Jacob 172
PLYMALE
w Anthony 167
w John 167
POAGE
James 158
William 158
POLER
Squire 163
POLLY
Hiram 162
POOLY
Charles 168
PORE(Poor)
Elisha 161
Mrs.Elizabeth 160
Ferdenand 160
PORTER
w Alexander 168
David 164
Jarrell 166
John 168
William 164
POTEET
John 158
Skelton 161
PRICE
Cornelius 167
Neely 162
PRESTON
w Thomas 169
QUEEN
w Absalom 168
w James 168
w Walters 168
RATLIFF
Fredrick 169
w Jeremiah 169
Thomas 170
w William 169
RAY
Creed T. 159
Elias 159
Isaiah 159
Mrs.Levina 172
Luke 171
William 166
RECE(Reese)
Abia 161
Thomas 160
REED
w Thomas 169

REYNOLDS
Griffin 161
James 160
Simon 164
Zekiel 165
RICE
James H. 171
RICHARDS
Ludwell 172
RICHEY
Luther 160
RIGG(s)
Charles B. 172
w Jarrett 171
Joseph 163
Thomas 159
ROACH
William 184
ROBERTS
Alexander 172
Alexander B. 164
Anderson 185
Elisha 158
w Ezekiel 170
Gaberiel 164
Harrison 163
Howell 163
Isaac 189
James 164
James 165
w John H. 158
Pleasant 164
Roda 163
Thomas 165
Williams 164
ROBERTSON
George 160
w Jesse 170
w John 170
w Joseph 170
w Richard 170
ROFFE
Ingram 160
James 166
Joseph 166
ROGERS
William 166
ROMAN
w James 168
ROSE
Joseph 164
ROSS
Covington 168
Granville 162
James 160
James K. 162
Robert 168
RUSSELL
w James 167
John 159
St.Mark 167

RUTHERFORD
Alexander 162
Thomas 162
William 162
w William 171
SAMUELS
John 163
SANDRIDGE
Reuben 160
SANFORD
Walker 165
SAUNDERS
Sampson 172
SAXTON(Sexton)
Abraham 161
John 161
SCALES
Lyman 167
Peter 158
SCISSON
Charles 170
SEAMONDS
Adam 172
Elijah G. 180
William R. 159
SELBEE
Charles 170
SELLARDS
w Cornelius 163
SELLERS
Anthony 169
SEVERN
Mrs.Osia 166
SHADWICK
Hiram 163
SHARP(E) 160
James 162
John W. 157
SHEFF
Andrew 166
John 166
William 166
SHELTON
Anthony 163
Elisha 165
Henry 168
James 172
John 165
SHERRIN
Alexander 159
SHOEMAKER
William 160
SHORT
William 170
SHY
Edward 161
Jeremiah 171
SIMMONS
William 161
SIMPSON
w Charles 163

SIRES(Syrus-Cyrus)
w Abraham 171
Daniel 172
James 160
John 171
Mailand(Syri) 163
w Smith 171
Thomas 172
w William 160
SITES
Christopher 165
John 166
SMALLRIDGE
John 163
SMITH
Ballard 165
w Eldridge 160
David 159
Dudley 157
*Mrs.Hannah 163
Harvey 165
w Henry 169
Henry 162
Henry 171
James 164
James 165
Jesse 161
w John 170
John 165
John M. 164
w John N. 162
Perscival 157
Peter 164
Ralph 166
w Robert G. 168
w Sarah 168
w Samuel 171
Mrs.Susan 172
Thomas 161
Uriah 161
William 171
w William J. 163
William M.K. 164
SNODGRASS
James 171
James 172
SPAULDING
w Flemming 170
William 170
SPEARSE
Mrs.El'beth 167
William 148
SPENCE
Job 188
SPERRY
w Benjamin 169
William 171

*Smith
Harrison 215

WITCHER
    Daniel   168
    Jeremiah   166
WOLCOTT
    Augustus   157
WOODS
    Nancy   159
WOOTTEN
    Simon   160
WORKMAN
    James   171
    Jesse   169
w Joseph   169
w Pleasant   169
WRIGHT
    Edward   161
    James   158
    John G.   157
    William Sr. 158
YATES
    Richard M. 160
    William P. 159
YELLY(Kelly)
w George   162
YONKER
    Abraham   162

       The names marked (w) are listed on the 1850 Wayne County Census. It is probable the other names on the Wayne pages (not marked) were also living in Wayne County in 1840, but have left by 1850.
Wayne pages in the 1840 Cabell Census:
       p4,5
       p12,13,14,15
       p27
       p29,30,31,32,33,34,35,36,37,38

THEAS TOO BABYS
THAT LIE HER
AIR NATHAN
CHAPMAN AND
MARY CHAPMAN
CHRIST DIED

AREA INCLUDED IN CABELL COUNTY

	Present Area	% Cabell	Year Created	Area Cabell
CABELL	282	100%	1809	282
BOONE	503	15%		75
LINCOLN	439	100%	1867	439
LOGAN	456	85%	1824	388
MINGO	424	85%		360
PUTNAM	346	5%		17
WAYNE	506	100%	1842	506

CABELL	1809	2067 sq miles
CABELL	1824	1227 sq miles
CABELL	1842	721 sq miles
CABELL	1867	282 sq miles

MAP page 254

The Size of Cabell County

Most of the counties in western Virginia began on a piece of paper before more than a handful of surveyors had seen the land. The parent county of all of West Virginia was Orange County created in 1738 with boundries that once included all the land west of the Appalachian Mountains, north to the Great Lakes, westward at least to the Mississippi and possibly to the Pacific Ocean and southward with no set boundary.

The eastern politicans continued to crave hugh sections of land into counties as settlers moved westward. Cabell's genealogy branches from Orange

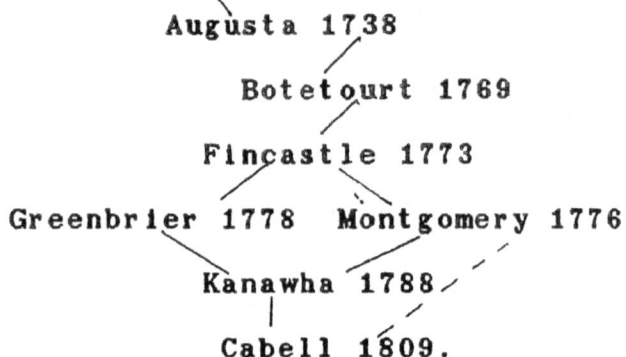

Augusta 1738

Botetourt 1769

Fincastle 1773

Greenbrier 1778   Montgomery 1776

Kanawha 1788

Cabell 1809.

Greenbrier and Montgomery counties were separated by the Kanawha River. Montgomery was on the south and a direct parent of Cabell, but when Kanawha County was created, it included land on both sides of the river and from both Greenbrier and Montgomery counties.

640 acres = 1 sq mile
Cabell 1809-2067 sq mile = 1,322,880a
Cabell 1824-1227 sq mile = 785,280a
Cabell 1842- 721 sq mile = 461,440
Cabell 1867- 282 sq mile = 180,480

1830 Census of Cabell County

Original was taken alphbetical-marriages are not definite
a person with this name was married

Adams, Elizabeth
   m-Robert Hereford 1834cc
Adkins, Alexander
   m-Sally Bragg 1828cc
Adkins, Bartlet
Adkins, Brison
Adkins, Catherine
Adkins, Charity
Adkins, Charles
   m-Polly Schott 1821cc
Adkins, Edward
   m-Gincy Bartram 1821cc
Adkins, Enoch
   m-Margaret Stokes 1827cc
Adkins, Frank
   m-Winnie Stanley 1830cc
w Adkins, Hamilton
   m-Jane Lovejoy 1826cc
Adkins, Hezekiah
   m-Sally Childers 1821cc
Adkins, Hezekiah
     s/o Berry
w Adkins, Hezekiah Sr.
Adkins, Isam
   -Polly Miller 1827cc
Adkins, Isaiah
   m-Nancy Bowen 1822cc
w Adkins, Jacob Jr. 1827cc
   m-Catherine Fernatt
w Adkins, Jacob Sr.
   m-Dicy Adkins 1822cc
Adkins, Jesse
SEVERAL JOHN's
w Adkins, John
w Adkins, John
Adkins, John R.
Adkins, Littleberry 1821
   ?Delfty Adkins LCoh
w Adkins, Littleberry
Adkins, Luke
   m-Sinthia Smith 1838cc
Adkins, Mark
   m-Caty Lovejoy 1820cc
w Adkins, Parker
   m-Jane Holt 1822cc
Adkins, Parker
    (New River)
Adkins, Reuben
Adkins, Richard 1828cc

w Adkins, Sherrod
w Adkins, Sherrod
    (Black)
w Adkins, William
Adkins, William
Allford, Mary LCoh 21-24
   (Hatfield or Rowley)
   w/o James or Stephen)
Allison, William
Allison, John
Ansel, Martin
Ansel, Melcor
Arthur, Thomas
w Artrip, William
Ashure, R. Isaac
w Bailey, Hugh
w Bailey, John
   m-Sally Plyes 1824cc
Ball, Nancy
Ball, Robert 1817LCoh
   m-Sarah Wilson
Ballern, James
Ballinger, Absolom
   m-Thinia Hazlett 1829cc
Balsell, William
w Barbour, Elisha
Barret, Andrew
   m-Dicy McComas 1818cc
Barrett, James
Barrett, John
   m-Nancy Adkins 1811cc
Bartrum, David
Bates, Elizabeth
   m-Calvin Harlan 1831cc
Bates, James
Battern, Stephen
Beaty, Samuel
Beaueick, Anderson
Beauick, Elijah
Becket, James
Becket, John
   m-Nancy King 1821LCoh
Becket, Josiah 1820LCoh
   m-Henrietta King
Becket, Thomas
Becket, William
   m-Sandal Roberts 1824cc
Bellamy, Berry L.
w Bellamy, John
w Bellamey, Mathew K.
w Bellamy, William S.

w = Wayne County Census 1850

1830

Bellamy, William W.
Beuhring, Fredrick G.L.
Biggs, Robert P.
Billups, Edward
    m-Dosha Wilgus 1822LCoh
Billups, James
Billups, Luke
w Billups, Richard
w Billups, Samuel
Billups, Thomas
Billups, William
Black, Adam
w Black, James
Blackimore, Dawson
    m-Jane Thompson 1830cc
Blair, John
Blake, Isaac
Blake, James
Blake, Jeremiah
Blake, Peter
Blake, Pinnell
Blankenship, Jesse
Blue, William
w Blose, Hiram
    m-Mariah Ferguson 1829cc
w Blose, Isaac   1828cc
    m-Prudence Ferguson
Blose, Valentine
Booten, Asa m Francis Spurlock
w Booten. Asa Jr. Roxanna Spurlock
Booten. Asa Sr.
    m Rebecca Davis d/o Daniel
w Booten, Rueben
w Booten, Reuben Sr.
w Booten, Simpson
    m-Joan Bowen 1827cc
Boothe, Elizabeth
    m-Sinclair Booten 1832
Boothe, Furgison
    m-Lucinda Perdue 1820cc
Boothe, Jonathan
    m-Celia Walker 1828cc
Bowen, Abner
w Bowen, Hugh
Bradshaw, Charles
Bradshaw, Jacob
Bradshaw, Lewis
Bradshaw, Skelton
    m-Mary V.McCoy 1819LCoh
    m-Rebecca Ferguson 1829cc
Bradshaw, William
Bragg, Jacob
Bragg, James
Bragg, Michael

Brewer, Thomas
Briant, John
Brown, Benjamin
    m-Nancy Bartram 1827cc
Brown, Benjamin
Brown, James
Brown, John
w Brown, Richard
Browning, Elijah
Brumfield, Byrd ?2nd LCoh
Brumfield, Henderson
Brumfield, William
Brumley, William
Buffington, James
    m-Eleanor Lane 1822cc
Buffington, Thomas
Buffington, William
Bumgardner, Jacob
Bumgardner, Philip
Burk, Esam
Burk, Michael
Burket, Fredrick ?2nd LCoh
Burnhart, Peter
Burns, Andrew 1829cc---
Burns, Francis
    m-Zillia Alford 1828cc
Burns, James
Burns, John
    m-Eleanor Jorden 1816cc
Burns, Peter
Burns, Peter
w Buskirk, Thomas Van
Butcher, Hannah
    m-Andrew Curtis1831cc
Butcher, James
    m-Cynthe Arthur 1824LCoh
Butcher, Mary
Butcher, Sarah
Butcher, Thomas J.
Butcher, William 1826cc
    m-Elizabeth Brumfield
Buzzard, Martin
    m-Rhoda Johnson 1848cc
Byas, John
Byes, Roland
Byas, Roland Sr.
Calloway, Elijah
Calloway, George
Calloway, Isaiah
Cameron, John
Campbell, John-
Campbell, John
    m-Hagar Lett 1827LCoh

1830

Campbell, John Jr.
    m-Martha Harmon 1829cc
Canterbury, John
    m-Nancy Newman 1829
w Carpenter, John
    m-Francis Smith 1841
Carroll, James T.
Carrol, Joseph O.
w Carter, Eaens
    m-Kessick Ray 1829cc
Carter, Hiram
Carter, John
Cartwill, Eleanor
    m-Willis Fields 1830cc
Cartmel, Henry
Cartmil, Thomas
w Casey, Jonithan
    m-Polly Kirby 1811cc
Chadwick, Hiram
Chandler, Thomas
Chaney, Abel
Chanske, Abraham
Chapell, Henry
Chapman, James
Chapman, John
Chapman, John Sr.
Chapman, John L.
    m-Julia Blackmore 1821
Chapman, Mahlon
Chapman, Philemon
Chapman, William
Chapman, William P.
Childers, Royal
Childers, Thomas
Clark, Aaron
Clark, Ezekiel
Clark, James
    m-Martha Lambert 1818LCoh
Clark, Samuel A.
    m-Nancy Lambert 1811cc
Clark, William
    m-Louisa Callihan 1824LCoh
Coffman, Ralph
Collins, John
Conner, Andrew
Conner, James
Conner, William
Conrad, David
    m-Catherine Black 1838MM
Cook, Andrew
Cook, Solomon
Cooper, Abab
    m-Mary Bradley 1823cc
Cooper, Silas
Condon, James M.

Copley, James
Copley, William
Cornwell, Benjamin
Cornwall, John
Cox, James
    Miriam Hilyard 1821cc
Cox, William
Cox, Zachariah
Crantz, Jacob
Crocket, Asher
    m-Nancy Spurlock 1828cc
Crocket, Peter
Crum, James
Crump, George
Curmenes, Linsey
Damron, Augusten
w Damron, George
w Damron, Moses
w Damron, Richard
w Damron, Samuel
Davis, Benjamin
Davis, Daniel m Elizabeth Stephenson
Davis, Daniel Jr.
    m-Mary Douthat 1817cc
Davis, James
Davis, James M.
Davis, Paul
Davis, Samuel 1812cc
    m-Lucretia Stephenson
Davis, Samuel M.
w Davis, William 1812cc
    m-Elizabeth Stephenson
Dean, Benjamin
w Dean, Jacob
    Elizabeth Burks 1827cc
Dean, John
    Julia Spurlock 1828cc
Dean, John
w Dean, Joseph
    m-Elizabeth Ferguson 1821cc
Dean, Samuel
    m-Sarah A.Spurlock 1828cc
Dearing, John
Deatly, John
w Defoe, James
    m-Nancy Cox 1813cc
Defoe, Polly
Dennison, James
Dennison, Thomas
Dial, John
Dial, Ransom
Dial, Thomas

Dick,Joseph

1830

m-Eleanor Butcher 1822cc
Dillon,Elizabeth
Dodridge,Enoch
Doolittle,Ambrose L.
Donithan,Martin
w Donithan,Rachael
Drake,Henderson
w Drown,Benjamin
Dunbar,Epraim
Dundas,Henry T.
Dundas,John
Dundas,Thomas
Duncle,Catherine
Duncle,William
m-Elizabeth Lee 1823LCoh
Durton,Elizabeth
Edwards,Joseph
m-Sally McComas 1822cc
Ellmore,Edward
Ellmore,William
Emmons,James
Eplain,Henry
m-Jane Adkins 1823cc
Eplain,Lydia
Evans,Benjamin
Evelsizer,Jacob
Everett,John Jr.
Everett,John Sr.
Everett,Nathan
m-Sally Reese 1814cc
Fields,Lavenia
Fields,Willis A.
m-Eleanor Cartmill 1830cc
Files,John
Fitspatrick,Isaac
m-Jane Sample 1814cc
Ford,James
Franklin,Edward
Frazier,Elizabeth
Frazier,George
w Frazier,Hasting
w Frazier,John
w Frazier,Lewis
Frazier,Micajah
Frazier,William
Fry,David
m-Christina Adkins 1820cc
Fulkison,Joseph
Fulkison,Peter
Fuller,Joseph
Fuller,Sylvester
Fullerton,William
Furgeson,Abraham
m-Nancy Vaugh 1821cc

w Furgeson,Edmond
m-Motley L.Adkins 1831cc
Furgeson,Jacob
Furgeson,James
Furgeson,James
w Furgeson,John
m-Eliz Mccoy 1817 LCoh
w Furgeson,John Sr.
Furgeson,Joseph
w Furgeson,Kelley
m-Ansley amoss 1821cc
Furgeson,Milton
Furgeson,Samuel
m-Patsey Stephenson 1810cc
Furgeson,Samuel J.
m-Amy Lynn 1818cc.
Furgeson,Thomas
w Furgeson,William
m-Lucinda Vaughn 1827cc
w Furgeson,William Sr.
Gallager,James
Gallaspy,Thomas
Gardner,Joseph
m-Rebecca Gilkison 1828cc
Gardner,Joseph
Barboursville
Gardner,Joseph
Guyandotte
m-Elizabeth Brown 1829cc
w Garret,Benjamin
Garret,Harvey
Garret,Leroy
m-Elizabeth Allison 1819LCoh
Garret,Robert
Gilkison,John
m-Delilah Drown 1823cc
m-Permely Roberts 1829LCoh
w Gilkison,Thomas
Graham,Ezekiel
Griffith,Jesse
Griffith,Samuel
Guinn,Andrew 1827cc
m-Rachael Harshbarger
Hager,George
Hagley,Peter
w Hampton,Anthony
w Hampton,Henry
m-Jane Thompson 1818cc
w Handley,Isaac
Handley,Sampson
Haney,William
Hanly,Robert
Hannon,John

1830

Harbour, David
    m-Mary Spurlock 1787Mt
Harbour, Jesse
    m-Jane Newman 1828cc
ω Harmon, Thomas
Harmon, Polly
Harmon, Solomon
Hasharger, John
    m-Ann Doolittle 1832cc
Hashbarger, David
Hatfield, Adam
Hatfield, Andrew F.
    m-Rachael Clark 1823cc
Hatfield, George
    m-Jane Swan 1821cc
Hatfield, Isaac
    m-Polly Clark 1823LCoh
Hatfield, James
    m-Zerilda Dunlap 1822cc
Hatfield, John
    m-Susan Brumfield 1823cc
Hatfield, Thomas
ω Hatton, Elijah
    m-Elizabeth McGinnis 1818cc
Hatton, Johnston
ω Hatton, Philip
ω Hatton, Samuel
ω Hatton, William
    m-Rebecca Hallery 1819cc
Hawthorn, Micajah
Hazlet, Alexander
ω Hazlet, Peter
    m-Sarah Rutherford 1827cc
Hazlet, Robert
Heath, Izrael
Heath, James
    m-Sarah Jorden 1823cc
Heath, Jonas
    m-Peggy Barrett 1828cc
Heath, Richard
Heath, William
    m-Nancy Sanford 1818cc
Henderson, Duncan
Henderson, John
    m-Elivira McComas 1828cc
Henderson, William
Hensley, John
ω Hensley, Samuel
    m-Katherine Leftridge 1817LCoh
ω Hensley, Samuel
ω Hensley, Solomon
Henwood, Joshua
    m-Anna Knight 1820LCoh
Hereford, James H.
Herndon, Valentine

Hisey, John
Hite, Jacob
Hite, John
Hite, William
    m-Jane Hawkin 1820cc
Holderby, Absalom
Holderby, Robert
Holdryde, John D.
    m-Sally Chapman 1819cc
Hollenbaugh, Martin
Hollenburg, C. John
Holley, Joseph
ω Holt, Nathan
Holten, Charles
Holten, George
    m-Sarah Holley 1820LCoh
Holten, James
Holten, Joseph
Holten, Phoebe
Holten, Samuel
Holten, William
Hoover, Rudolph
Hopbarn, James J.
Hopkins, Cornelius
Howard, Clarbourne 2nd LCoh
Hudson, John
    m-Margaret McCray 1818cc
Hudson, Lewis
Huggard, Catherine (Black)
    m-Andrew Huggard 1794 KCM
Hull, Hiram D.
    m-Sally Burket 1828LCoh
Hull, James
Hull, Martin
Hull, William
Humphrey, Elias
Hunter, Sally
Hunter, Samuel
Hutchinson, Hannah
Jackson, Randal
Jarred, David
Jarrel, James
Jarrel, Janes
Jarrel, John
Jefferson, Henry
Jenkins, Bennet KCM
    Rebecca Swan 1812
Jenkins, Carey
Jenkkins, Levi
Jenkins, William
Job, Henry ---1831 LCoh
Job, Jacob
Johnston, Benjamin
Johnston, Benjamin

188

Johnston, Burwell
Johnston, George
Johnston, George
    Tyler Creek
Johnston, James
    m-Mary McGinnis 1822 LCoh
Johnston, John
    m-Mary Campbell 1824LCoh
Johnston, John
w Johnston, John
    Bear Creek
w Johnston, John
    Buffalo
Johnston, Margaret
Jones, Gabriel
Jones, John
    m-Lusindy Webb 1825LCoh
Jorden, Andrew
Jordan, James
    m-Penny Lee 1810cc
Jorden, John
Joy, John
Keaton, George
Keaton, Roland
    m-Lucinda Conner 1828cc
Keenan, Patrick
    Kelley, Adam
Kelley, Stephen
w Keser, Christian
    m-Peggy Blose 1816cc
Kesee, John
Ketchum, Jesse
Kile, Samuel
Kile, Thomas
Kilgore, George
Kilgore, Jeremiah
    m-Nancy Fullerton 1821LCoh
Kilgore, Thomas
King, John C.
    m-Catherine McComas 1822LCoh
Kirby, John
Knight, Abner
Knight, Abner, Jr.
Knight, Issabella
Knight, James
Kouns, George W.
Kouns, Jacob
Laidley, John
Laidley, Thomas
Lambert, Elijah
    m-Elizabeth Wilson 1827cc
Lambert, Ezekiel
    m-Polly Ferguson 1819cc
Lambert, James
    m-Maria Cumpston 1827LCoh

Lambert, Jeremiah
Lambert, Philip
    m-Margaret Jones 1822cc
Lambert, William
Latoulle, Victor
Legg, James
Lemay, James
    m-Nancy Huggert 1811cc
Leonard, James
Lett, Adam
Lett, Joseph
w Lett, Nance
w Likens, Gooden
    m-Martha Vaughn 1817cc
Love, Daniel
Love, William
Lovejoy, Mary
Lovejoy, Rebecca
Lovejoy, William
w Low, Carr
    m-Sarah Withrow 1827cc
Low, Elizabeth
Low, Jacob
Low, James
Lower, Elizabeth
Lower, Henry
Lowes, Eva
Lucus, William
Lucus, William Sr.
Lunceford, Lewis
Lusher, Margaret
Lusher, Nancy
w Luther, Henry
Maddy, Henry
w Malcom, Joseph
Markum, Jacob Jr.
Markum, Jacob Sr.
Markum, John
w Markum, Joseph
Markum, Josiah
Markum, Moses
Markum, Thomas
    m-Malinda Ferguson 1828cc
w Marrs, Andrew
Martin, Benjamin
Martin, Elizabeth (Earls)
    Oty Martin 1822 LCoh
Mather, John
    & Lickman
Mather, Madison
Mather, Ralph
Mather, William
Maupin, Thomas

1830

Maupin, Thomas Jr.
Mays, George
McClasky, John
    m-Arie Roberts 1818 KCM
McCollister, Andrew
McCollister, Edward
McCollister, Richard
McCollister, Richard
McCollister, Samuel
McCollister, Samuel
McCollister, Thomas
McClure, Strother
    m-Jane Cartmill 1828cc
McComas, Charles
McComas, Elisha
McComas, George
    m-Catherin McConnell 1818LCoh
McComas, Hiram
McComas, Isaac
McComas, James
McComas, Jesse
McComas, John s/o John
    Edith Johnson 1822cc
McComas, John
McComas, John Sr.
McComas, Maxey
McComas, Riaphes
McComas, Thomas
McComas, William
    m-Elizabeth McComas 1818cc
McCormack, David
McCormack, James Jr.
    m-Hannah Wright 1830cc
McCormack, James Sr.
w McCormack, Levi
McCoy, William
McGinnis, Allen
McGinnis, Edmond
McGinnis, James Jr.
McHenry, James
w McHenry, John
McQuerter, James
McQuirter, Mary
Meadows, John
    m-Ruth Alford 1822cc
Merrit, George
    m-Levina Turley 1826cc
Merrit, Jacob
Merrit, John
    m-Sally Wentz 1812cc
Merrit, Lerose
Merrit, Margaret
Metcalf, Abraham
Metcalf, Solomon

Michard, Joseph
Miller, Andrew
Miller, James
    m-Elizabeth Stowers 1821cc
Miller, William
    m-Mary Crocket 1829cc
Mines, Isaac
w Moor, Fredrick
Moor, Martin
Moor, Thomas
    m-Elizabeth Stephenson 1817cc
Morgan, John
Morris, Armstead
Morris, John
Morris, Sarah
Morris, Sherrod
Morris, William
    m-Sally Spurlock 1812cc
Morris, William
Morrison, John
Morrison, Patrick
Morrison, William
Murray, John
w Napper, Edmond
w Napper, Moses
w Napper, Patrick
w Napper, Thomas
w Nelson, William --LCoh 1831
Newman, Alexander
Newman, Grenville
Newman, James
Newman, John
Newman, John
    Mud River
w Newman, Joseph
w Newman, Joseph
Newman, Leroy   1845MM
    m-Elizabeth Atkinson
Newman, Peter
Newman, Peyton
Newman, Russell
Newman, Vincent
Nickolas, John L.
Noble, William G.
    m-Martha Newman 1819cc
Nowel, Winston
Olliver, James
w Osburn, Edmund
w Osburn, John
Parker, James
Parks, Joseph
Parsons, Samuel
Parson, William
Partlow, Elizabeth

1830

Partlow, Henry
' Patten, David
Paul, Daniel
Payne, Harrison
    m-Polly Mccomas 1813cc
Payne, William
w Perey, David
Perey, Hiram
Perry, James
Perey, Jesse
w Perry, John
w Perey, Martin
Perry, Richard
Perey, Solomon
Perey, Solomon
w Perey, William
W Perry, William
Peter, George
Peter, Jacob
Peyton, Charles
Peyton, Charles Sr.
Peyton, Henry
Peyton, Henry Sr.
Peyton, John
w Piles, John
    m-Nancy Bloss 1824cc
Pincon, John
Pine, Alexander
    m-Patsey Barbour 1834cc
Pinnell, James
Plank, Christy
Plumley, Mathias
Plymel, James
w Plyman, Anthony
    m-Polly Ferguson 1827cc
Plyman, Gaberiel
    m-Polly Hatfield 1828cc
w Plyman, John
    m-Rebecca Ferguson 1819cc
Poage, William
Poindexter, Alburtus
Polly, Hiram
Poor, Robert
Pore, Thomas
    m-Rhoda Smith 1822cc
w Porter, Alexander
Porter, David & William
Porter, John
Porter, John
Porter, William
Poteet, James
    m-Lucinda Turner 1829cc
Poteet, Sarah
Powell, Thomas A.

Pumley, Mathias
w Purdue, Isaiah
    m-Lucinda Lett 1816
w Purdue, James
    m-Sarah Lett 1819cc
w Queen, Absalom
w Queen, Walter
Radcliff, Richard
Radcliff, Thompson
Radcliff, William
Ray, Andrew
Ray, Benjamin
Ray, James
Ray, John
    m-Tabitha Partlow 1819cc
Ray, Lavenia
Reace, Abia
Reace, Allen
Reace, Joseph
Rece, Austin(Rice)
Reynolds, David
Reynolds, Ezekiel
Reynolds, Griffin
Reynolds, James
Reynolds, John
Reynolds, Luke
Reynolds, Simeon
Ridge, John
Riggs, Charles
Riggs, Joseph
    m-Ann Wintz 1829cc
Roberts, Alexander
Roberts, Henry
Roberts, Henry
Roberts, Isaac
Roberts, John
Roberts, Michael
    m-Susan Dennison 1830cc
Roberts, Pleasant
Roberts, Orra
Roberts, William
Robison, Joseph
Robison, Richard
Roffe, Ingram
Rogers, George
Runions, Joseph
    m-Rebecca Adkins 1827cc
Russell, Charles
    m-Mahalia Kelly 1828LCoh
Russell, Daniel
    m-Lucy Lane 1829MM
Russell, David
    m-Julia Bennet 1819MM
Russell, Henry

1830

wRussell, James
    Camp Creek
Russell, John
Russell, Lewis
Russell, Meredith
Russell, Saint Mark
   m-Margaret Morrison 1820cc
Rutherford, Elliot
Rutherford, Joseph
   Frances hazlett 1817cc
Rutherford, Robert
w Rutherford, William
Samuels, John
Sandridge, Reuben
Sanford, Walker J.L.
   m-Sarah Brumfield 1818cc
Saunders, Martha
Saunders, Sampson
   m-Ann Guin 1821cc
Scales, Nathaniel
Scales, Peter
Scauley, George
Seamonds, Elijah G.
Seamonds, William
Sexton, Elizabeth(Black)
   m-William Sexton 1801KCM
Shelton, Anthony
Shelton, James
Shelton, John
Short, Samuel
Short, Thomas
Shortridge, Levi
   m-Elizabeth Love 1831cc
Shy, Edward
Simmons, William
   m-Polly Kilgore 1823cc
Sites, Christopher
Smallridge, John
Smith, Byrd
   m-Betsey Boothe 1829LCoh
Smith, David
Smith, Dudley D.
w Smith, James
Smith, James
   m-Martha Snodgrass 1823cc
Smith, Jesse
SEVERAL John's
Smith, John
   Guyandotte
w Smith, John
   Sandy River
w Smith, John N.
-Smith, Peter
-Smith, Ralph

w Smith, Samuel
Smith, Sarah
   m-John Cook 1840cc
Smith, Thomas
Smith, William
   m-Tabitha Halls 1820LCoh
Snodgrass, James
Snyder, William
Spears, John
w Sperry, Benjamin
w Spurlock, Burwell
Spurlock, Daniel
w Spurlock, Jesse
   m-Cinthia Booton 1829cc
Spurlock, John
Spurlock, Judah
Spurlock, Lucy
w Spurlock, Stephen
Spurlock, William
Staley, Jacob
   m-Elizabeth Burks 1846cc
w Staley, Joseph
w Staley, Stephen
Stanley, Elizabeth
   m-James Nicely 1841cc
Stephenson, Benjamin
   m-Mourning Low 1827cc
w Stephenson, Benjamin
Stephenson, Daniel
   m-Martha Smith 1834cc
Stephenson, George
w Stephenson, Gilbert Sr.
   m-Dorice Peyton 1827cc
Stephenson, Jeremiah
Stephenson, John Jr.
Stpehenson, John Sr.
Stephenson, Mark
Stephenson, Mary
Stephenson, Nancy
Stephenson, Sarah
Stephenson, William
Steven, Joseph
Stith, Hannah
v Stith, John
Stokes, Brice
Stone, John
Strath, Leonard
Stratton, Cornelius
Stribling, Thomas
Strother, Philip
w Strother, Stephen
Strupe, Melcer
Strupe, William

1830

w Stuart, William
    m-Eleanor Walker 1817cc
Stuck, Jacob
    m-Betsey Baird 1821LCoh
Swan, Hezekiah
Swan, Leven
Swan, Thomas R.
W Syrus, Abraham
Syrus, James
W Syrus, Smith
Syrus, Thomas
W Syrus, William
    m-Rebecca Boulton 1813cc
Tacket, Luanda
Teal, John
Templeton, James
    m-Jane Morrison 1823LCoh
Templeton, John
w Thacker, Harrison
    m-Louise Merrix 1836cc
Thacker, Reuben
Tharp, James
Tomlin, Isam
Thompson, Elias
Thompson, John 1820cc
    m-Eleanor Hutchinson
Thompson, John
Thompson, John N.
Thompson, Patterson, W.
Thompson, William
Thornburg, Solomon
Toney, James
Toney, Jesse
    m-Elizabeth Smith 1819cc
Toney, John
Trout, Abraham
Tull, William 1817LCoh
  m-Hannah Cyle (Kyle)
Turley, Arthur F.
Turley, Emmerson
Turley, James
Turner, John
Turner, Joseph
Vaugn, John
    m-Luddie Crabtree 1812cc
Vaugn, Thomas
w Vaugn, William
Walker, Charles
Walker, John
Walker, Julius
Walters, Hiram
Walters, Jack
Ward, John
Washington, Samuel Geo.
w Watts, Ambrose
  m-Jane Swearingen 1818cc

Watts, Elias
Waugh, Thomas
Webb, James
w Webb, Samuel
Webb, Susannah
Wellington, Erastus
w Wellman, David
W Wellman, James
    m-Nancy Wilson 1822cc
W Willman, John
w Willman, Robert
    m-Mahala Short 1829cc
Wells, Hiram
Wells, Jane
Wells, Moses
Wells, William
Wheeler, James
Wheeler, John
Wheeler, Josiah
Wheeler, William
White, Overton
Whitlock, William H.
    m-Nancy Derrick 1817cc
Wiatt, Thomas
    m-Rachael Burnside 1784 KCM
Wigatt, Thomas
Wilcox, Moses
    m-Elizabeth Derny 1825LCoh
w Wilson, Alexander
    m-Sally Ball 1822cc
w Wilson, Charles
    m-Hannah Garrard 1822cc
w Wilson, James
Wilson, Mary
Wilson, Stephen
    m-Sarah Gillen 1827LCoh
Wilson, Stephen
    m-Agnes Witcher 1810cc
Wince, Joseph
Wince, Philip
Wince, Wendle
Witcher, Daniel
Woods, James
Woods, John 1825LCoh
    m-Susannah Buffington
Workman, Jacob
w Workman, Joseph
w Workman, Pleasant
Workman, Stephen
Wright, William
Yates, Richard
Yates, William
Young, George W.

MALES

0-5	5-10	10-15	15-20	20-30	30-40	40-50	50-60	60-70	70-80	80-90	90-100	100
562	417	362	310	465	251	177	92	62	21	3	1	1

total 1830-5,884

FEMALES

0-5	5-10	10-15	15-20	20-30	30-40	40-50	50-60	60-70	70-80	80-90	90-100
540	487	341	310	383	237	149	81	45	15	4	1

1840 Cabell County, Virginia Slave Schedule

slave owner	male 0-10	10-24	24-36	36-55	55-100	100+	female 0-10	10-24	24-36	36-55	55-100	100+	total
Adams,Nathaniel							3	1					4
Adams,Peter		1											1
Adkins,Ezekiel Sr.	2						4		1				7
Adkins,Izaiah								1					1
Adkins,Littleberry	1		1					2	1				5
Bellomy,Ezekiel								1					1
Bellomy,Mathew Jr.		1											1
Bellamy,William L.											1		1
Bellamy,William W.	1						1	1					3
Beuhring,F.G.L.	1	1		1			1	2					6
Billups,William	1							3					4
Black,Adam	1						1	1	1				4
Black,James	1						1	2					4
Blake,Pinnel		1											1
Brown,Benjamin	1	2	1		2			2		2			10
Brown,John		1											1
Brown,Samuel			1					1					2
Brown,Thomas	1	1					1	1					4
Buffington,William	1	3		1			3	1	2				11
Cammeron,John D.	1												1
Chapman,George			1					1					2
Chapman,Mrs.Frances		2					1		1				4
Cox,Mrs.Elizabeth											1		2
Dean,John	1	2					1		1	1			6
Doddridge,William								1					1
Donathan,Rachel			1										1
Douthat,William	3	2	1	2			5		2	1	1		16
Duke,John	1												1
Dundass,Thomas									1	1			2
Everett,John Jr.	2	2	2	1	1			3		1			12
Ferguson,James		1						1					2
Fulkerson,Joseph	2						1						3
Garrott,James	1				1		1	1					4
Giles,Samuel							1						1
Gilkerson,John	1		1				1		1				4
Gwinn,Andrew	2	1					2	1					6
Hanley,Isaac E.								1					1
Hanley,Thomas		1											1
Hannon,John	2	1					1	2		1			7
Harbour,David							2	1					3
Hatten,Samuel			1							1			2
Hite,William	1							1					2
Holderby,Absolum			1										1
Holderby,James	2		2				2	1		1			8
Holderby,Robert										1			1
Jenkins,William	2	4		3	2	1	8	7	2	8			37
Johnson,Samuel			1										1
Jordan,Thomas L.	1						1						2
Kelly,Mrs.Mary	1	1											2
Kertley,Jeremiah								1					1

NANCY (UP) died 1844 (Cox, Mrs. Elizabeth)

MARIAN (GBCB) (Hannon, John)

37 ⌐ (Jenkins, William)

(HANNON, E.) MASON CO.? LEWIS + WIFE ELIZABETH (GBCB)
esom

(HANNON, JESSE) + MORIAH

JENKINS - (GBCB)
ELVIRA - Nelly
PEGGY - LUCINDA

1840 Cabell County, Virginia Slave Schedule

slave owner	male 0-10	10-24	24-36	36-55	55-100	100+	female 0-10	10-24	24-36	36-55	55-100	100+	Total
Kertley,Joseph	1	1					4	1	1				8
Kirtley,Thomas	1	1		1			1	1					5
Kilgore,Jeremiah	3							1					4
Kilgore,Thomas	3	2	3				3		2				13
Kinsloving,James				1	1					1			3
Lacy,David								1					3
Laidley,John	1			1					1				3
Lane,Mrs.Penelope									1				1
Latulle,Lewis								1					1
Latulle,Peter							1			1			2
Lett,Nance	1	1	1				2		1				6
Lour,Andrew		1					2		1				4
Lour,Mrs.Elizabeth	2	1	1				3	2					10
Loar,Mrs.Mary Ann							1						1
Love,Daniel			1				1		1	1			4
Love,William	2	1	1				1	1					6
Mathews,William								1					1
Maupin,Mrs.Margaret		1	1					1	1				4
Maupin,Thomas		1						1					2
Mayse,Lewis							1	1					1
McCallister,Malcolm								1					7
McCallister,Thomas	1	1		1			3		1				7
McComas,William	3	1	1				1	1	1	1			9
McCormick,George		2											2
McCorkick,John		2						1					3
McCormick,Levi		1						1					2
McCormick,Mrs.Mary Ann									1				1
McGinnis,Allen	3	1					1		1				6
McKeand,Willis	2						5	1					8
McMahan,Wayne								1					1
Merris,William									1				1
Merritt,John		1		1				1					3
Moore,Frederick	2	2	2				2	1	1				10
Moore,Martin	4	4		1			3	3	2				17
Morgan,Elijah H.	1			2			1						4
Morris,Charles		1					1						2
Morris,John	1	4	2	1			5	5	1	1	2		22
Olliver,James			1					2					3
Payne,Dr.William		1											1
Perry,William											1		1
Plymale,John		2								1			3
Porter,David				1									1
Porter,John							1	1	1				3
Ratliff,Thomas								1					1
Rece,Abia	2	1					2		1				6
Roberts,John H.		1						1					2
Russell,John		1	1						1				3
Rutherford,Thomas		1							1				2
Samuels,John	1							1		1			3
Sanders,Sampson	9	8	5	2	3		4	3	1	3	1		39

1841 OP-PHI als.1856

BRIGHT C6BC

1840 Cabell County, Virginia Slave Schedule

	male						female						
slave owner	0–10	10–24	24–36	36–55	55–100	100+	0–10	10–24	24–36	36–55	55–100	100+	
Scales, Peter		1											1
Shadwick, Hiram	1						1	1			1		4
Shelton, James	4	3	1				3	1	3				15
Simmons, William							2		1				3
Sires, William								1					1
Smith, John	2						1			1			4
Smith, Percival S.		1					1						2
Spurlock, Burwell		1											1
Spurlock, Daniel		1						1	1				3
Spurlock, Stephen			1						1				2
Stewart, Robert							1						1
Stone, James		1						1					2
Stone, Mrs. Gracie								1					1
Summers, George W.		1						1					2
Summers, Ferdinand F.	1										1		2
Thacker, Harrison						1							1
Thompson, Robert N.B.								1					1
Thornburg, Solomon	2	2		1				1		1			7
Varnum, Moses								1					1
Walker, Urban					1						1		2
Wellman, Robert									2				2
White, James	1						2		1				4
Wiley, Robert	1												1
Williams, William		2											2
Wilson, John	1												1
Wilson, Stephen	3						1		1				5
Witcher, Jeremiah		2	2								1		5
Wolcott, Augustus S.		2					2	1					.5
Wright, John G.	1	1					1	1	1				.5
Yates, William P.		1	1				1		1				'4

(WHITTON, B) MASON? Sely (GBCB)
(T. WAUGH) Mahala (GBCB)
(J. WARDEN) Alice (GBCB)

Wm P. Yates (Cem)

Nelson 1789–1854
Henry 1837–1851
Emily 1797–1830
Andrew 1842–1843
George 1844–1846
inf 1847
Harriet 1796–1848

1830 Cabell County,Virginia Slave Schedule

	male						female							
	0–10	10–24	24–36	36–55	55–100	100+	0–10	10–24	24–36	36–55	55–100	100+		
slave owner														
Adams,Elizabeth		3											3	
Adkins,Bartlett									1f					1f
Adkins,Hezekiah Sr.							1						1	
Adkins,Isaiah							1						1	
Adkins,Parker							2f		1f					3f
Adkins,Reuben		1					2	1					4	
Adkins,William								1f						1f
Allison,John	1			1			1	1					4	
Beaty,Samuel							1		1				2	
Bellomy,John								1					1	
Bellomy,Mathew H.	2						1		2				5	
Beuhring,F.B.L.		1		1			1						3	
Billups,Edward	1						3	1					5	
Billups,Thomas								1					1	
Billups,William	2				1		1	2			1		6	
Black,James							3	1					4	
Blake,Adam	1						1		2				4	
Blake,Isaac	2	2					1						5	
Blake,Peter	1												1	
Booten,Asa Sr.			1				1		1				3	
Booten,Reuben Sr.	2												2	
Buffington,James		1		1			2	1	1				6	
Buffington,Thomas			1					1		1			3	
Buffington,William	4		1					1					6	
Bragg,Jacob									1f					1f
Brown,Benjamin	4	1		1			2	2	2				12	
Brown,Richard	5	2	3				2	2	2				16	
Burk,Evan								1					1	
Butcher,Mary	4			1			1		2				8	
Cartmill,Thomas			1										1	
Chadwick,Thomas				1					1				2	
Chapman,Philemon									1				1	
Chapell,Henry		2	2						1f				4	1f
Coffman,Ralph		5	2										7	
Conner,James		1	2				3	1	1				8	
Cox,James							1			1	1		3	
Dean,John	2						1	2	1				6	
Dennison,Thomas		1											1	
Dundas,Thomas								1		1			2	
Edwards,Joseph		1											1	
Everett,John Jr.	1	3		1			1	2	1				9	
Everett,John Sr.	1		3					1			1		6	
Everett,Nathan					1								1	
Fields,Lavenia							1	1					2	
Fulkerson,Joseph								1					1	
Fulkerson,Peter	2						2						4	
Fullerton,William			2	1					1	1			5	
Gallaher,James		1											1	
Gardner,Joseph (b'v)		1							1		1		3	

1830	male						female							
	0	10	24	36	55		0	10	24	36	55			
slave owner	10	24	36	55	100	100+	10	24	36	55	100	100+		
Gardner,Joseph(Guy)								2		1			3	
Graham,Ezekiel	1	1		2		(1)			1	1			7	
Gwinn,Andrew			1f					1					1	1free
Hampton,Anthony									1				1	
Hannon,John	2						3	1	1				7	
Hatton,Samuel		1											1	
Hazlett,Alexander		1											1	
Hensley,Samuel	1												1	
Hite,Jacob	1	1					2	1					5	
Hite,John	1							1					2	
Hite,William	1	1		1									3	
Holderby,Robert	1	1					1	1		1			5	
Holley,Joseph	2f	1f		1f			2f	1f		1f			8f	
Holten,Charles	3f		1f				3f	1f		1f			9f	
Holton,George		1f							1f				2f	
Holten,James			1f				1f	1f					3f	
Holten,Joseph			1f				5f		1f				7f	
Holten,Phoebe	1f								1f	1f	2f		5f	
Holten,William		3f	1f				1f	1f		1f			7f	
Hull,James	2								1				3	
Hull,Martin		1					1						2	
Jarred,David	3			1			2	2	1				9	
Jenkins,William	6		1	2	2		8	4	6	4			33	
Job,Jacob		1	1										2	
Kilgore,George							1						1	
Kilgore,Jeremiah								1						
Kilgore,Thomas	3	4					5	2	1				15	
Kirby,Joseph							4	1					5	
Kouns,George W.	2	1			1			1					5	
Kouns,Jacob	3	4	3	3					1	1	1		16	
Laidley,John	1			1				2					4	
Lett,Nance	1	1					1	1		1			5	
Letulle,Victor			1										1	
Love,Daniel		1						2					3	
Love,William		1						1					2	
Lower,Elizabeth	4	1					2	1	1				9	
Lower,Henry								1					1	
Maupin,Thomas	1	3						2		1			7	
Maupin,Thomas Jr.		1						!					1	
McCollister,Thomas	1		1					1					3	
McComas,Elisha	3			2			1	1					7	
McComas,George							1						1	
McComas,Moses									1				1	
McCormick,James Sr.	1	3			1			3		1	1		10	
McGinnis,Allen A.	3						1						4	
McGinnie,James Jr.		1						1					2	
Merrit,Jacob		1											1	
Merritt,John									1f				1f	
Merritt,Lerose	1	1			1		2	1		1			7	
Merrix,William								1					1	
Michard,Joseph		1											1	

1830	male						female							
	0	10	24	36	55		0	10	24	36	55			
slave owner	10	24	36	55	100	100+	10	24	36	55	100	100+		
Miller,Ralph								1					1	
Moor,Fredrick	2	3					3	1					9	
Moor,Martin	2	2		2			4	1	2				13	
Morris,John	1	1		1						2			5	
Morris,Sarah	2	1			1								4	
Newman,Greenville		1											1	
Oliver,James		1											1	
Parks,Joseph					1f				1		1f		1	2f
Perdue,James	1												1	
Perdue,Isaiah	1								1				2	
Plyman,Anthony	1												1	
Plyman,John	2								1				3	
Powel,Thomas W.									1				1	
Rece,Abia	1												1	
Rece,Austin		5	1						1				7	
Russell,Daniel							1		1				2	
Russell,John		2	1					1					4	
Russell,Lewis			1										1	
Samuels,John		1					1		1				3	
Sanders,Martha	1	1		1			2	1		1			7	
Sanders,Sampson	6	3	5	1	1		2	3	2	1			24	
Scales,Peter				1				1					2	
Shelton,Anthony							1	1					2	
Shelton,James	1	2					1	1					5	
Short,Samuel	2									1			3	
Shortridge,Levi	2		1				1	2					6	
Simmons,William	1												1	
Smith,John(Guy)	1				1		4		2				8	
Synder,William		1						1					2	
Spurlock,Burwell	1	1					1		1				4	
Spurlock,Daniel		1					1			1			3	
Spurlock,Lucy	1f	1f												2f
Spurlock,Stephen		1	1					1	1	1			5	
Stone,John		1											1	
Strother,Stephen							1						1	
Thompson,John	2	3						1		1			7	
Thornburg,Solomon	2		1						1				4	
Turner,Joseph	3f													3f
Turner,Joseph	1												1	
White,Overton							1	1					2	
Williamson,John							1	1		1			3	
Wilson,Stephen	2	1											3	
Witcher,Daniel	2	1	2							1			6	
Yates,William		1						2					3	

total black														
slave	116	94	39	26	13	1	94	89	49	31	9		total	561
free	10	5	5	2	1		14	5	5	7	2			56
total	126	99	44	28	14	1	108	94	54	38	11			617
Barboursville	2	2	2	2			1	3	3	1				

1820 Cabell County, Virginia Slave Schedule

slave owner	male 0-14	male 14-26	male 26-45	male 45+	female 0-14	female 14-26	female 26-45	female 45+	total	
Adkins,Littleberry						1			1	
Adkins,Sherrod	1								1	
Adkins,Thomas							1		1	
Artrip,William			1						1	
Barnett,Edward			1						1	
Baty,James						1			1	
Billups,Thomas							1		1	
Booten,Reuben							1		1	
Bowen,Hugh		3							3	
Brown,Benjamin		1	1						2	
Brown,Richard	2	3	2				1		8	
Buffington,Thomas	1		1						2	
Buffington,William						1	1	1	3	
Burton,Allen	1			3			1		4	
Burton,John		1				1	1		3	
Catlett,Alexander	1								1	
Chapman,Chadwalder	2	1							3	
Chapman,Philemon	1	2	1			1	1		6	
Cox,James		1	1						2	
Dingess,John		1				1			2	
Dingess,Peter					2	1			3	
Dingess,William	4	2			1	1			8	
Dole,Jemima					2	3	1		6	(5 are mulatto)
Donathan,Elijah					2				2	
Douthat,Margaret	2	1			1		1		5	
Dundass,John	1		1				1		3	
Estes,Joel	2	1							3	
Everett,John Jr.	2	2	1			1			6	
Everett,John Sr.		3			1		1		5	
Farley,Nimrod							1		1	
Ferguson,Samuel	1	1		1					3	
Fulkerson,Joseph					1				1	
Fulkerson,Peter					1				1	
Fullerton,William	1	1	2		1	1	1		7	
Harmon,Molly (Harmon)	2					2		1	5	
Hatton,George Jr.	1				1				2	
Hensley,David			1						1	
Hensley,Nancy					1	1			2	
Hensley,Robert			1						1	
Hinch,Samuel	1	1				1			3	
Hite,Jacob	1	2			3		1		7	
Hite,William	3			1	1		1		6	
Holderby,James	1				1		1		3	
Hull,Martin	1					1			2	
Jarrett,David					2	1			3	
Jerell,Mildred					2		1		3	
Joab,Jacob	1	1					1		3	
Kilgore,Thomas	5	1			2	2			10	
Laidley,John					1				1	
Leah,Shelton					1				1	

1820 slave owner	male 0-14	14-26	26-45	45+	female 0-14	14-26	26-45	45+	
Lett,Nantz	2				1		1		4
Love,William	1								1
Low,Elizabeth	3				2	1	1	ω	7
Martin,Benjamin	1						1		2
McCormick,Moses	1	1				1	1		4
McGinnis,Edmund					3			1	4
McMahon,John	2				1	1			4
Milkey,John	1								1
Moore,Frederick	1	1	1				1		4
Moore,Jefferson	2		2				2		6
Mopen,Thomas(Maupin)	1				2		1		4
Nicholas,Wilson C.	14	8	7	2	6	8	4	3	46
Prichard,James							1		1
Ratliff,David	1								1
Russell,Mark	2	1	1		3		1		8
Rutherford,John	1				1	1			3
Sanders,Sampson	5	4	2	1	4	4	1		21
Sharp,Leonard	1								1
Short,Samuel					1	1			2
Shortridge,Levi					1				1
Smith,John	1		1			2			4
Spurlock,Burwell					1				1
Spurlock,David					1		1		2
Spurlock,Stephen	1	1			1	1			4
Spurlock,William								1	1
Stallings,Griffith		1			2	1			4
Stuart,Absolum					1				1
Thomas,Henry			1		1				2
Toney,Jesse							1	1	2
Toney,William						1			1
Ward,Jeremiah	2		1		2	1		1	7
Warth,Alexander	1				1				2
Wellman,John	1					1			2
Wilson,Stephen	1				1	1			3
Witcher,Daniel	1	1				1			3

1820 Cabell County
852 households
 85 slave holders   10%
    25 had 1
    46 had 2-5
    12 had 5-10
     2 over 20 slaves

Catlet's = Catlettsburg,KY   Scales Tavern = 6th St.HTGN
Short's = Louisa,KY   Buffington's = 30th St.HTGN
Trout's Hill = Wayne,WV   Prospect Point=   Hill HTGN
Stoke's Mill = Lavalette   Morris Tavern = Milton
McComas Salt Works=Salt Rock Conner's Tavern=Culloden
          HTGN=Huntington

CABELL COUNTY 1820
-JOHN WOOD'S MAP-

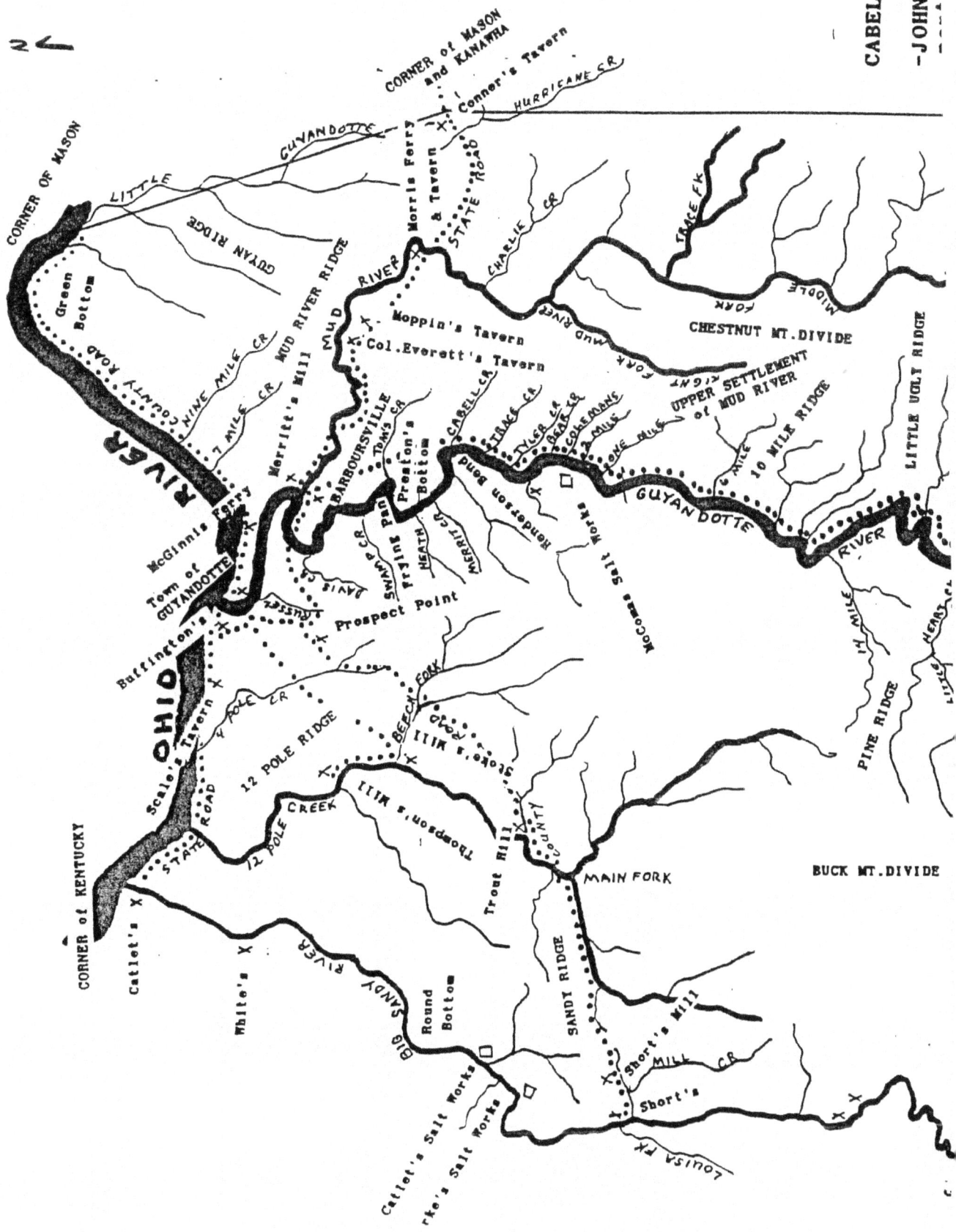

REVOLUTIONARY SOLDIERS IN 1840 CENSUS

John Adkins Sr.	84
Valentine Blose	82
Thomas Chandler	78
Asher Crocket	81
Adam Crom	85
John Everett Sr.	87
James Gillingwater	74
John Leslie	79
William Mead	78
Robert Rutherford	77
John Stephenson	79
Peter Sullivan	85

OLDER CITIZENS OF THE 1830 CENSUS

Roland Bias Sr.	90
Micajah Frazier	80
Robert Garret	80
John Johnson	100-Bear Ck
Cornelius Hopkins	80
James Emmons	80
Lerose Merrit	80
Edmund Osburn	90
Judah Spurlock	80
Thomas Smith	80

The Dusenberry Mill reproduced from original painting
of MRS. O.E. BIRD

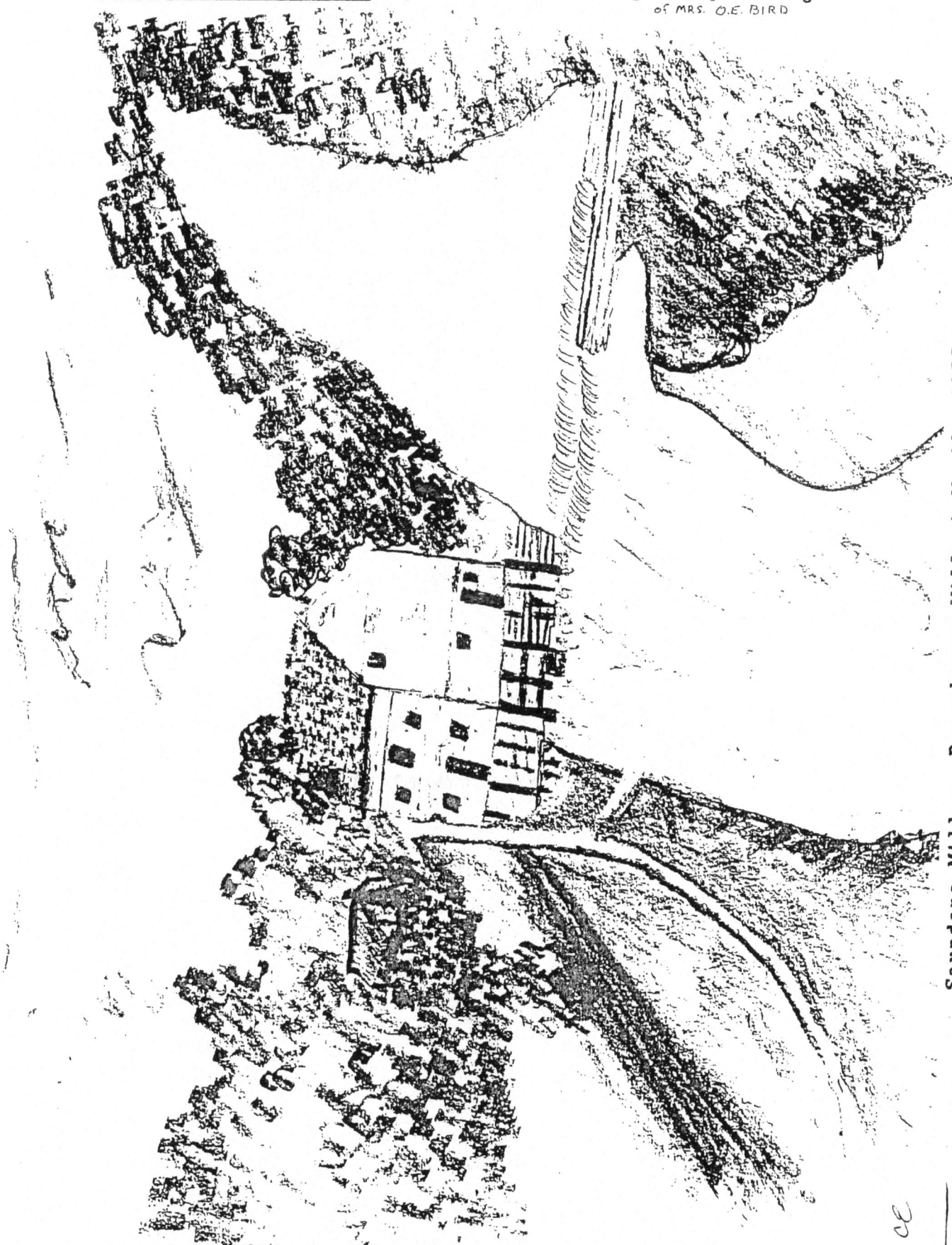

OCCUPATIONS LISTED IN THE 1820 CENSUS
OTHER THAN FARMER

BAKER	X
BLACKSMITH	XXXXX
BRICKLAYER	XX
CARPENTER	XXXXX
CABINETMAKER	XX
COOPER	XXXX
DISTILLER	X
HANDYCRAFT	XX
HATTER	XXX
SADDLER	XX
SHOEMAKER	XX
STONEMASON	X
TAILOR	XX
TANNER	XX
WAGONMAKER	X

EMPLOYMENT OTHER THAN FAMER

1820 OCCUPATIONS	15	1850 OCCUPATIONS	60
PERSONS EMPLOYED	35	PERSONS EMPLOYED	138

1820 Cabell County Census
cc = Cabell County   B = Barboursville   G = Guyandotte
marriages are added as reference not fact
cc=Cabell, Va   CCA or A=ccAnnals   MM=Mason, Va   GaOh=Gallia, OH
Gb=Greenbrier, Va Mt=Montgomery, Va   Gpky=Greenup, KY
KCM=Kanawha, Va   Taz=Tazewell, Va   LCoh=Lawrence, OH

w cc Adams, William
    | Adkins, Archibald
    | m-Polly Adkins   1820cc
    | Adkins, Barlett
    | Adkins, Brison
    | Adkins, Charity
    | Adkins, Hezekiah-Nancy Spears 1819cc
    | Adkins, Jacob
    | Adkins, Jesse
    | Adkins, John
    | m-Christina Adkins 1819cc
w | Adkins, John
X | Adkins, Joshua
w | Adkins, Littleberry
    | Adkins, Luke
X | Adkins, Mark
    | m-Caty Lovejoy 1820cc
w X | Adkins, Parker
    | m-Jane Holton 1822cc
    | Adkins, Reuben-Agnes Price 1805Mont
    | Adkins, Richard
w X | Adkins, Sherod Sr.
X | Adkins, William
w | Adkins, William
    | Alford, George
X | Allin, Henry |
    | Allison, William
    | Amoss, Arisha(McGinnis)
    | m-John Amoss 1811
    | Amoss, Asa
    G   Anderson, William (Tailor)
   cc   Ancill, Martin
    | Ancill, Melchor
    | Arthur, James
    | Arthur, Thomas
    | Artrip, John
w | Artrip, William
    | Artrip, John
    B   Baber, John
   cc   Bailey, Caleb
w | Bailey, Hugh
    | Bairding, John
    | Bairding, Joseph |
    | Baker, David
    | Laker, Henry
    | Baldwin, John
w | Ball, James
    | Ball, Robert-Sarah Wilson 1817LCoh
X | Ballard, John
    | Ballard, John Jr.
X | Ballard, Phillip

w cc Ballomy, John
    | Barnheart, Peter
    | Barnheart, Peter Jr.
    | Barrett, Andrew-Dicy McComas 1818cc
    | Barrett, Edward
    | Barrett, James
    | m-Saray Hatfield 1802/3 KCM
    | Barrett, John
    | m-Nancy Adkins 1811cc
    | Barrett, Joseph-Polly Sample-12c
    | Barrett, Samuel
    | m-Carissa McComas 1819cc
    | Barton, William   ·
    | Bartrum, David
    | m-Rebecca Blue   1810cc
    | Bartrum, James
    | m-Delila Wilson 1813
w | Bartrum, John
w | Bartrum, Stephen
    | Bates, Daniel (1830 Elizabeth)
    | m-2nd Polly Johnson 1819
w | Baty, James
    G   Battezel, William(hatter)
    B   Bennett, Michael
X cc Bias, James
    | Bias, John
    | m-Sally Rea 1819cc
X cc Bias, Odediah
    | Bias, Roland
    | m-Dicy, Brumfield 1813cc
    | Billups, Richard
    | Billups, Thomas
    | Billups, Thomas
    | Black, Adam
    G   Blajet, Luther
   cc   Blake, Isaac
    | Blake, Jeremiah
    | Blake, John
    | Blakenship, Conley
    | Blakenship, George
    | Blakenship, Jesse
    | Blakenship, John
    | m-Agnes, Short 1802 KCM
    | Blakenship, Nancy
    | Blakenship, Peter
    | Bloss, (Blows), Valentine
    | Blue, Richard
    | Booth, Charles
    | Booth, Ferguson
w | Booten, Asa, Jr.
    | Frances Spurlock 1813cc

v = Wayne County Census 1850
X = Logan County Census 1830

1820

w cc Booten, Asa
w ' Bootin, Reuben
   '
   ' Bowen, Abner
w ' Bowen, Hugh-Elizabeth Owen 1805Mont
   ' Bradshaw, Charles
   ' Bradshaw, John
        Rebecca Stephenson 1817cc
   ' Bradshaw, Shelton-Mary McCoy 1819Loh
   ' Bradshaw, William
   ' Bragg, Jacob
   ' Briant, John
   ' Brown, Benjamin-Matilda Scales CCA
   ' Brown, James-Catharine Foster 1790Mt
   ' Brown, John-Jane Wurnel 1819MM
   ' Brown, John
w ' Brown, Richard-Sarah Haney CCA
   ' Brown, Thomas W.(bricklayer)
   ' Brumfield, Byrd
   ' Brumley, William
   ' Buffington, Jonathan
   ' Buffington, Thomas-Anne Cline '75A
G ' Buffington, William-
           Nancy Scales CCA(both)
B Beuhring, F.G.L.(Distiller)
cc Beckett, James
        m-Hannah Lee 1814cc
B Bumgardner, Phillip
cc Burgess, Thomas
   ' Burk, Michael
   ' Burns, James
   '   m-Nancy Alford 1818cc
   ' Burns, John
   '   m-Eleanor Jorden 1816cc
   '
   ' Burns, Peter
   ' Burns, Roland
   ' Burton, Allen
   ' Burton, John
   ' Butcher, Samuel
   ' Butcher, William
   ' Briyin(Buyin), Joshua
B Caldwell, Cuff
        (carpenter-free black)
cc Calloway, Elijah
   ' Campbell, Thomas
   ' Camron, John
   ' Canterbury, Samuel
   ' Cardwell, Nathan
        m-Nellie McGinnis 1811cc
B Carnes, James
cc Carnes, Thomas
   ' Carpenter, Thomas
   ' Carroll, James
   ' Carter, Abner
   ' Carter, John (cabinet maker)

cc Cartmill, Henry
' Cartmill, Thomas-Nancy Compton
           1802Taz
' Casy, Benjamin(cooper)
' Catlett, Alexander
' Chandler, Abraham
' Chandler, Thomas
' Chapman, Andrew
' Chapman, Cadwallider
'   m-2Sally Cockburn 1816cc
' Chapman, Edward
' Chapman, John-Dicey Napper 1791Mont
' Chapman, John Jr.
'   m-Lucy Hudson 1816cc
'   Chapman, John Sr.
G Chapman, Philoman
' Chapman, Thomas
'   Lucy Morris 1802/3 KCM
' Chapman, Wm.-Sarian Estes-- MM
' Childers, Thomas B.
' Childers, Allen
' Childers, Allen Jr.
G Clapp, Thomas

cc Clark, Matthew F.
' Clark, Samuel
'   m-Nancy Lambert 1811
' Clark, Wm.Sr.-Jane Ferguson 1787Mt
' Clendenon, Robert A.
' Clevinger, Joshua
' Clive, Peter
' Cole, John R.-Isabell Woods 1810Mt
B Collins, Patrick-
        m-Nancy Griffy 1818LCoh
G Collins, Thomas C.
cc Collins, William
' Conley, Garland
' Conley, Isaac
'   m-Betsy Smith 4 apr 1811
' Conner, James
' Conner, Wm.Catherine Poff 1811Mt
G Cooper, Able
cc Cooper, Robert
' Cooper, Wm.Betsey Bumgardner 1808MM
' Copley, William
' Cornwell, Benjamin
' Cowen, Samuel
' Cox, James
' Cox, William
' Cox, William
' Cox, William
'   m-Sally White 1813cc
' Crawford, Isaiah
' Cremeans, Lindsey
'   m-Susan Brumfield 1802/3 KCM
' Crocket, Asher
'   m-Sarah Blankenship 1800Mt

1820

✗ cc Curry, Barnabas	ѡ cc Drown, Benjamin
¦ Curry, Robert	¦ Dugan, Hugh
¦ m-Susannah Runner 1792Mt	¦ Duncan, William
¦ Curry, Samuel	¦ m-Mary Dirk 1786Mt
¦ Dale, Jemima	¦ Dundass, John
¦ Dameron, Augustus	¦ Dunfuee, John
¦ m-Elizabeth Dearing 1812cc	¦ Dunkle, Henry
¦ Dameron, Edmund	¦ Dunkle, Jacob
¦ Dameron, Lazrus	¦ Dunlap, John
✗ ¦ Daniels, Ezekiel	✗ Elkins, Archbald
ѡ ¦ Davis, Benjamim	✗ Elkins, Daniel
ѡ ¦ Davis, Daniel	✗ ¦ Elkins, James
¦ m-Mary Douthat 1817cc	✗ ¦ Elkins, Richard
¦ Davis, Jesse	✗ ¦ Elkins, Zackrus
¦ Davis, John	✗ ¦ Ellis, Evan
¦ Davis, John W.	¦ Ellis, Philip
¦ Davis, Paul	G Emons, Mary
¦ Davis, William B.	cc Estes, Joel E'beth Bradley Franklin Co.
¦ Davis, William	¦ Everett, John -1st Sarah Woodson
¦	¦ 2nd-Sarah Dedman (CCA)
¦ Davis, William	¦ Everett, John Jr.
¦ Davis, William 1812cc	¦ Everett, Nathan
¦ m-Elizabeth Stephenson	¦ m-Sally Rece 8 feb 1816
¦ Davis, William	B Everett, Richamond (hatter)
¦ Dean, Benjamin	cc Ewins, (Evans)Richard
ѡ ¦ Dean, Joseph	cc Ewins(Evans, Thomas (carpenter)
¦ m-Nancy Russell 1816cc	¦ Farley, George
¦ Dean, Samuel	✗ ¦ Farley, Henry
¦ m-Polly Russell 1818cc	¦ Farley, John
¦ Dearing, Anthony	¦ m-Salley Puzey 1811cc
¦ Dearing, John	¦ 2-Polly Ferguson 1813cc
¦ Dearing, William	✗ ¦ Farley, Nimrod
¦ Defoe, Polly	¦ Farley, Thomas
¦	¦ m-Patsey Lester 1789Mt
ѡ ¦ Defore, James	✗ ¦ Farley, William
¦ m-Nancy Cox 1813cc	¦ 2-Elizabeth Chetwood 1816cc
¦ Defore, Levi	¦ Ferguson, Edward
¦ m-Pinnah Cox 1820cc	¦ Ferguson, James
✗ ¦ Dempsey, John	ѡ ¦ Ferguson, Joel
✗ ¦ Dempsey, Joseph	ѡ ¦ Ferguson, John
¦ Dempsey, Thomas	ѡ ¦ Ferguson, John
¦	¦ Elizabeth McCoy 1817 LcOh
¦ Dempsey, William	¦ Ferguson, Joshua
¦ Demsey, John	¦ Ferguson, Joshua
¦ Denison, Thomas	¦ Sarah Woods, 1811 GaOh
¦ Dial, John	¦ Ferguson, Samuel
¦ Dial, Ransom	¦ Ferguson, Samuel
¦ m-Nancy McComas 1810	¦ Patsey Stephenson 1810cc
¦ Dillion, Roland	¦ Ferguson, Samuel
✗ ¦ Dingass, John	¦ Ferguson, Samuel-Amy Lycan 1810cc
✗ ¦ Dingess, Peter	¦ Ferguson, Thomas
¦ Dingess, Peter Jr.	ѡ ¦ Ferguson, William
¦ m-Mary Stone 1820	¦ Ferill, Richard
✗ ¦ Dingess, William	¦ Fips, John (cooper)(Fills)
¦ Donathan, Elijah	¦ Fitzpatrick, Isaac
¦ Douthet, Margaret	¦ m-Jane Sample 29 mar 1814

cc Ford, James
    Elizabeth Fisher 1805 GpKy
Forth, John
    m-2 Nancy Jordan 1818
Forth, Robert
Francis, William
Franklin Edward
w Frasure, John
w Frasure, Lewis
    Elizabeth Ratcliff 1805 GpKy
Frasure, William
Fry, John
    m-Catherine Snodgrass 1823cem

Fryley, James
Fulkerson, Joseph
    m-Susannah Lane 1817cc
Fulkerson, Peter
Fullerton, William
Furguson, Henry
G Galliher, James
cc Gardiner, Joseph
B Gardner, Joseph
cc Garmeny, William
w Garrett, Benjamin
Garrett, Joseph
    m-Martha Hutchinson 1824cc
Garrett, Leroy
Garrett, Robert
Gay(Ray), Joseph
Gibson, Alexander
    Polly Patterson 1817cc
w Gilkeson, John-Jane Kesee 1823GpKy
Gilkeson, Nancy
Gillaspie, Thomas (blacksmith)
Gilpin, Samuel
Godbey, William
Gray, James
Green, Giles
Greenwood, William
Griffith, John
    Guinn, Polly 1819cc
Grove, Joseph
Guthrie, Robert
Gwinn, Andrew
Hagor, Allen
Hauger, Andrew
    m-Nancy Barker 28 oct 1813
Hauger, Catherine
Hager, Michael
(Hagley see Haygley)
Hail, John
    Nancy Ratcliff 1819cc
Hainor, George (Haynor-Hager)

Hall, James
Hamilton, John

w cc Hampton, Anthony
    (Jane Thompson 1811cc
    (Henry)
w Hampton, Henry
Hampton, Malinda (Shortridge)
    m-William Hampton 1802 KCM
Hampton, William
    Haney, William
Hannon, John (not Nat.)
    m-Mary White 1812cc
Harbour, David-Mary Spurlock 1787Mt
G Harden Stephen
cc Harmon, Molly
Harmon, Nicholas
cc Harris, Simon
Harrison, Harmon
Harshbarger, David (blacksmith)
Harwood, Joshua
Haskins, James
Haskins, Solomon
Haskins, William
Hatfield, Adam-Mary William 1799Mt
Hatfield, Andrew-Mary Marr 1798Mt
Hatfield, Isaac-Mary French 1788Mt
Hatfield, James
    m--Dolly Bias 1817cc
    m-Rebecca Brown 1819cc
Hatfield, John m-MARY McCOMAS 1788 Mt
Hatfield, John
Hatfield, William
    m-Anny Brumfield 1793Mt
w Hatten, Elijah
    Elizabeth McGinnis 1818cc
Hatten, George-Rhoda Kirby 1803Mt
Hatten, George Jr.
Hatten, John
Hatten, Philip
w Hatten, Samuel
w Hatton, William
w Hatton, William
w   m-Rebecca Hallery 1819
Haygley, Peter
Haynie, Hansford
Hayner, Fredrick
Hayner, Jacob
Hayner, James
Hayner, Lewis
Hazlett, Alexander
Heath, Isreal (stonemason)
Heath, William
    m-Nancy Sanford 4 Jun 1818
Henderson, William
Hensley, David
Hensley, Joseph
    m-Hannah Miller 1809 GpKy
Hensley, Nancy
Hensley, Robert

1820

w cc Hensley, Samuel	cc Jarrett, David (h'dyc'ft)
w ¦ Hensley, Solomon	¦ Jarrett, David
ℒ ¦ Hensley, William	¦ Jarrett, James
¦ Hensley, William	¦ Jarrett, James
¦ Hereford, William	¦ Jefferson, Henry (cooper)
m-Polly Cox 1814cc	¦ Jefferson, Henry
¦ Herndon, Valentine	ℒ¦ Jeffry, William
	¦ Jenkins, Bennett
cc Hilyard, George	m-Rebecca Swan 1812 KCM
¦ m-Sally Staley 1815cc	¦ Jerell, Mildred
¦ m-Betsy Knight 1816cc	¦ Jeral, Pryor (Jarrell)
¦ Hilyard, John	¦ Jewel, Solomon
¦ Polly P.Gray 1816cc	¦ Joab, Jacob
cc Hillard(Hilyard)Joseph	¦ Johnson, Benjamin
¦ m-Elizabeth Morris 1796 KCM	¦ Johnson, Benjamin
¦ Hillman, William	m-Theadocia Wilson 1794Mt
¦ Hinch, Samuel	¦ Johnson, Burwell
ℒ¦ Hinchman, William	¦ Johnson, George
¦ Hines, Elias	¦ Johnson, James-Rachael Copley 1786Mt
¦ Hisel, Thomas	¦ Johnson, Joseph-Martha Logan 1817CCA
¦ Hisey, John	¦ Johnson, Lewis
¦ Pricillas Hutchinson 1824LCoh	¦ Johnson, Nimrod
¦ Hite, Jacob-Sarah Scales CCA	¦ Johnson, Pattey (Perry ?)
¦ Hite, William-Elizabeth Brown CCA	¦ Johnson, Sugar
¦ m3-Jane Hawkin 1820cc	¦ Johnson, Thomas-Mary Reyburn 1793Mt
¦ Hodgison, John	¦ Jordan, Andrew
¦ m-Elizabeth Martin 1808 KCM	m-Polly Chapman 1802 KCM
G Holderbey, James-Lane/Wright CCA	¦ Jordan, James
cc Holdright, John D.	m-Penney Lee 1810cc
¦ m-Sally Chapman 1819cc	¦ Jordan, James Sr.
¦ Hollenbaugh(Hollenback), George	¦ Jordan, John
¦ Hollenbaugh, John	¦ Jordan, Jonathan
¦ Hollenbaugh, Martin (cooper)	m-Rachael McCray 1811cc
¦ m-Elinor Hampton 1811cc	¦ Jordan, William
¦ Hoozer, Randolph	¦ Keenan, Patrick
¦ Hosley, Julius	Susan Arbough 3 Jan 1810Gb
¦ Hubbord, David	Rebecca McComas 1818cc
¦ Hudson, John	¦ Keese, Richard
¦ m-Lilicia Rector 1813cc	¦ Keezer, Christopher
¦ Hudson, John Jr.	m-Peggy Bloss 1816cc
¦ m-Margaret McCray 1818cc	¦ Keezer, John
¦ Hudson, Lewis	¦ Kelly, Beal
¦ m-Maurmen Keeten 1809KCM	w ¦ Kelly, Joseph
	m-Elizabeth Stith 1817LCoh
¦ Huff, Gabriel	¦ Kenedy, Charles
¦ Hugart, Andrew	¦ Kidwell, Joseph
¦ Hugert, James	G Kidwell, Richard
¦ m-Agnes Patten 1821cc	
¦ Hull, Martin-Susan BuffingtonCCA	cc Kilgore, Thomas
¦ Hunt, James	¦ Kington, Francis
¦ Hunter, John	ℒ¦ Kirk, James
¦ Hunter, Sally	w ¦ Kirk, John
¦ Hunter, Samuel	¦ Kise, George(Casy ?)
¦ Hutchison, David	¦ Kishwer(?),Matthias
¦ Irwin, Patsey	¦ Kitchum, Jesse
¦ Jackson, William (carpenter)	¦ Kitchum, Phillip
¦ m-Susannah Pratt 31 Jan 1819	¦ Knight, Abner

1820

cc Knight, James 1802 Gb
    Margaret Cavendish
'   Knight, William
B   Laidley, John
        (Rachel Pettit 1808Gpky ?)
        Mary Scales Hite 1816 CCA
cc Lambert, Ezekiel
'   Polly Ferguson 1819cc
'   Lambert, Jeremiah-
'   Sarah Alsup 1788Mt
'   Lambert, William
'   Leak, Skelton
'   Legg, Devenport
'   Legg, James
'   Lelandos, Prosper(not Nat.)
'   Lemay, James
'   Nancy Huggert 1811cc
'   Lemmons, William
'   Lemons, Elijah
'
'   Lett, Joseph
'   Susannah Pauley 1817cc
w' Lett, Nantz
G   Letulle, Victor(baker)
cc Littey, Robert
'   Love, Charles
'   Love, Daniel
'   Cynthia Chadwick 1818GpKy
'   Love, William
'   Elizabeth Hampton 1829GpKy
'   Lovejoy, Josephus
'   Lovejoy, Michael
'   Lovejoy, Michael Jr.
'   Lovejoy, Rebecca
'   Low, Elizabeth
'   Low, Henry
'   Low, Jacob
'   Low, James
'   Low, Jesse
'   Low, Mary
x' Lucas, John
'   Lucas, William-Elz.Price 1782Mt
'   Lunsford, John
w' Luther, Henry
w' Lykins, Goodwin (not Nat.)
'   Martha Vaughan 1817Gb
'   Mabe, Philip
'   Mady, Henry
'   Mansfield, Isaac
'   Marcum, Jacob
'   Marcum, John
w' Markrum, Joseph
'   Marcum, Moses
'   Marcum, Stephen
'   Mars, James
x' Marrs, John
'   Martin, Benjamin
'   Martin, Jesse

cc Maxey, Benjamin
'   Mayo, James
'   Jane Garrett 1812cc
'   McCallister, James
'   Mary Smith 1820cc
'   McCallister, thomas
G   McCleland, George (taylor)
cc McClocky, John
'
'   McComas, Charles
'   McComas, Elisha
'   Anna French 1792Mt
'   McComas, George
'   McComas, Isaac
'   McComas, Jese
'   Judith Napper 1789Mt
'   McComas, John
'   m-Mary Barnes 7 Jan 1813
'   McComas, John
'   m-Catherine Hatfield 1786Mt
'   McComas, John
'   McComas, Moses-Lucy Napper 1793Mt
'   McComas, Thomas-Mary Aldrich 1779Mt
'   McComas, William-Mildred Ward CCA
'   (Dicy Chapman 1797Mt)
x' McComas, William
'   Elizabeth McComas 1818cc
'   McCormack, David
'   McCormick, Eli
'
'   McCormick, Elizabeth
'   McCormick, James
w' McCormick, Levi
'   McCormick, Moses
G   McCoy, William (tanner)
        Nancy Bradshaw 1817cc
x cc McDonald, Jonas
'   McGinnis, Celia
'   McGinnis, Edmund
'   McGinnis, James (cabinetmaker)
'   McGinnis, Samuel
G   McMahon, John
cc McMilion, John
x' McNealy, David
'   McNealy, Richard
'   McNealy, Robert
'   Nancy Christian 1812cc
'   McNealy, Samuel
'   McWhater, James
x' Meade, Samuel
'   Meadows, John
'   Merritt, George
'   Merritt, John
'   Sally Wentz 1812cc
'   Merritt, Lerose
'   Merritt, Obediah
'   Merritt, Pelington
x' Miller, Abraham

1820

✗ cc Miller,Abraham	cc Odair,John
ı Miller,Andrew	W ı Osburn,Edmund
ı Miller,Andrew	W ı Osburn,John
ı Miller,Embly	ı Cynthia Ferguson 1817cc
ı Miller,George	ı Overstreet,Dabney
✗ ı Miller,James	ı Jane Rodgers 1812
ı Miller,James	ı Owens,William
✗ ı Miller,John-Nancy Rece 1816GpKy	ı Nancy Crease 1797 KCM
✗ ı Miller,John	ı Page.Lucy
ı Miller,Lydia	ı Paine,Harrison
ı Miller,Moses	ı Polly McComas 1813cc
ı Miller,William	ı Parker,Joseph
ı Elizabeth Frick 1792 KCM	ı
ı Ester Henderson 1816 GpKy	ı Parsons,Samuel
ı Mimms,Martin	ı Parsons,William
W ı Moore,Fredrick	ı Partlow,George
ı Moore,Jefferson	ı Partlow,Joshua
ı Moore,Martin	ı Patten,David
ı Morris,Achilles	ı Patterson,Littlebury
ı Morris,John	ı Patterson,William
ı Mary Ann Coleman 1796 KCM	ı Pauley,William
ı Morris,Levi	ı Payne,William
, Morris,Thomas	ı Peanipeld,William
ı Abigail Scales 1814cc	ı Pearson,Simon (blacksmith)
ı Morris,William D.	W , Perdue,Isaiah
W ı Morris,William	ı Lucinda Lett 1816
, Morris,William	W ı Perdue,Sarah(Lett)
ı Sally Spurlock 1812cc	ı James Perdue 1819
ı Mecky Brown 1819cc	✗ ı Perry,Henry
ı Ann Shelton 1820cc	✗ ı Perry,James-Pheby Pickens 1802Taz
ı Morris,William Jr.	ı Perry,Jesse
ı Morrison,John	ı Elizabeth Cartmill 1820cc
ı Morrison,Patrick	W ✗ ı Perry,John
ı Ann Scales 6 may 1819	ı Perry,Richard
ı Morrison,Rachael	ı Perry,Solomon Jr.
ı Morrison,William	ı Miram Cartmell 1818cc
G Moss,Peter (carpenter)	W ı Perry,William
cc Mosser,Thomas	W ı Perry,William
ı Morrmann,Charles	ı Peterman,Jacob
✗ ı Mountz,David	ı Lucy Stewart 1818cc
✗ ı Mullins,Nathaniel	ı Peter,Matthew
ı Murner(?),James	ı Peyton,Charles
ı Murphey,John-Nancy laken 1819Gpky	ı Peyton,Henry
ı Murphey,John	ı Peyton,Henry Jr.
W ı Napper,Thomas	ı Peyton,John F.
ı Newman,John	ı Susannah Payton 1812cc
ı Sally Garrett 1814cc	ı Peyton,Jonathan
ı Newman,John	✗ ı Philips,Henry
ı Newman,Joseph	ı Pickens,Peter
ı Newman,Leroy	✗ ı Pine,James
ı Newman,Peyton	ı Plymale,John
ı Nicholas,W.C. (Wilson Cary)	ı Rebecca Ferguson 1819cc
ı Night,Libbey	ı Pore,Robert
ı Noble,William G.(lath Operator)	ı Pore,Thomas
ı Martha Newman 1819cc	ı Porter,John

1820

	Left column		Right column

cc Porter, William
    Poteet, James
ı Price, James
ı Price, John
ı Prichard, James
ı   Elizabeth Stewart 1818cc
ı Pryor, Jeral
ı Rabb, David (blacksmith)
G Rainey, John
cc Rally, Isum
ı Ratliff, Daniel-
ı   Stacy Fraziar 1805GpKy
ı Ray, Benjamin
ı Ray, James
ı Ray, Jesse
ı Ray, John
ı   Tabitha Partlow 1819cc
ı Ray, Joseph (Gay)
ı Rece, Abia
ı   Elizabeth Harmon 1808 KCM
ı Reece, Allen
ı Rece, Joseph
ı Reynolds, John
ı Richards, William
ı Riggs, Charles B.
ı Ritter, Hugh M.
ı Roberts, Green
ı Roberts, Isaac
w ı Roberts, John
ı Roberts, Pleasant
w ı Robertson, Joseph
ı Robertson, William
ı Roffe, Ingram
ı Rogers, George
G Rose, Eramus
cc Ross, Samuel
ı Rubey, John
ı Rubey, Samuel
G Runner, Isaac (blacksmith)
cc Runnion, Adam
cc Russell, John-
ı   Susan Miller 180/3 KCM ?
ı   Rebecca Buffington 1820cc
ı Russell, Mark
ı   Ester Dean 1811cc
ı Rutherford, Griffith (tanner)
ı Rutherford, John-
ı   Sally Scott 1813GaOh
⤬ B Rutherford, Joseph (hatter)
cc Rutherford, Robert
ı   Frances Hazelett 1817cc
w ı Rutherford, William
ı Sailsberry, Elijah
ı Samples, James
ı Samples, John
ı   Sarah Barrett 1812cc
ı

cc Sampson, Thomas
    Sanders, Sampson
ı Sanford, Robert (shoemaker)
ı Sandford, Walker
ı   Sarah Brumfield 1818cc
ı Savoirs, Heiney
ı Sanson, John
ı Saxton, William
ı Scales, Nathaniel
ı Seamonds, Elijah G.
ı   Keeton s/o Justin Sandridge CCA
ı Serus see Syrus (Cyrus)
ı Sharp, Leonard
ı Shelton, Abraham
ı Shelton, James
ı   Susannah Hannon 1809 KCM
ı Shelton, John
ı Shelton, John
ı Shelton, Joseph
ı Shelton, Samuel
ı Shelton, Stephen
ı Shepherd, Jesse
ı Shirkey, John
ı Short, Samuel
ı Short, Thomas
ı Shortridge, Levi
ı   Love, Elizabeth 1813cc
ı Shy, Edward
ı Simmons, Ephraim
ı Smallridge, John
ı   Mary Bell 1820cc
ı Smith, Adam
ı   Polly Garrett 1810cc
⤬ ı Smith, Benjamin
⤬   Martha Stratten 1817cc
⤬ ı Smith, George
w ı Smith, James
ı Smith, Jesse
⤬ G Smith, John
ı   Elizabeth Vaughn 1813cc
w⤬ cc Smith, John
ı   Eliza Fuller 1809cc
ı Smith, Jordan
ı Smith, Mary
ı Smith, Peter
ı
w ı Smith, Samuel
⤬ ı Smith, Thomas 1794 KCM
ı   Elizabeth Young
ı Smith, Thomas
ı   Mary Deal 1819cc
w⤬ ı Smith, William
ı   Sarah Hatfield 1811cc
ı Snodgrass, James
ı Southerland, Alexander
ı

1820

cc	Spears,George	cc
	Elizabeth Miller 1818cc	
	Spears,John	
	Catherine Peyton 1802/3 KCM	
	Sperry,Benjamin	
	Winney Artrip 1793Mt	
w	Sperry,Obdiah	
w	Spurlock,Burwell-Sallie Morrison	
	Spurlock,Daniel	w
	Spurlock,George	
	Elizabeth Clore 1791Mt	
	Spurlock,John	
	Polly Dean 1819cc	
	Spurlock,Juda	
	Spurlock,Mary	
w	Spurlock,Stephen-Nancy Amoss CCA	
	Spurlock,William	
	Frances Morris 1809 KCM	
	Stafford,John	
	Strailey,Charles M.	
	Stailey,Daniel	
	Stailey,Jacob	
w	Stailey,Stephen	
	Stailey,Stephen Jr.	
	Stallings,Griffith	
	Stallings,Isaac	
	Stallings,Josiah	
	Stallings,Samuel	
	Stanley,George	
	Stanley,Joseph	B
	Stanley,William	cc
	Starr,Elizabeth	
	Stater,James	
	Staton,Charles	
	Stephen,Joseph (saddler)	
	Stephens,Elijah	
	Stephens,Francis	
	Stephens,Gilbert	
w	Stephenson,Benjamin	
	Stephenson,Jeremiah	
	Nancy Duncan 26 feb 1818	
	Stephenson,Mark	
	Stewart,Andrew	
	Stewart,William	
	Eleanor Walker 16 Jan 1817	
	Stith,Harmon	
w	Stith,John	
	Stokes,Brice	
	Stokes,James	
	Stokes,John	
G	Stone,John (bricklayer)	
cc	Stone,John	
	Straton,Joseph (see Staton)	
	Mary Henderson 1819cc	
	Stroope,Melchor	

cc	Stroope,William
	Peggy Merritt 1817cc
	Stuart,Absolum
	Swan,Levin C.
	Swan,Thomas
	Swan,Thomas
	Swearinger,Leonard
w	Syrus,Abraham
	Syrus,Frances
	Syrus,Isaac(Serus
	Syrus,Thomas
	Tacket,John
	Sarah Heilyard 1800 KCM
	Taylor,Maryann
	Thacker,Reubin
	Nancy Allen 1797Pittsly Co.
	Tharp,James
	Thomas,Henry
	Thompson,James
	Elizabeth Thintapn 1789 KCM
	Thompson,John (handycrafts)
	Thompson,John 1820cc
	2?-Elender Hutchinson
	Thompson,Robert
	Thompson,William
	Thompson,William
	Thorn,Michael (hatter)
	Martha Peters 1820
	Thornburg,Solomon (blacksmith
	Toney,James
	Elizabeth Smith 1819cc
	Toney,Jesse
	Toney,John
	Mary Ferguson 1808 KCM
	Toney,Squire
	Nancy Brown 1813cc
	Toney,william
	Trout,Abraham
	Tull,William
	Tulley,Clayboren
	Tunt(?),Fredrick
	Turley,Floyd
	Turley,James
	Elizabeth Stark 1804 KCM
	Turley,John
	Turner,Adam
	Turner,Francis
	Turner,George
	Turner,Joseph
	Turner,William
	Tyree,William
	Vance,Abner
	Vance,James

1820

Xcc Vance, John

X Vance, Richard
X Vance, Susanna
X Varney, Andrew
| Vaughn, John
| Luddie Crabtree 1812cc
w | Vaughn, Thomas
| Vinson, James
| Walker, Charles
| Walter, Hyram G.
| Ward, Benjamin
| Ward, Jeremiah (110y)
| Ward, John
| Ward, Richard
| Ward, Roland (saddler)
| Ware, Philip
| Warth, Alexander
w | Watts, Ambrose
| Watts, Eleanor
| Watts, Elias
| Webb, James
G Webb, Nathaniel (shoemaker)
| Webb, Robert
w | Webb, Samuel-
| Polly Frashur 1809 GpKy
w | Welman, James
w | Welman, John
| Wheeler, Elizabeth
| Wheeler, James
| Wheeler, Joseph
| Wheeler, William
G Wheelright, Nathaniel
cc Whipple, John
X | White, Benjamin
| Nancy Goodwin 1787 Amherst
X | White, Benjamin H.
X | White, James
| Lucy Elkins 14 Jul 1814
X | White, James
| White, John
|
X | White, William
| Nancy Foster 1813GpKy
| Whittlock, William
| Nancy Derrick 1817cc
| Whitton, Ransom
| Wilch, James
| Wilson, Charles
| Wilson, James
| Patsy Rusel 1802/3 KCM
| Wilson, John
| Kathrine Donnally 1802 KCM
| Wilson, Robert
| Polly Russell 1802/3 KCM
| Wilson, Samuel (carpenter)
| Wilson, Samuel

cc Wilson, Stephen
. Agnes Witcher 1810cc
| Wilson, William
| Wince, Joseph (Wintz)
| Wince, Philip
| Wince, Windle
| Windship, Samuel
| Wishong, John
| Wishong, Leonard
| Witcher, Caleb (wagonmaker)
| Witcher, Daniel
| Withers, John
| Woods, John
| Polly Osburn 1817
| Woosley, David
| Workman, Jacob (Wartman ?)
| Wyatt, Thomas (same ??)
| Rachael Burnside 1784 Gb
| Hanna McClallister 1811GaOh
| Yopp, Charles
|

For some reason the 1820 Cabell
Census did not arrive in Washington
until late 1821. There is letter
at the end of the census return.

Free White males	2,362
Free White females	2,147
Male slaves	206
Female slaves	186
Males of color-Free	2
Females of color Free	7
TOTAL	4,910

1809 public buildings of Cabell laid out at mouth ouf Guy. in field of Wm. Holderby -p61 BK I

OHIO STREET

William Buffington 2

Robert Holderby 3
Wm. Merritt

John Smith Henry & Charles Lewis 4

COURT STREET

Wm. Anderson 5
James F. Johnson Wheelwright & Simmons 6

Edmund McGinnis 7
Abraham Miller 8

1 2 3 | 25 26 27 | 1 2

Ward 12

John Smith Daniel Witcher 11

Daniel Witcher Daniel France 10
Buffington 14

Sylvester Fuller 9
James McGinnis Jr 15

4 | 24 | 4

8 | 23 | 5

Jacob Job Sr 6 | 22 | 6

mmons 13

DDLE STREET (BRIDGE)

18 Galliher

e Ward 19 Rodgers

17

16

7 | 21 | 7

8 | 20 | 8

9 | 19 | 9

20

21

22

BUFFINGTON STREET

26

25

24 Thomas Clap

James Galliher 23
John B. Hereford

10 | 18 | 10

11 | 17 | 11

27 ington

28

29

Jas Galliher 30
Pilamon Chapman

12 | 16 | 12

Spangler 34
Galliher

33 Edmund Morris

32

31 Richard Crump

13 | 15 14 | 13

Original Town 1809

Additions 1850-1866

GUYANDOTTE, VIRGINIA 1809

208

S 55° E 50p   4 feet 6 inches

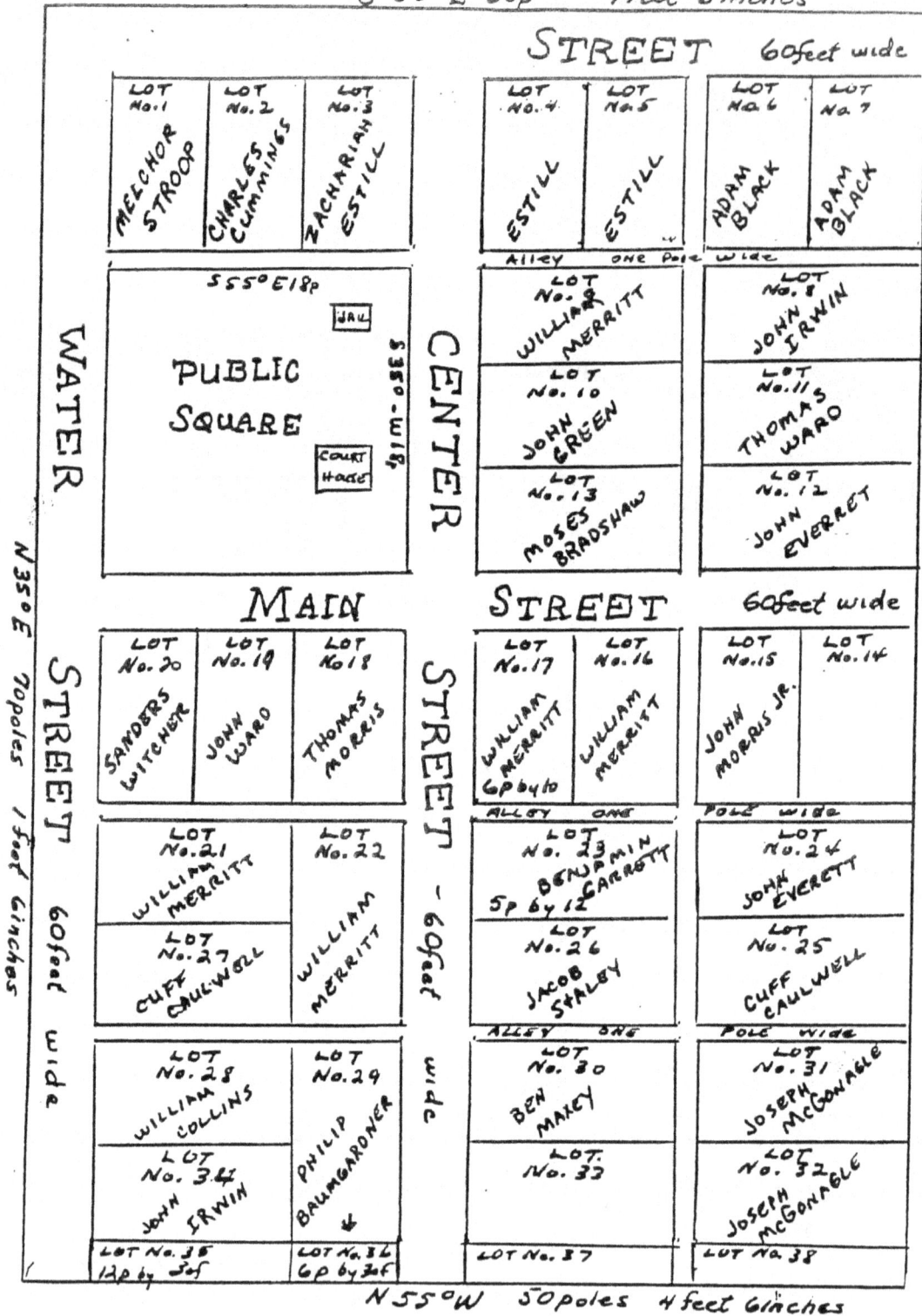

STREET   60 feet wide

| LOT No.1 MELCHOR STROOP | LOT No.2 CHARLES CUMMINGS | LOT No.3 ZACHARIAH ESTILL | LOT No.4 ESTILL | LOT No.5 ESTILL | LOT No.6 ADAM BLACK | LOT No.7 ADAM BLACK |

S 55° E 18p

JAIL

PUBLIC SQUARE

S 35° W 18 p

COURT HOUSE

WATER STREET

CENTER STREET

N 35° E 70 poles 1 feet 6 inches

60 feet wide

Alley   one pole wide

LOT No.9 WILLIAM MERRITT	LOT No.8 JOHN IRWIN
LOT No.10 JOHN GREEN	LOT No.11 THOMAS WARD
LOT No.13 MOSES BRADSHAW	LOT No.12 JOHN EVERRET

MAIN   STREET   60 feet wide

| LOT No.20 SANDERS WITCHER | LOT No.19 JOHN WARD | LOT No.18 THOMAS MORRIS | LOT No.17 WILLIAM MERRITT 6p by 40 | LOT No.16 WILLIAM MERRITT | LOT No.15 JOHN MORRIS JR. | LOT No.14 |

Alley   one   pole wide

| LOT No.21 WILLIAM MERRITT | LOT No.22 WILLIAM MERRITT | LOT No.23 BENJAMIN GARROTT 5p by 12 | LOT No.24 JOHN EVERETT |
| LOT No.27 CUFF CAULWELL | | LOT No.26 JACOB STALEY | LOT No.25 CUFF CAULWELL |

Alley   one   pole   wide

| LOT No.28 WILLIAM COLLINS | LOT No.29 PHILIP BAUMGARDNER | LOT No.30 BEN MAXEY | LOT No.31 JOSEPH McGONAGLE |
| LOT No.34 JOHN IRWIN | | LOT No.33 | LOT No.32 JOSEPH McGONAGLE |

| LOT No.35 12p by 3 of | LOT No.36 6p by 3 of | LOT No.37 | LOT No.38 |

CENTER STREET — 60 feet wide

N 55° W   50 poles   4 feet 6 inches

PLAN of TOWN of BARBOURSVILLE

By William Buffington, County Surveyor

LAID out for WILLIAM MERRITT

1814

FIRST PROPERTY OWNERS

"A Chapter of Early Cabell County History"
The Herald-Advertiser, Huntington, WV December 2, 1928

—By MARY McKENDREE JOHNSON—

ritt's Mill, once a famous old landmark at the mouth of the Mud river, figured in the early life of C...

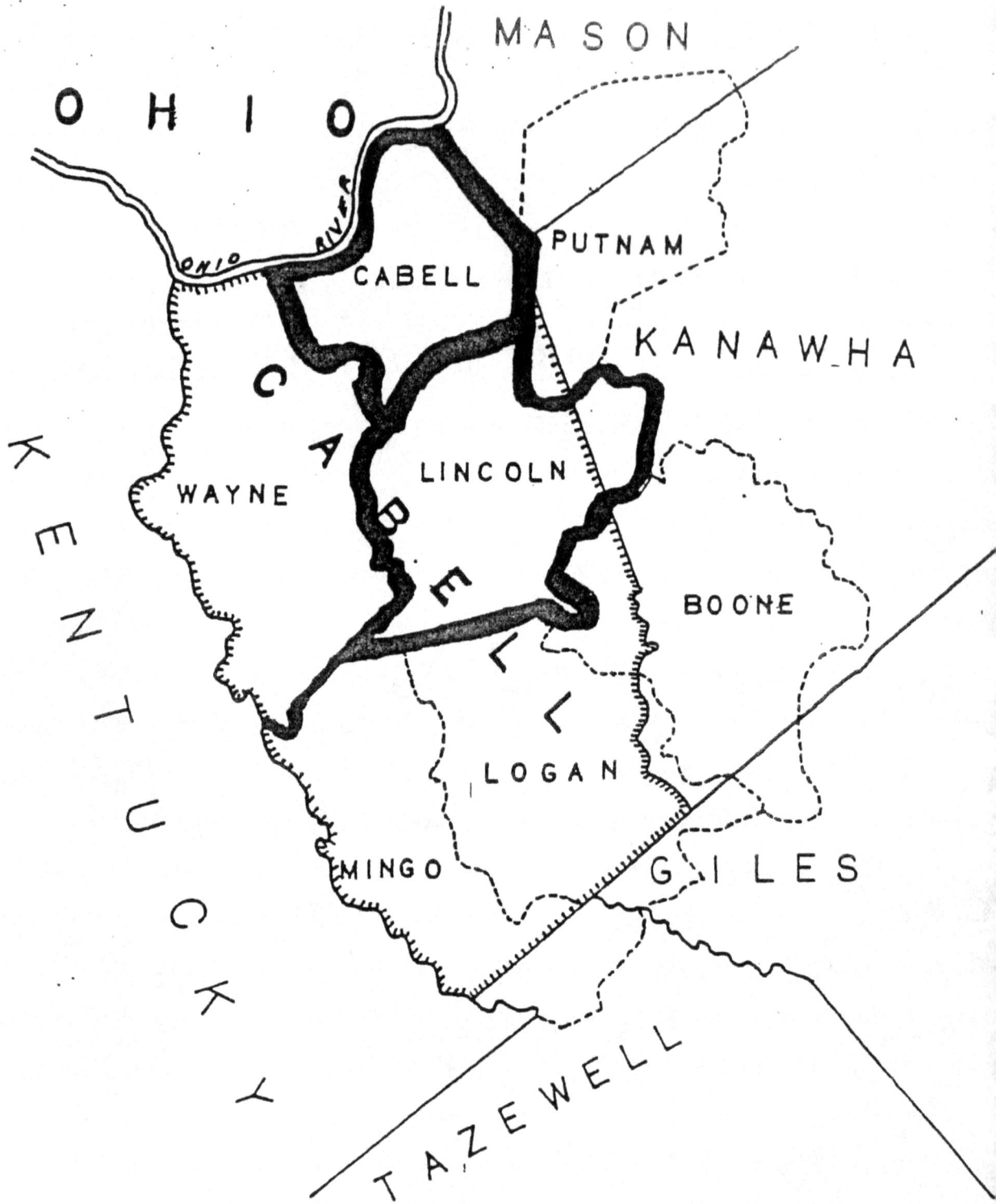

CABELL COUNTY'S EXTENT 1810-1820

- - - - Present county boundaries
,,,,,,,,,,,1810-1820 boundaries

THE CENSUS DID MAKE MISTAKES

1820	1830	1840
William Adams	not listed	William Adams
6 Barrett	3 Barrett	no Barrett
Robert Guthrie	not listed	Robert Guthrie
William Hinchman	not listed	William Hinchman
5 Marcum	7 Markum	2 Markum
not listed	Martha Saunders	died

This is just a small sample of the mistakes. Several important people were missed in these census as well as the 1850 census.

In 1850 Martin Moore #13 is listed as a slave holder; he is not listed on the regular population schedule.

#532 and #536 are partially duplicated.
#532 and #533 are neighbors ? together ?

The Size of Cabell County

Most of the counties in western Virginia began on a piece of paper before more than a handful of surveyors had seen the land. The parent county of all of West Virginia was Orange County created in 1738 with boundries that once included all the land west of the Appalachian Mountains, north to the Great Lakes, westward at least to the Mississippi and possibly to the Pacific Ocean and southward with no set boundary.

The eastern politicans continued to crave hugh sections of land into counties as settlers moved westward. Cabell's genealogy branches from Orange

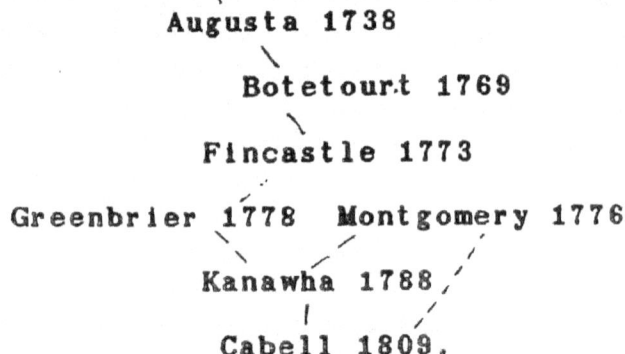

Augusta 1738

Botetourt 1769

Fincastle 1773

Greenbrier 1778   Montgomery 1776

Kanawha 1788

Cabell 1809.

Greenbrier and Montgomery counties were separated by the Kanawha River. Montgomery was on the south and a direct parent of Cabell, but when Kanawha County was created, it included land on both sides of the river and from both Greenbrier and Montgomery counties.

AREA verses POPULATION	
640 acres = 1 sq mile pop = population	
1809-2067 sq mile = 1,322,880a - 3,680pop 1810	
1820-	4,910pop 1820
1824-1227 sq mile = 785,280a	
1830-	5,884pop 1830
1840-	5,954pop 1840
1842- 721 sq mile = 461,440a	
1850-	- 5,710pop 1850
1867- 282 sq mile = 180,480a	

CABELL COUNTY 1815 TAX LIST
from Sigfus Olafson

as used in ABSTRACTS OF DEED BOOK II 1814-1819 CABELL COUNTY, VA/WV
by this author

Cabell County was organized in 1809. The 1810 and 1815 tax lists were used by Olafson to recreate the 1810 census. Spellings can vary greatly.

Bias, James
, Obediah Sr.
, Obediah
, Roland
Black, Adam
Blankenship, Archibald
, George W.
, Jesse
, William
Bloss, Valentine
Bolt, Isaac
Bolt, James
w Booton, Asa Sr.
w , Asa Jr.
, Laban
w , Reuben
Booth, Charles
Bostic, Manoah

Adair, John
Adams, Charles
Adams, Robert
Adkins, Hezekiah
, Isaac
, Jacob
, Jesse
w , Littleberry
, Randolph
, Reuben
w , Sherrod
x , Sherrod-the upper
w x , William
Aldridge, James
w Bowen, Hugh
Aldridge, Robert
Bowles, William
Alford, George
Boyd, Alexander
Alford, James
Bradshaw, Moses
Amos, John
Brammer, Edmund
Ansell, Martin
, James
Ansel, Melcher
, John
Arthur, Thomas
, Joseph
Artrip, John
Brandon, Stewart
w Artrip, William
Brewin, William
Austin, Thomas
Brown, Benjamin
w Bailey, Hugh
, Elijah
Ball, John-in valley
w , Richard
Ball, John-on Sandy
, William
Ballard, Elijah
Brumfield, Byrd
x , John Sr.
, James
, John Jr.
, William
x , Phillip
Bryant, John
Baker, Henry
, Joseph
Barker, William
, Lawrence
Barnes, John
Buffington, Jonathan
Barnhart, Peter
, Thomas Sr.
Barrett, Andrew
, Edward
, Thomas Jr.
, James
, John
, William
, Joseph
Bumgardner, Phillip
, Samuel
Burk, Michael
Bartram, David
Burns, John
, James
Burns, Peter
w , John
Burress, William
w , Stephen
Burton, John
Bates, Daniel
Caldwell, Cuff
Bean, Stephen
Cardwell, Nathan
Beckett, James
Cartmill, Henry
Bellamy, John
Carter, John
Casey, Jonathan

Chapman, Andrew
, Cadwallader
w , Edward
, George-Ohio
, George-Guyan
, Henry
, John Sr.
, John Jr.
, Joseph
w , Thomas
Childers, Thomas
Christian, Allen
Clark, Samuel F.
Clark, William
Clapp, Thomas
Cogburn, Sally
Collins, John
Collins, Paul
x Conley, Garland
, Isaac
, Thomas
Conner, William
Cornwell, John
Cornwell, Wesley
Cox, James
, William
, William-Sandy
Cremeans, Burton
Cummins, Charles
Daggs, Reuben
Dameron, Augusta
, Cyrus
, Onesipherous
Daniel, Edmund
Davidson, George
w Davis, Benjamin
w , Daniel
, Jesse
, Paul
, Samuel
, Thomas
, William
, William
, William
Dean, Benjamin
Defoore, James
x Dempsey, John
, Thomas
, William
Dennis, John
Derton, Peter(Deering)
Dial, John
x Dingess, John
x , Peter
, Peter Jr.
, William
Dial, Ranson

x LOGAN
W WAYNE

Doddridge, Josiah
Donathan, Elijah
Douthitt, Daniel
Douthitt, Margaret
w Drown, Benjamin
Dunkle, Henry
x Elkins, Daniel
xx   , James
    , Richard
    , William
    , Zacheus
x Ellis, Evan
    , Spencer
    , Philip
Ellison, James
Emmons, Cyremus
Estes, Joel
Evans, Ferrell
Evans, James
Everett, John Sr.

    , John Jr.
    , Nathan
Fannon, John
x Farley, Henry
Ferguson, James
w   , John Sr.
w   , John Jr.
    , Joshua
    , Samuel Sr.
    , Samuel Jr.
    , Sam. son-Jol
    , Thomas
w   , William
Ferrell, John
Ferrell, Richard
Finney, John
Ford, James
Forth, John
France, Daniel
France, Henry
Franklin, Edward
w Frazier, Lewis
Frazier, William
Friley, James
Fudge, Jacob
Fulkerson, Peter
Fullerton, James
Fullerton, William
Gallaher, James
w Garrett, Benjamin
    , Benjamin Jr.
    , Lewis
    , Joseph
    , Robert

w Gilkerson, John
    , Nancy
    , Thomas
Ginnit, James
x Godbey, William
Gragston, John
Graham, Jonathan
Gray, James
Greenwood, William
Griffith, John
Groves, Joseph
Gullett, Christopher
Gullett, Daniel
Guthrie, Robert
Hager, Allen
    , James
x   , Michael
Hagley, Peter
w Hampton, Anthony
w   , Henry
    , William
Hannan, John
Harbour, David
Harrison, Obed
    , Hannah
    , Simeon
Hatcher, Farley
Hatcher, Henry
Haskins, William
Hatfield, Adam
    , Isaac
    , John
    , Thomas
Hatton, Asa
    , John
w   , Phillip
w   , Samuel
w   , William
Hayden, Jeremiah
Hayner, Cathrine
    , Fredrick
    , Jacob
    , James
    , Mary & Polly
Haynie, Henrie
Haynie, William
Hays, John
Hazlett, Alexander
Hazelwood, Pleasant
Heath, Isreal
Heaton, Patterson
Helphistine, Henry
Henderson, William
Hensley, Daniel
w   , Samuel
w   , Solomon
    , Stephen

Herdon, Valentine
Highsey, John
Hillyard, Jonathan
Hillyard, Joseph
Hinch, Samuel
x Hinchman, William
Hite, Jacob
Hite, William
Hodgison, John
Holderby, Absalom
    , James
    , Robert
    , William
Hollenbeck, George
    , John
    , Martin
    , Marin Jr.
Holt, John
Holt, Newton
Hoozer, Rudolph
Hoskins, James
Hoskins, James
    , John
Howard, David
Howard, John
Howe, Chester
Huddleston, Abram
    , Daniel
    , Stephen
Hudson, John
Hudson, Lewis
Huggart, Andrew
Hull, Martin
Hunter, Samuel
Irwine, John
Irwine, Thomas
Jarrell, Benjamin
x Jeffery, William
Jenkins, Bennett
Johnston, Benjamin
    , Martha
    , Nimrod
    , Sugar
    , William
    , Jonathan
Jones, Thomas
Jordan, Andrew
    , Charles
    , James Sr.
    , James Jr.
    , John
Kelly, Stephen
Keyser, Christopher
Keyser, John
Kezee, Richard
Kilgore, Thomas
Kimberling, Adam

L LOGAN
W WAYNE

Laffoon, Daniel
Laidley, John P.
Lambert, Hannah
Lambert, Jeremiah
Leftwich, Sally
Lemay, James
Leonard, Rufus
Love, Charles
Love, William
Lower, Henry
Lower, Peter
Lycan, Jacob G.
Marcum, Jacob
, James
, Josiah
Mansfield, Isaac
Maxcey, Ben
Maxcey, Jonathan
Mayab, Phillip
Mayo, James A.
McCallister, Richard
McCallister, Thomas
McComas, David
, Elisha
, Elisha
, Isaac
, Jesse
, John
, John Sr.
, Moses
, Stephen
, Thomas
, William
, William
, Wm. (son John
McCormick, James
, Levi
, Lewis
, Moses
McGinnis, Achilles
, Edmund
, James
, John
, Pyrrhus
, Samuel
McGonigle, Joseph
McKinney, William
McMahon, John
McNeely, David
, James
, John
, Richard
, Robert
McWhorter, John

Merritt, George
, John
, Lerose
, Obadiah

, Pellington
, William
Miller, Abraham
, Abraham Jr.
, Embly
, James
, William
, William
Moorman, Charles
Morgan, Elizabeth
Morris, Achilles
, Ambrose
, Edmund
, John Sr.
, John Jr.
, Levi
, Thomas
, Thomas A.
, William
, William D.
Morrison, Patrick
Morrison, William
Muncey, James
Muncey, Samuel
Neal, Daniel
Newman, John
, John
, Leroy
, Peyton
, William
Nicholas, Wilson C.
Overstreet, Dabney
Parker, Joseph
Parker, Samuel
Parsons, Samuel
Parsons, William
Partlow, George
Patton, David
Pauley, Harrison
Payne, Richard
Payne, William
Perdue, Isaiah
Perry, Henry
, John
, Solomon
, William
Peters, Matthew
Peyton, Charles
, Henry
, Henry Jr.
, John
, Jonathan
, William

Pewsey, James
Phillips, Henry
Pine, James
Poore, Robert
Poore, Thomas
Porter, Alexander
, John
, William
Poteet, James
Reece, Abia
, Allen
, Joseph
Reuby, Samuel
Rigg, Baptist
, Joseph
, Stephen
Robertson, Joseph
Robertson, Richard
Rodgers, George
Rodgers, John
Roffe, Ingram
Ross, Robert
Row, William
Runner, Isaac
Runyon, Adam
Russell, John
, John
, Lewis
, Mark Sr.
, Mark Jr.
, Phillip
, Thomas
, William
, William
Rutherford, Francis
, Robert Sr.
, Robert Jr.
, Thomas
, William
Salmons, James
Sample, George
Sample, John
Samuels, John (atty)
Sanford, Robert
Sansom, John
Sanders, Sampson
Sanders, Martha
Saxton, William
Scales, Nathaniel

, Noah
, Peter
Shannon, William
Sharp, Leonard
Sheets, Leonard

Shelton, John
Shelton, Stephen
Short, Samuel
Short, Thomas
Simmons, Sarah-wid.
Slaughter, Andrew
Smiley, Samuel
Smith, Adam
x   , Benjamin
         , Benjamin
         , Ezekiel
w   , James
         , Jesse
xx   , John
wx   , John
         , Peter
         , Ralph
xx   , Thomas
xx   , William
x   , William
    Snodgrass, James
            , Robert
            , Samuel
    Southerland, Alexander
    Sparr, John
    Spears, John
    Speers, Paul
    Speery, Benjamin
    Sperrt, Samuel
w   Spurlock, Burwell
            , Charles
            , Daniel
            , George
            , Jesse
            , Stephen
            , William
    Stafford, Absalom
    Staley, Jacob
w   Staley, Stephen
    Stallings, Isaac
            , Jacob
            , Josiah
    Stephenson, Alexander
            , Alex. Jr.
w   , Benjamin
            , Elijah
            , Gilbert
            , John
            , John Jr.
    Stewart, Absalom
            , Charles
            , Mitchell
            , Ralph
    Stith, James
w   Stith, John
    Stokes, Brice
    Stokes, James

xx Stone, John
x   Stratton, Joseph
    Stroop, Melcher
    Swann, Benjamin
          , Levin
          , Thomas
    Swan, Thomas (Guyan)
    Swearingen, Leonard
    Syres, Abraham
         , Frances-wid.
         , Thomas
         , William
    Tabor, Robert
    Talbot, James
    Talley, Grief
x   Taylor, Mary Ann
    Thompson, John
            , Juda
x   , William
    Thornburg, Solomon
    Tiller, William
    Toney, Edmund
         , Jesse
         , John
         , Leah
         , Squire
x   , William
    Tull, Wm. & Agnes
    Turley, Atha
          , James
          , John
    Turner, James
          , Martha
    Vanhoose, John
    Vanhoose, Levi
    Vanosdall, William
    Vaughn, John
w   Vaughn, Thomas
    Vinson, James
    Walker, Charles
          , Daniel
          , Henry
    Wallace, John
    Wallace, Timothy
    Walls, Jacob
    Walton, Nancy
    Walton, William
    Ward, Benjamin
        , George
        , John
        , Jeremiah
        , Phillip
        , Thomas
    Webb, Robert
w   Wellman, James
           , John
           , Jeremiah

    Wheeler, James
           , Joseph
           , William
x   White, Benjamin
x   , James
         , John
x   , William
    Wilgus, James
    Williams, Hiram
    Williamson, Alden
    Wilson, Charles
          , James
          , Robert
          , Stephen
    Wentz, Jacob
         , Phillip
         , Windle
    Witcher, Daniel Sr.
    Wishon, John
    Woosley, David
    Workman, Jacob
           , James
           , Joseph
    Wray, Benjamin
        , James
        , Jesse
    Witcher, Daniel Jr. o

CABELL COUNTY 1810 TAX LIST
from Sigfus Olafson
as used in ABSTRACTS OF DEED BOOK II 1814-1818 CABELL COUNTY, VA/WV

Cabell County was organized in 1809. From 1809 until 1820 it included all or part of Boone, Lincoln, Logan, Mingo and Wayne and a small section of Putnam. Cabell's first census of 1810 was destroyed. The 1810 and 1815 tax lists were used by Olafson to recreate the 1810 census. Some of the names on these lists never resided in Cabell although they did earn property in the region.

Adams, Robert
Adkins, Berry
Adkins, Hezekiah
Adkins, Jacob
Adkins, James
Adkins, Sherod
Adkins, Sherod(Little)
Adkins, Spencer
Adkins, William
Aldridge, James
Allsberry, Charles
Amos, John
Amos, Martin
Amos, Samuel
Ansell, Melker
Armstrong, John
Artrip, William
Austin, Michael
Austin, Thomas
Baker, Henry
Ball, John
Ballard, Jesse
Ballard, Micajah
Ballard, Stephen
Barhart, Jacob
Barhart, Peter
Barnes, John
Barrett, Edward
Barrett, John
Barton, William
Bartram, David
Bartram, John
Bartram, Stephen
Bean, Stephen
Bellamy, Benjamin
Bellamy, Ellet
Beller, Elias
Benson, Samuel
Bias, James
Bias, John
Bias, Obediah Sr.
Bias, Obediah
Blankenship, William
Blue, Cornelius
Blue, Samuel
Bloss, Phetha

Boalt, Isaac
Boalt, James
Boothe, Charles
Booton, Asa
Booton, Laban
Booton, Reuben
Bostick. Manoah
Boyd, Alexander Sr.
Boyd, Alexander
Brammer, Edward
Brammer, John
Brewer, Isaac
Brown, Henry
Brown, James
Brumfield, Bird
Brumfield, George
Brumfield, William
Brown, Richard
Bryan, John
Bryan, Lawrence
Buffington, Jonathan
Buffington, Thomas
Buffington, Thomas Jr.
Buffington, William
Burcham, John
Burns, Peter
Burris, William
Burris, William
Burton, John
Camell, Elias
Cardwell, Nathan
Carter, John
Cartmill, Henry
Casey, Johnathan
Chapman, Cadwallader
Chapman, Haney
Chapman, John
Chapman, John
Chapman, Thomas
Christian, Allen
Christian, Allen
Christian, Thomas
Clap, Thomas
Clark, Samuel
Clark, William
Clevenger, Levi

Collins, Lewis
Conley, Garland
Conley, Isaac
Conley, Thomas
Cornwell, Wesley
Cox, John
Cox, William
Cremeans, Burton
Cremeans, Higgs
Cremeans, Lindsey
Cremeans, Moses
Cremeans, Reuben
Crump, Hanley
Crump, Richard
Dameron, Augustus
Daniel, Edmund
Davidson, George
Davis, Benjamin
Davis, Daniel
Davis, Paul
Davis, Thomas
Davis, William
Davis, William
Dearing, John
Dennis, John
Dial, Ranson
Dingess, Peter
Dingess, William
Donothan, Elijah
Douthit, Daniel
Douthit, Margaret
Droddy, Ezekiel
Dunbar, William
Dunkel, Henry
Durton, Peter
 (Derton, Deering)
Elkins, Absalom
Elkins, Daniel
Elkins, James
Elkins, Richard
Elkins, William
Elkins, Zachariah
Ellis, Spencer
Ellis, Uriah
Ellison, James
Emmons, Cyreneous
Epling, John
Erwin, Thomas
Estes, Joel
Estill, William L.
Evans, Ferrell
Farley, Henry
Ferguson, John
Ferguson, Samuel
Ferguson, Sr.

Ferguson, Thomas
Ferguson, William
Ferrell, Richard
Ford, James
Forgy, Hugh
Forgy, James
France, Daniel
France, Henry
Friley, James
Friley, Samuel
Fudge, Jacob
Fullerton, James
Fullerton, John
Fullerton, William
Fuson, William
Garrett, Benjamin
Garrett, Benjamin
Garrett, Isom
Garrett, Joseph
Garrett, William
Gilkerson, Nancy
Godbey, William
Grant, John
Grant, Vinson
Grant, William
Gray, James
Gray, Joseph
Greenwood, William
Griffith, John
Gumby, Daniel(negro)
Guin, John
Hager, Michael
Hager, Philip
Hagley, Peter
Hampton, William
Haner, Fredrick
Haner, Jacob
Haner, Lewis
Haney, Henry
Hannan, Esom
Hannan, John
Harbour, David
Harrison, John
Harrison, Obadiah
Harvey, William
Hatcher, Edward
Hatcher, Farley
Hatcher, Henry
Hatfield, Adam
Hatfield, Andrew
Hatfield, Isaac
Hatfield, John
Hatfield, Joseph
Hatfield, Thomas
Hatfield, William
Hatfield, William Jr.

Hatton, Asa
Hatton, John
Hatton, Samuel
Hatton, William
Hayman, Hezekiah
Hazelett, Alexander
Heath, Isreal
Helverson, Henry
Henry, James
Henry, John
Higgins, John
Hillyard, Jonathan
Hillyard, Jonathan
Hillyard, Joseph
Hillyard, Thomas
Hisey, John
Hite, Jacob
Hite, Martin
Hite, Wesley
Hodge, John
Hogan, David
Hogan, James
Holderby, William
Holderby, William Sr.
Holland, Michael
Hollenbeck, George
Hollenbeck, John
Hollenbeck, Martin Sr.
Hollenbeck, Martin Jr.
Hoskins, Levi
Hoskins, William
Hoskinson, James
Howard, Edward
Howe, Chester
Howell, James
Huddleston, Daniel
Huggard, Andrew
Hulwin., Thomas
Hutchinson, Hanna
Hutson, Lewis
Jarrett, David
Johnston, Benjamin
Johnston, Perry
Johnston, Perrin W.
Johnston, Sugar
Jones, John
Jones, Thomas
Jourdan, Andrew
Jourdan, James Sr.
Jourdan, James Jr.
Jourdan, John
Jourdan, Jonathan
Jourdan, William
Kelly, Stephen
Kezee, Richard
Kilgore, Thomas
Kirk, James

Lambert, Job
Lane, Charles
Lane, William
Lankford, Robert
Lee, John
Lee, Sarah
Lore, Henry
Lore, Peter
Marcum, Jacob
Marcum, James
Marcum, Josiah
Marcum, Moses
Marcum, Stephen
Marcum, William
McComas, David
McComas, Elisha
McComas, Isaac
McComas, Jesse
McComas, John
McComas, John Jr
McComas, Moses
McComas, Thomas
McComas, William
McCown, John
McCoy, David
McCoy, Theophilus
McGinnis, Edmund
McGinnis, Samuel
McNeely, David
McNeely, John
McNeely, Richard
McNeely, William
Merritt, John
Merritt, Lerose
Merritt, Obadiah
Merritt, William
Miller, Embley
Miller, Hugh
Miller, William
Moore, Ronal
Morgan, Simon
Morris, Edward
Morris, John Sr.
Morris, John
Morris, William
Morrison, Charles
Morrison, William Sr
Morrison, William
Mounts, David
Muncey, Samuel
Nance, Daniel
Nance, Thomas
Napier, Thomas
Neal, Daniel
Neal, Samuel
Nelson, Samuel
Newman, Leroy

Newman, Peyton
Nicholas, Wilson Cary
Nuil, John
Parsons, Colwell(widow)
Parsons, William
Pauley, Edward
Payton, Henry
Payton, John
Payton, Jonathan
Peary, Solomon
Peary, William
Perdue, Isaiah
Peters, Matthew
Phillips, Henry
Pine, James
Pine, Squire
Porter, Alexander
Prate, Jesse
Puthoff, Henry
Puzey, James
Randal, Daniel
Randal, John Sr.
Randal, John
Rea, James
Rea, James(OHIO)
Read, John
Reece, Abiah
Reece, Joseph
Reuby, Samuel
Rice, Allen
Rice, Ezekiel
Riffe, Abraham Sr.
Riffe, Abraham
Riffe, Gabriel
Riggs, Baptist
Riggs, Stephen
Ripley, Berry
Ripley, John
Robertson, John
Robinson, Richard
Robinson, - - -
Roffe, Ingram
Rogers, George
Rogers, John
Russell, Isaac
Russell, Jeffery
Russell, John
Russell, Mark
Russell, Owen
Rutherford, Reuben
Rutherford, Ribert
Rutherford, Thomas
Salmons, James
Sample, George
Sanders, Sampson

Sansom, John
Saxton, William
Scales, Nathaniel
Scales, Noah
Scales, Peter
Shelton, James
Shelton, John
Shelton, Joseph
Shelton, Robertson
Shelton, Samuel
Short, Samuel
Short, Thomas
Sias, Isaac
Simmons, John
Sirus, Abraham
Sirus, Fanny
Sirus, Thomas
Sidmore, Micajah
Slaughter, Ezekiel
Smiley, Samuel
Smith, Constantine
Smith, James
Smith, John
Smith, John(Ohio)
Smith, John
Smith, William Sr.
Smith, William Jr.
Snell, Jacob
Snodgrass, James Jr.
Snodgrass, Robert
Snodgrass, Samuel
Spears, James
Spears, John
Spears, Paul
Sperry, Benjamin
Spurlock, Burwell
Spurlock, Charles
Spurlock, Daniel
Spurlock, David
Spurlock, George
Spurlock, Jesse
Spurlock, Stephen
Spurlock, William
Stafford, John
Stallings, Jacob
Stephens, Gilbert
Stephens, John
Stephens, Zachariah
Stephenson, Alexander
Stephenson, Robert
Stephenson, Samuel
Stephenson, William
Stewart, Absalom
Stewart, Charles
Stewart, James

Stewart, John
Stewart, Ralph
Stokes, Brison
Stokes, Mary
Stone, John
Stout, John
Strupa, Melker
Sutherland, Alexander
Swearingen, Leonard
Tallery, Grief
Taylor, Fredrick
Taylor, John
Thompson, Patton
Thompson, William
Tiller, William
Toney, John
Toney, Squire
Toney, William Sr.
Toney, William
Trent, John
Tule, Richard
Turley, John
Vaughn, Thomas
Walker, Patton
Walker, William
Wallace, Agnes
Wallace, John
Walton, Nancy
Walton, William
Ward, Jeremiah
Ward, Thomas
Ware, Phillip
Wellman, Jeremiah
Wellman, John
White, Benjamin
White, James
White, John
Wilks, James
Williams, Joseph
Williamson, Alden
William, John
Wilson, James
Wilson, Robert
Wilson, William
Wintz, Phillip
Wintz, Windle
Wishbon, John
Witcher, Daniel
Witcher, Daniel
Witcher, Samuel
Wood. Mathew
Woodward, Slyvester
Woosley, David
Workman, Jacob
Workman, James
Workman, Joseph

1810 residents

Amos,Martin   -Frances Bellamy   1811cc
Blackburn,Polly-Henry Puthoff   1810cc
Blue,Samuel   -Sarah Janes   1811cc
Bostick,Manoah -Jensy Scales   CCA
Broon(Brown),James-Mariah Hall   1819cc
Collins,Lewis   -Nancy Lee   1811cc
Cremeans,Birtow-Polly Adkinson   1811cc
Davidson,George-Polly Pepper   1804Mont
Elkins,Richard -Nancy McGuire   1787Mont
Epling,John   -Pattice Parsons 1801Mont
Ferguson,John   -Margaret McKennee 1789Mont
Ferguson,Thomas-Rachel Munsey   1790Mont
McComas,David   -Cloe Bailey   1787Mont
Russell,Jeffery-Elizabeth Brown   CCA (110yr)
Scales,Nathaniel-Mary Frances--   CCA
Scales,Peter   -Ann Minor   Orange Co.CCA
Stewart,Absolum-Susannah Smith   1793Mont
Stewart,James   -Nancy Burgess   1798Mont
   Bryan,Lawrence-Elizabeth Morris 1797(4) KCM
   Hilyard,Joseph - Mary Morris 1796 KCM

1815 Residents

Atkins,Isaac   -Betsey Atkins   1811cc
Amos,John   -Arrisba McGinnis 1811cc
Beckett,James   -Margaret Peden   1794Mont
Bowles,William -Nancy Harrison   1814cc
Brumfield,James-Elizabeth Rece   1818GpKy
Cartmill,Henry 5 listings 1780's Botetourt
Chapman,Cadwallader-Sally Cockburn1816cc
Hilyard,Jonathan-Catharine Row   1811cc
Howe,Chester   -Nancy Drown   1819cc
Huddleston,Adelcha-Mary Row   1813cc
Huddleston,Stephen-Betsey Row   1814cc
Hudson,John   -Lilicia Rector   1813cc
McGinnis,Pyrrhus-Betsey Barnes   1812cc
Neal,Daniel   -Peggy Griffith   1810cc
Overstreet,Dabney-Jane Rodgers   1812cc
Parker,Samuel   -Nancy Russell   1814cc
Patton,John   -Nancy Walton(wd) 1817cc
Payton,William -Nancy Poage   1813cc
Russell,John-Rebecca Buffington   1820cc
Rutherford,Thomas-Mary Collins   1806Gpky
Stephenson,John-Mary McKinney   1815Gpky
Syrus,William   -Rebecca Boulton   1813cc
Wellman,Jeremiah-Ann Randle   1813cc
Workman,Joseph -Elizabeth Elkins   1813cc
Walton,George   -Nancy Campbell   1814cc

MARRIAGES from MARIETTA,WASHINGTON CO.OH
Buffington,William - Sarah Hughes 25 dec 1798
Hollenbeck,Chasper- Lucy Sherman Booth 2 jun 1801
Petit,John G. - Lucy Woodbridge 20 apr 1795
Stroud,William - Mary Lindsey 6 feb 1798

APPENDIX

BIBLIOGRAPHY

Adkins,Carey & Chafin-1850 Census of Cabell County
    Huntington,WV 1987
Albermarle County,VA Marriage Book I
Botetourt County,VA Marriages Book I
Cabell County Deed Books I,II,III,IV
Cabell County Marriage Book I
Cabell County Court Records 1810-1850
Dusenberry,W.C. Diary 1855-1872
Eldridge,C.-Cabell County Cemeteries -Volumes I,II,III
    Chesapeake,OH 1990-92
Eldridge,C.-Extinct Towns of Cabell County
    Chesapeake,OH 1982
Franklin County,VA Marriage Book I
Gallia County,Ohio Marriage Book 1803-1850
    Gallia County Historical Society 1983
Greenbrier County,VA Marriage Book I
Greenup County,Kentucky Marriage Book I
Guyandotte Herald, 1853-1855 Guyandotte,VA
    West Virginia University Newspaper Study
Kanawha County Marriage Book Book I
Lambert,Fred B. Manuscript Collection
    Special Collections Marshall University,WV
Lawrence County,Ohio Marriage Book 1817-1862
    Donna L.Murdock,Ironton,OH
Mason County,VA Marriage Book I
Montgomery County,VA Marriages Book I
Proctor,E.P.-Articles on early Cabell County
    published Herald Advertiser 1928-1929
Sigfus Olson-1850 Census of Cabell County
    on file Marshall University
Tazewell-Archives of the Pioneers of Tazewell
    County,VA-Marriages 1800-1820
United States Census 1820,1830,1840,1850
Wallace,G.S.,"Cabell County Annals and Families"
    Garrett & Massie, Richmond 1935
Worell,A.L."Over the Mountain Men-Their Early Court
    Records in Southwest Virginia- Balitmore 1976

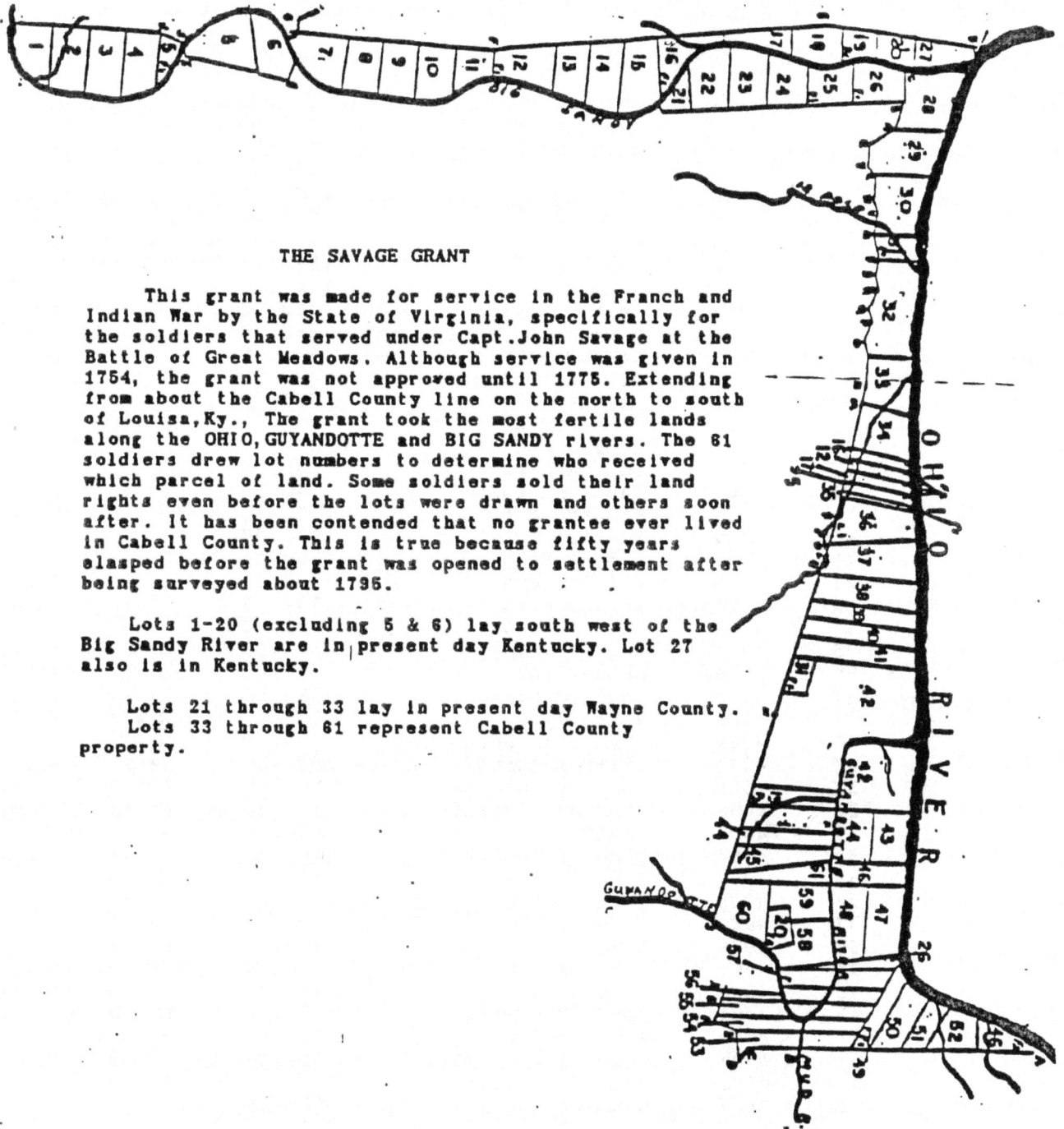

THE SAVAGE GRANT

This grant was made for service in the French and Indian War by the State of Virginia, specifically for the soldiers that served under Capt.John Savage at the Battle of Great Meadows. Although service was given in 1754, the grant was not approved until 1775. Extending from about the Cabell County line on the north to south of Louisa,Ky., The grant took the most fertile lands along the OHIO, GUYANDOTTE and BIG SANDY rivers. The 61 soldiers drew lot numbers to determine who received which parcel of land. Some soldiers sold their land rights even before the lots were drawn and others soon after. It has been contended that no grantee ever lived in Cabell County. This is true because fifty years elapsed before the grant was opened to settlement after being surveyed about 1795.

Lots 1-20 (excluding 5 & 6) lay south west of the Big Sandy River are in present day Kentucky. Lot 27 also is in Kentucky.

Lots 21 through 33 lay in present day Wayne County.
Lots 33 through 61 represent Cabell County property.

THE SAVAGE GRANT

Appendix B

VALUE OF THE 1775 REDIVISION OF SAVAGE GRANT

LOT #	ACRES	PATENTEE	VALUE	
1	400a	Nathan Chapman	$788.75	
2	400a	George Hurst	808.50	
3	500a	John Smith	953.12	
4	400a	George Malcomb	707.68	
5.	600a	Richard Trotter	2322.50	Edward McCarty
6	500a	Richard Smith	1550.00	
7	400a	Robert Jones	1356.00	Henry Hampton
8	400a	Charles James	1125.00	
9	400a	John Kincaid	1125.00	
10	400a	Mathew Doran	928.50	John Morrow/Rutherford
11	400a	Richard Balton(Boston)	884.50	John Morrow/Rutherford
12	400a	John Franklin	1290.00	
13	400a	William Johnston	898.50	
14	400a	William Jenkins	365.50	
15	400a	James Ludlow	652.50	John Poage
16	400a	Edward Goodwin	1469.75	
17	400a	John Gnolson	1285.00	
18	400a	James Latrott	940.50	John Poage
19	400a	Richard Morris	600.00	
20	362a	William Copeland	1000.00	
21	400a	Daniel Staples	552.00	
22	400a	William Bailey	590.00	Charles Brown
23	400a	Thomas Moss	581.00	
24	400a	Phillip Gatewood	587.00	
25	400a	Henry Bailey	1312.00	Charles Brown
26	400a	Mathew Cox	602.63	David Spurlock
27	400a	Charles Smith	2524.63	H.Catlett/Easton
28	400a	John Huston	3650.63	Charles Morgan
29	400a	Christian Baumgardner	3500.00	Charles Morgan
30	400a	William Carnes	3000.00	Daniel Leet
31	400a	William Coleman	1161.25	Achilles Rodgers
32	400a	John Maid(Mead)	3900.25	James McCormack
33	400a	James Ford	400.25	James McCormack
34	400a	Timothy Conway	4000.00	James McCormack
35	400a	John Wilson	1235.25	Mangus Tate
36	400a	John Wilson	4000.25	(" " ?)
37	400a	James Samuels	4000.25	Henry Hampton
38	400a	Daniel Paul	4000.25	Henry Hampton
39	400a	William Lowry	3454.25	Edward Sniggers
40	400a	John Bishop	2845.25	Van Swearengin
41	400a	Angus McDonald	2371.50	hinself
42	3428a	John Savage	15960.25	William Buffington
43	400a	William Broughton	727.50	Edmund Taylor
44	600a	Edmund Waggoner	2140.50	Edmund Taylor
45	400a	Mathew Jones	609.50	

redivision of savage grant (con't)

46	4J0a	Wm.Johnston	689.50	for himself
47	400a	David Gorman	425.50	Edm.McGinnis/Larue
48	400a	Nathaniel Barrett	601.50	Edm.McGinnis/Larue
49	600a	Robert Tunstall	1908.75	John Morrow/Rutherford
50	600a	Robert Langdon	1647.50	John Morrow/Rutherford
51	400a	Jousha Jorden	1742.50	John Morrow/Rutherford
52	400a	Edward Evans	2295.50	John Morrow/Rutherford
53	400a	John Ramsey	834.75	John Morrow/Rutherford
54	400a	Michael Sculley	950.75	John Morrow/Rutherford
55	400a	Marshall Pratt	1845.50	(Jhn Morrow/Rutherford)
56	400a	James Given(guinn)	1707.50	(John Morrow/Rutherford)
57	400a	William Hagan	1508.50	(Wm.Morgan) ****
58	400a	James Cammack	715.50	Edm.McGinnis/Larue
59	400a	Patrick Galloway	750.50	Edm.McGinnis/Larue
60	500a	Hugh McCoy	*26.25	Edm.McGinnis/Larue
61	400a	Joseph Gatewood	924.50	Gabriel Throgmorton

SAVAGE CLAIMENTS AS OF 1795
IN CABELL COUNTY

LOTS 33,34	James McCormack	800a
35,36	Mangus Tate	800a
37,38	Henry Hampton	800a
39	Edward Sniggers	400a
40	Van Swearengin	400a
41	Angus McDonald (original)	400a
42	William Buffington (surveyor)	3428a
43,44	Edmund Taylor	800a
45	Mathew Jones (original)	400a
46	William Johnson (original)	410a
47,48		
58,59,60	Edmund McGinnis/Isaac Larue	2100a
49,50,51		
52,53,54		
55,56,57	John Morrow/Robert Rutherford	3800a
61	Gaberiel Throgmorton	

Some of the families of the patentees must have come
west even after they sold their warrants.
Names still found in the area: Chapman,Smith,Malcom,
Jones,Kincaid,Johnston,Jenkins,Morris,Bailey,Cox,
Baumgardner,Wilson,Samuels,Paul,Barrett,Langdon,Jorden,
Pratt,Gwinn,Cammack and McCoy.

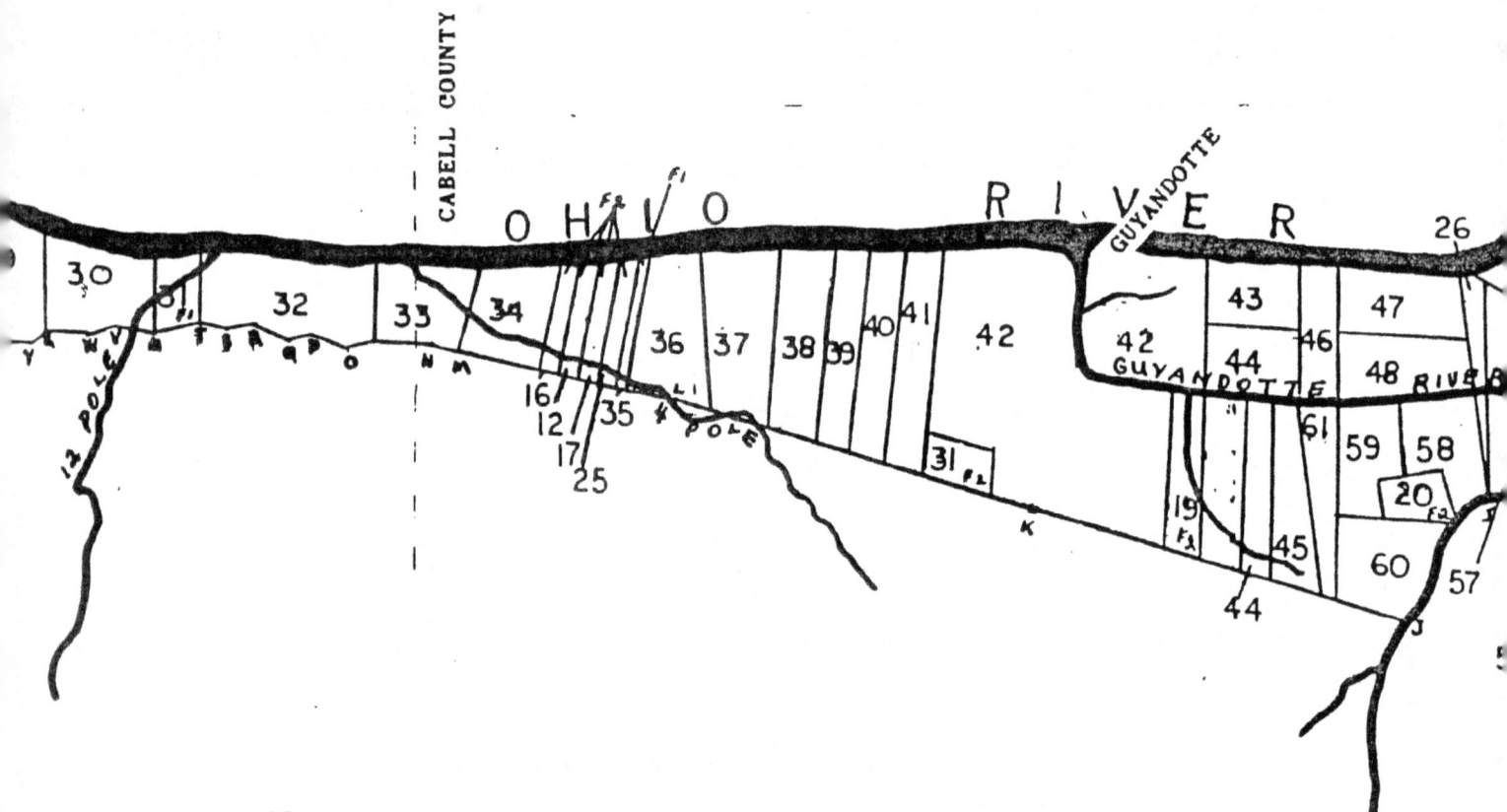

CABELL COUNTY

O H I O   R I V E R

GUYANDOTTE

30

31

32

33

34

36   37   38   39   40   41   42

16   35

12

17

25

31

43   47

42
GUYANDOTTE

44   46

48   RIVER

61

59   58

19

45

20

44

60   57

26

POLE

12 POLE

48-SAVAGE-BUFFINGTON   33-34 JAMES McCORMACK

37-38 HENRY HAMPTON   49-56 JOHN MORROW-ROBERT RUTHERFORD

58-60 EDMUND McGINNIS

CABELL COUNTY SECTION OF THE SAVAGE GRANT

INDEX for CABELL COUNTY CEMETERIES
taken from 3 volumes of

CABELL COUNTY CEMETERIES
by Carrie Eldride

Volume I   -north of Teays Valley
Volume II -south of Teays Valley
Volume III -Huntington city limits

numbering system
#12=Volume I--#S12=Volume II--#H12=Volume III

CEMETERY INDEX (con't)

S62A-R.Bias	-Tyler Creek
S64A-WW Morrison	-head/Tom's Ck
S67 -A.Beckett	-Fudges Creek
S69 -McCallister	-Fudges Creek
S70 -J.Morrison	-Salt Rock N
S73A-B.L.Perry	-Tyler Creek
S73B-J.B.Bias	-Tyler Creek
S74 -W.Morrison	-Tyler Creek
S76A-Baker	-Madison Creek
S76B-Gue	-Smith Creek
S80 -Clay	-Bowen Creek
S90 -Porter	-Salt Rock
S93B-Holton	-Salt Rock
S95A-Cremeans	-Madison Creek
S98B-S.Midkiff	-Salt Rock
S99 -Gill	-Salt Rock
S99A-Scites	-Salt Rock
S99D-E.McComas	-Salt Rock
S99E-Keenan	-Salt Rock
S99F-Shelton	-Salt Rock
H2 -Wright	-east R60
H3 -Everett Jr.	-Guy
H4 -Pats Branch	-Guy
H6 -Guyandotte	-Guy
H8 -Highland	-Guy E
H10-Spring Hill	-20th St
H12-Paine	-16th St
H16-Hull	-Central City

NAME CHANGES

Studying the history of an area can be both rewarding and frustrating. One of the first problems encountered is the the many differnt names that all appear with only one location. Unless the area was an offical incorporated town or cemetery, the local people tended to change the name quite often. Cemeteries acquired the name of the "last" person buried there although burials may have begun one hundred years before.

Towns named the most important resident. Present day Martha is so named because a woman named Martha Eskridge had a store in the early part of the twentieth century, but the site has also been Bloomingdale, Ashland, Love, Dusenberry Mill, Saunders Mill and Estis Mill.

Do not panick if you cannot location a certain "town". Check old road maps, atlases and post office records as well as court house records and you will find the name you seek plus several more unsuspected names.

CENSUS LOCATIONS
Identified if verified
west to east

It may be assumed that houses between the verified houses are in the same location, although there are exceptions. It is probable that some census information was second hand.

Barboursville   717-760 --- 990,991,994,995,1011

B'ville/north   40-42,159-160---378-380,923

B'ville East   375,376,385,387,389

Fudge Creek   155,247,259,260,383,386,492-494

Blue Sulphur   80,666,922,1008

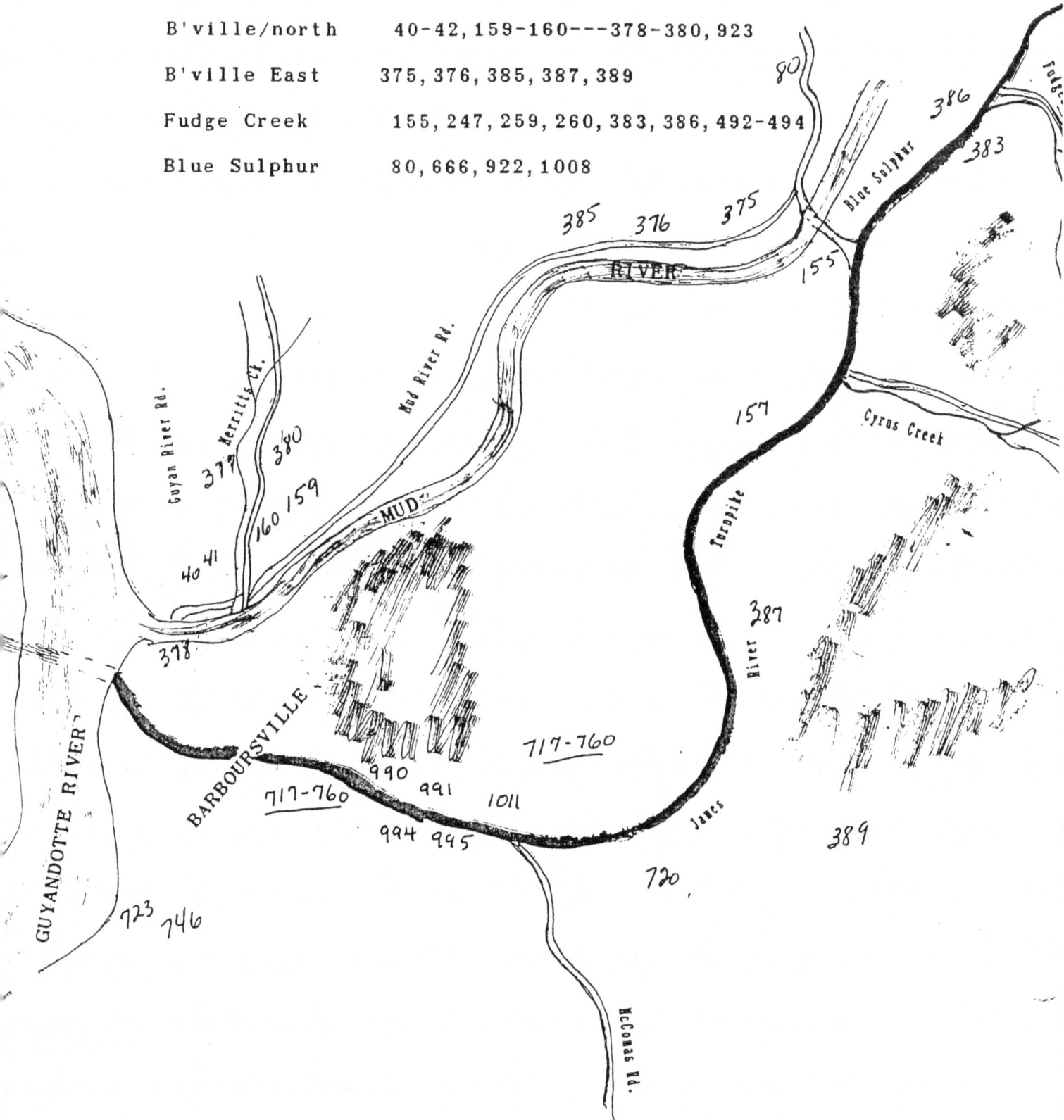

CENSUS LOCATIONS
identified if verified
east to west

Long Level(county line) 289,292,656,660

Mud Bridge(Milton) 264-272,278-282,298,299,521

Ball's Gap   607-613

Yates Crossing   1-8,35-39

Poore's Hill   13,14,80 --- 302,303,306 --- 1012

Howells Mill   22-33 --- 670

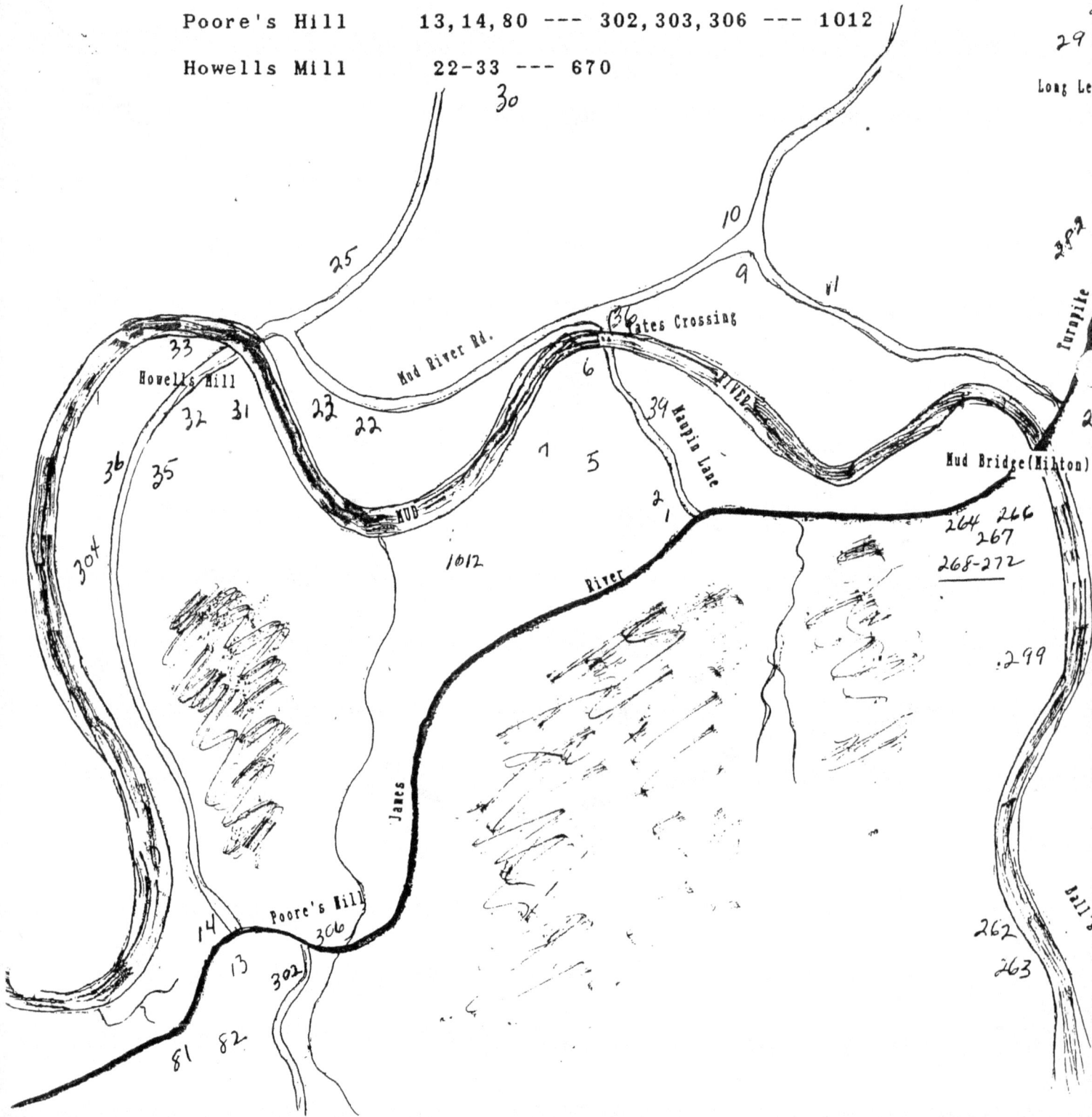

CENSUS LOCATIONS
identified only if verified
west to east

Spurlock Ck   198-208

Union Ridge/   209,214,220,224-225,228-236
  Barkers Ridge

Greenbottom
  E to county line 169,170,178-180,186-188,194-196

7 Mile   58-78   ----   151,162-167,839,841

River-Cox's Landing 53-56

Little 7 Mile   43-50

OH-Cox's Landing   53-56

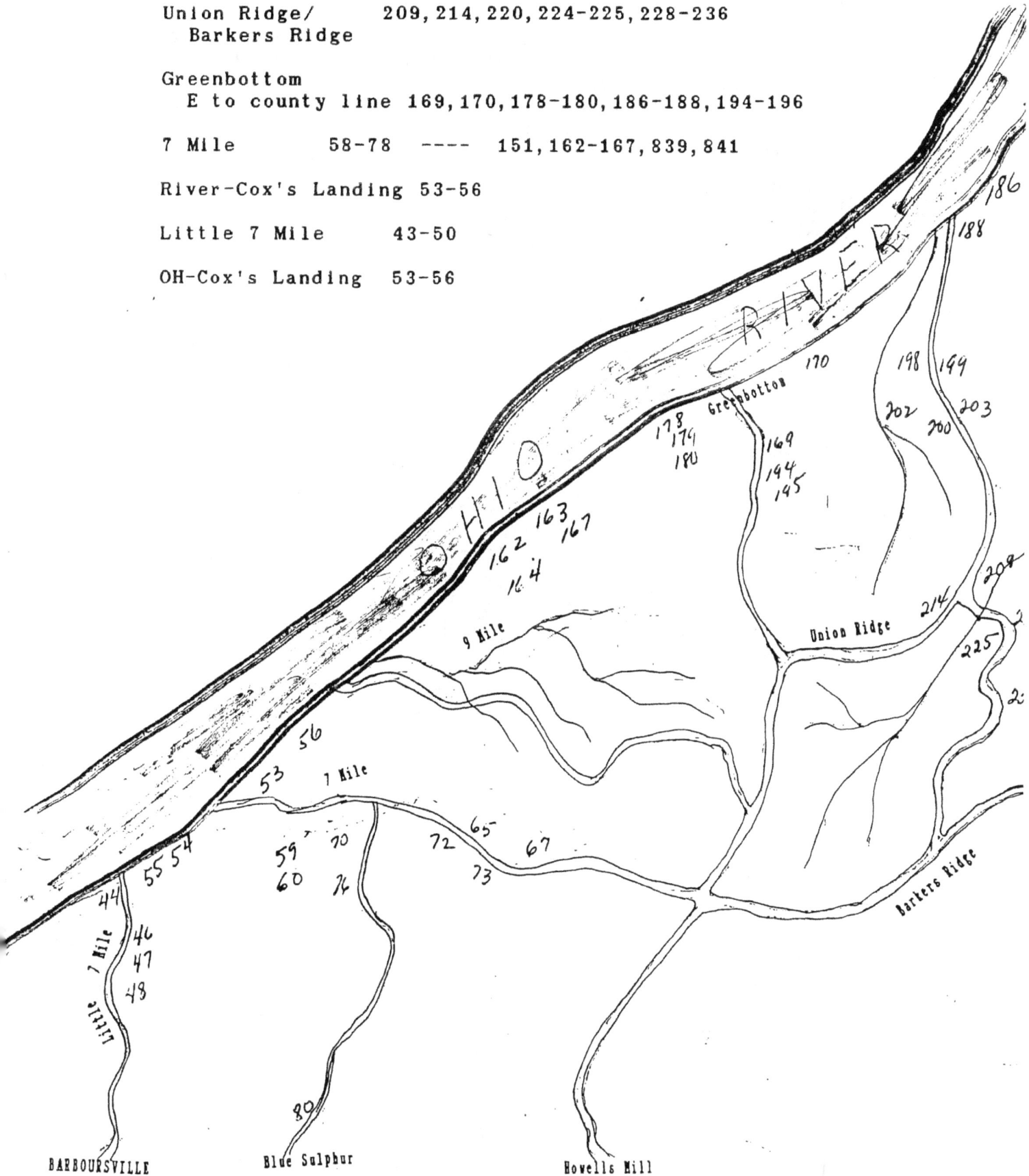

CENSUS LOCATIONS
identified if verified
north to south

```
Bloomingdale/Martha   392,395-399,404-407
Tom's Creek 410,414,418,420
Roach        106-110 --- 308,314-318,422,429-433
Salt Rock   111-114 -- 143-147 -- 334,439-443,460,482,614
Tyler Creek    103,104 -- 330,484,488,492-494,499
Heath Creek     86-92,149-153
Madison Creek/Bowen Creek 100-102,115-121,133-136,528-533
Raccoon          123-132
Lincoln County ?   137
```

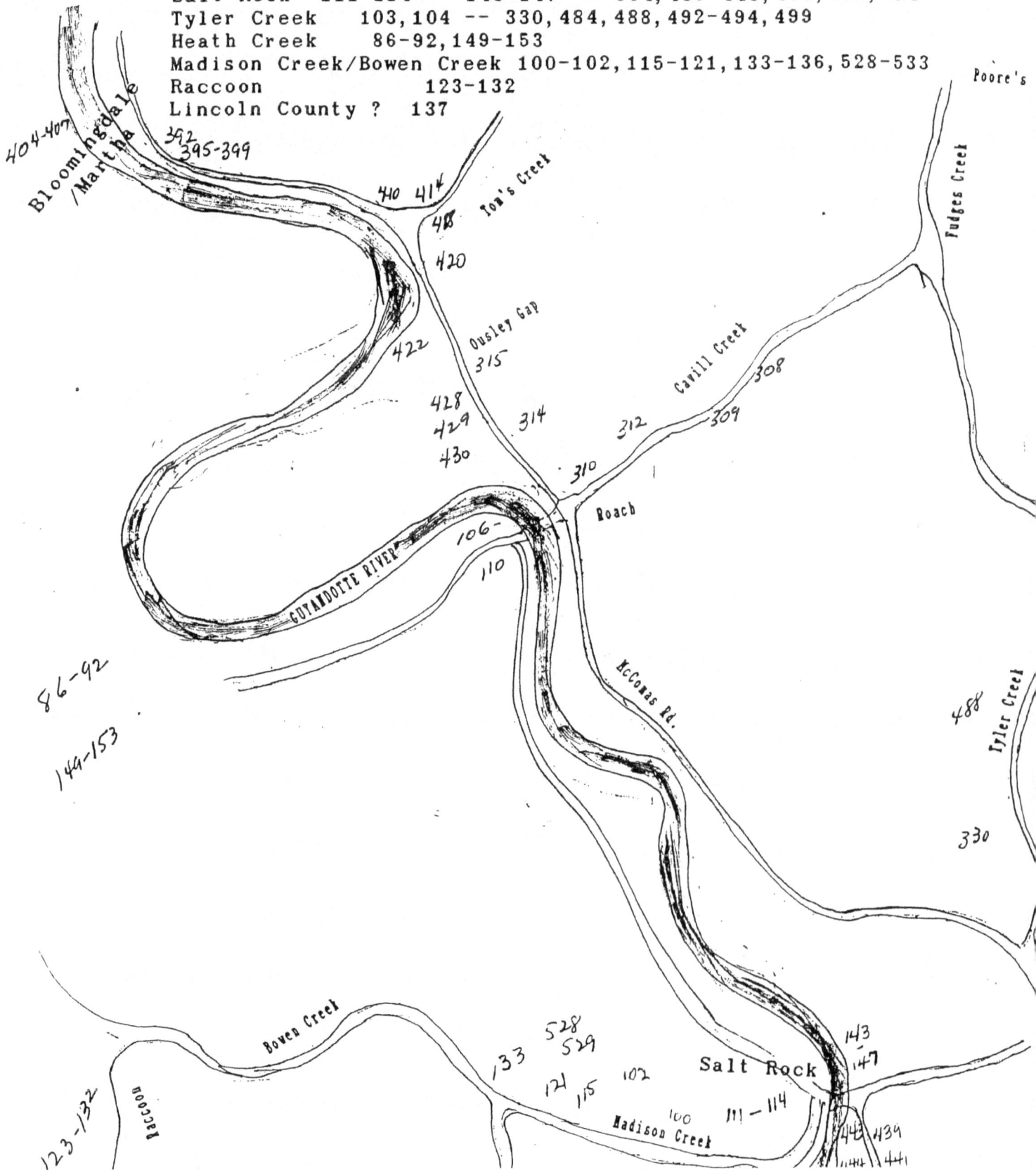

CENSUS LOCATIONS
indentified if verified
west to east

West End-Central City 900-907,911,912,914

Ohio River W/Guy   765,887,915,919,940-944,962,967-978

Guyandotte   768-835

4 Pole/Bowen Ridge 344,590,591,857,865-869,877,880

Pea Ridge West/Davis Creek   693,699,709,714-716,846,856,926
   (east end B'ville)

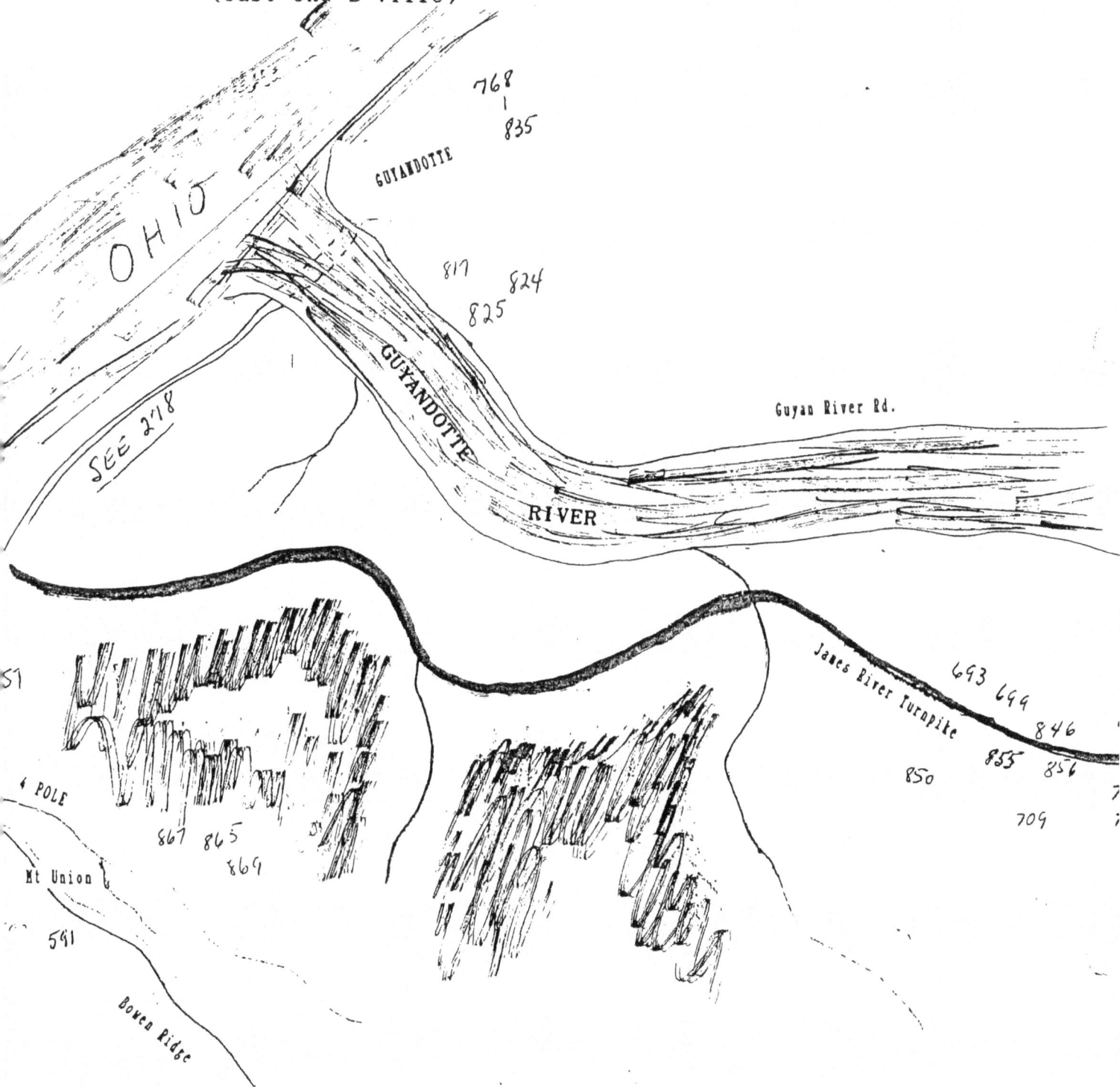

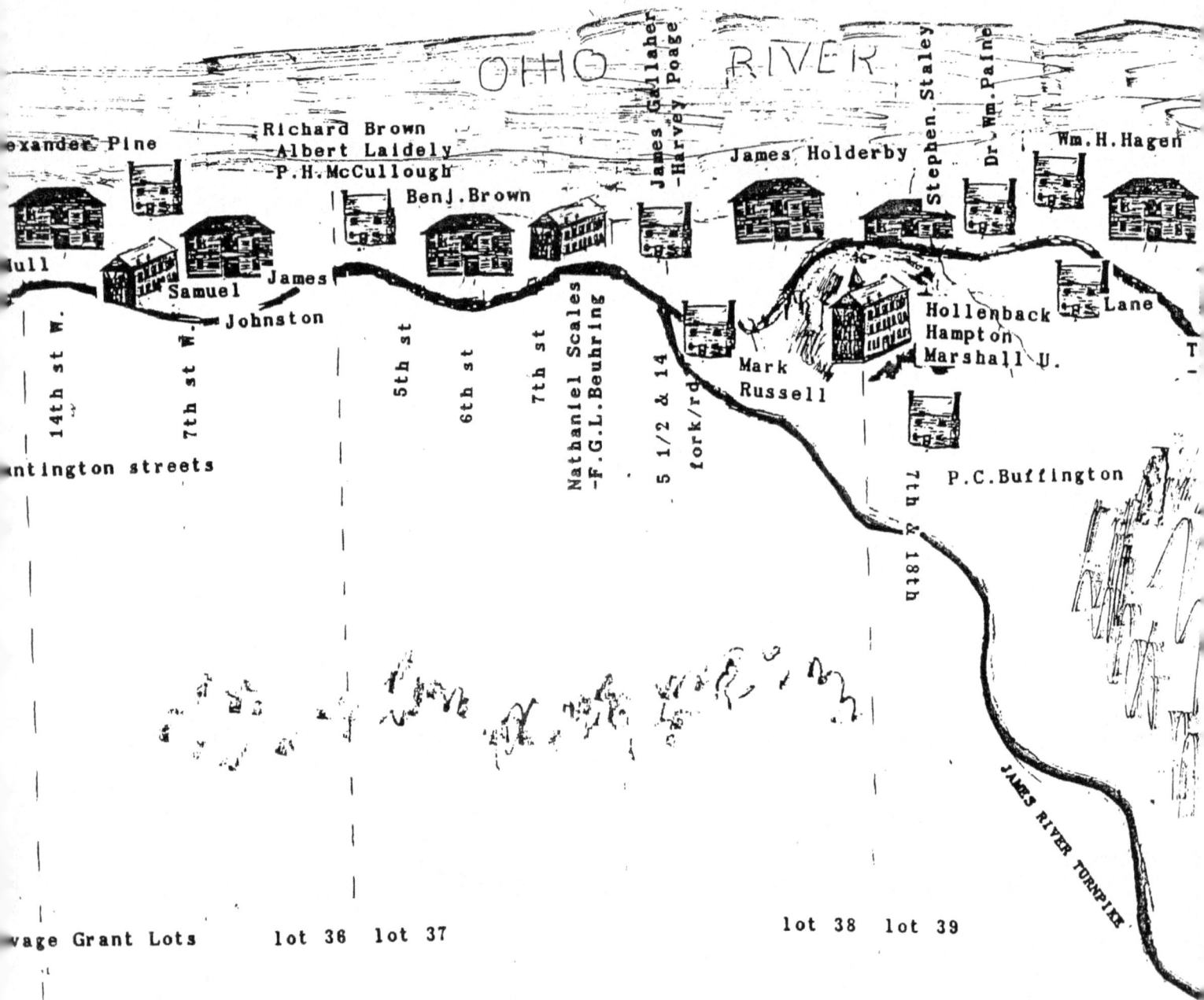

OHIO RIVER

Alexander Pine

Richard Brown
Albert Laidely
P.H.McCullough
Benj.Brown

James Gallaher
Harvey Poage

James Holderby

Stephen Staley

Dr.Wm.Paine

Wm.H.Hagen

Hull

Samuel
Johnston

James

Mark
Russell

Hollenback
Hampton
Marshall U.

Lane

14th st W.

7th st W.

5th st

6th st

7th st

Nathaniel Scales
-F.G.L.Beuhring

5 1/2 & 14
fork/rd

7th & 18th

P.C.Buffington

Huntington streets

Savage Grant Lots   lot 36   lot 37   lot 38   lot 39

JAMES RIVER TURNPIKE

SETTLERS ALONG THE OHIO WEST OF GUYANDOTTE

822 Head of Household-x822 extra person in household
(no number)-member of Household

BECKER see (-ner)		**BEXFIELD**		**BIAS** (con't)		**BLAKE** (con't)	
715Albrecht	92	220 Richard	33	William	20	388 John W.	53
Fredrick	92	**BIAS**		William	21	Margaret	33
Joanna M.	92	Absolum	66	William	58	x732Margaret	94
Matilda	92	Adele	20	William	66	Margaret A.	28
Mildred W.	92	America	20	William C.	18	Martha	53
BECKETT		111 Anderson	21	**BILLUP**		Mary E.	28
America	81	Angeline	20	Alexander	41	Nancy	53
Andrew L.	58	Brodaus D.	66	284 Andrew	41	Nancy(Kni)	28
Charles	43	Charlotta	66	Charles W.	41	170 Pinnell	28
494Charles	65	Clarissa	20	James J.	41	Peter	53
Emily	58	Corneluis	17	John	41	389 Sarah	53
Emslay	43	Corneluis	67	Mary(Wil)	41	**BLANKENSHIP**	
Hannah L.	64	Criseby	20	**BLACK(E)**		Abigail	110
848James	64	94 Daniel	18	997 Adam	126	Arabella	103
618James	81	Dicey	20	Adam C.	71	Charllotte	103
Lennis C.C.	64	Drusilla	20	Adam K.	37	x354Elizabeth	49
Louisa	43	Elizabeth	66	241 Andrew	36	822 Enoch D.	103
Louisa J.	65	Emerline	20	246 Ann (e)	36	George L.	110
Mary	43	Emily P.	58	251 David	37	George V.	110
299Moses	43	Emily T.	17	Eliza	72	866 Ira	110
Sarah	81	Enos	21	Elizabeth	126	John T.	110
Susannah	65	Evermont	21	Emberson	37	Lockey(Sh)	110
Tabitha	81	Hugh	20	George A.	71	Lelia	110
Virginia	81	103 James	20	Hulda	36	Leonard	103
William	81	James	66	Isabel H.	126	Louisa	103
BECKNER		James	67	548 James C.	71	Martin T.	110
Irene	111	James A.	26	John	126	Orella	110
John C.	111	88 James F.	17	John J.(e)	36	x354 Ralph	49
Lydia	111	James P.	66	John W.	72	Samatha O.	110
879Mary	111	152 James R.	26	Katy	37	872 Samuel	110
Stephen	111	Janetta	18	Lavicy A.	37	Samuel J.	110
BEECHAM(BURCHAM)		Jerrimiah	58	Lucy W.	71	William J.	110
Amanda	29	498 John	66	Margaret	36	**BLOOM(Blume)**	
Andrew	29	Julia A.	18	Mary	36	X1015 Ivan	172
Elizabeth	29	511 Larkin	67	Mary	37	**BOILING(Bolling)**	
174George	29	Lavania	20	Mary H.	71	x911 John	115
John	29	Lindsay	67	Permelia A.	71	**BOOTH**	
Mary A.	29	Lindsey M.	58	Rufus T.	126	Ballard	24
Melvina	29	Linvilla	21	Ruth	36	Elevey	25
Sampson S.	29	Margaret	20	Sarah C.	71	James	24
BELL		Marietta	66	Sarah E.	37	144 John	25
x638James	83	Martha(Mit)	20	Virginia	126	Martha	24
x638John	83	Martha J.	66	996 William	126	Mercy	24
BELANEY(mey)		Mary	66	William	72	Nancy	25
Armstead	115	Mary A.	26	**BLAKE**		x482 Nathaniel	64
Charles	115	x425 Matilda	58	Albert C.	34	Rachael	24
Eliza A.	115	Mears	20	Albert E.	53	139 Samuel	24
Ellenor	115	Melvil	66	x959 Andrew	121	William	24
908John	115	x153 Merian	26	Christian	34	**BOWEN**	
Malissa	115	Nancy	21	Edna	53	Adelaid(Te)	10
Micena A.	115	503 Nancy A.	18	Fredrick	28	Amanda J.	23
Nancy E.	115	Obadiah	66	x959 George	121	Ann	32
Phebe F.	115	Obadiah	67	223 Isaac	53	Elizabeth	23
Samuel T.	115	Polly	20	Isaac	34	Ezekiel	10
BEUHRING		103 Roland	20	James M.	34	201 Ezekiel	32
Corenora	119	425 Rolen	58	x959 James M.	121	Jane A.	10
944Fredr.G.L.	119	Rutha(Chi)	67	218 Jeremiah	33	Jefferson	31
Melcina	119	Sarah	17	Jerrmiah	34	134 Malinda	23
Nora	119	Sarah	66	Johannah	34	Nancy J.	23
		Sarah E.	18				
		Thomas	67				
		x153 Thomas A.	26				

CADENBACK
760 Joseph 97
CAMPBELL
Charles H. 98
763 Cyrus 98
Elizabeth 48
Elizabeth 98
346 John 48
John M. 98
Mary 98
Robert 98
Sarah A. 98
CARDWELL
Amanda 112
889 Manoah 112
Mary E. 112
Olivia 112
Sarah 112
CARPENTER
x640 Lewis 83
Mary 13
x640 Tabitha 83
49 William 13
CARROLL
Adam Z. 71
Amanda A. 74
Charles B. 74
Cynthia 74
514 James T. 68
547 Jas.T.Jr. 71
John A. 74
Margaret 68
Martha J. 71
564 Samuel 74
William A. 68
William H. 74
CARTER
Catherine 109
Charles 103
815 Henry 103
862 Hiram 109
James 103
James J.L. 109
Mary 103
Nancy 109
38 Silas 11
CASEY
Jemima 113
Louisa 59
Marietta 59
435 Mary 59
896 William 113
CASPELMAN
Caroline 102
801 W. 102
CHADISON
948 George 120
Henry 120
Mary 120
Olivia 120

CHAMBERS
Elizabeth 75
576 Fredrick 75
190 Robert 31
Sylvester 75
CHAPMAN
Albert 79
Alexander 118
America M. 38
452 Andrew 60
Armintha 79
Casey A. 126
Catherine 40
Cenantha 38
Cynthia 43
Cynthia 60
Eli 79
Elijah 116
Elizabeth 38
Elizabeth 60
Elizabeth 105
Elizabeth 126
Evelene 118
934 Frances 118
Frances J. 40
826 George 105
275 German 40
260 Green 38
751 Henry M. 27
Henry G. 126
Jackson 38
James 60
James H.K. 38
Jameson 79
John 38
301 John 43
John 60
607 John 79
1001 John 126
John M. 27
Julia(McC) 60
Leffanor 38
Lewis H. 27
607 Lucinda 79
Lucy 38
Lucy(Hud) 79
Martha 38
Martha 40
Martha 43
Martha 79
Mary 27
Mary J. 34
Mary M. 27
Milton 38
Minerva 38
Minta 43
Molly 43
Nancy L. 40
Nehamiah 38
Phebe 43
Polly 43
Polly 126

CHAPMAN (con't)
Rhoda 79
Rufus 40
Rutha 38
Sally 126
Sophia 38
Susan E. 27
Tazewell 43
Warren 38
138 William 11
260 William 38
William 79
1002 William 126
Willis 38
CHAPDU
788 Charles 101
Francis 104
818 Franklin 104
James 104
Mary 104
Olivia 101
788 Peter 101
Robert 104
Sarah J. 101
Seymor 104
CHILDERS
682 Abraham 88
Ann 17
Benjamin A. 17
Catherine 55
Elizabeth 17
Elizabeth 25
Elizabeth 88
Greenville 21
George W. 55
John M. 55
Mary J. 88
Melvil 17
Nancy 17
Patrick H. 55
85 Royal 17
404 Samuel 55
Sarah A. 17
Sarah E. 55
147 Spencer 25
Telithia 17
Thomas 17
William 55
William F. 25
William L. 17
CHRISTIAN
Mary A. 101
794 Thomas 101
CHURCH
George 27
Henry L. 27
John W. 27
159 Octavius 27
Margaret 27

CLARK
Andrew T. 106
Charles R. 98
839 Daniel 106
David 106
Edgar B. 100
Elizabeth 98
Emeline A. 100
Emily 106
Evan 106
Frances 33
George P. 100
Harvey 106
766 Henry 98
221 Howard 33
Jane 106
Johnnah 33
John A. 100
John T.R. 98
Lavenia 106
Lilly R. 33
Mary E. 100
514 Nancy 68
784 Peter 100
Philemun 100
Philina M. 33
Phillip F. 33
Rachael 106
Rinaldo 98
x784 Silas M. 100
Virginia 33
William 103
x969 William 123
William F. 33
COBOURN
697 John 90
Sarah L. 90
COFFEE
George 106
836 Jacob 106
Mary J. 106
COLLINS
Aaron 13
Abigail 83
Alan W. 16
Amanda 16
Anna 19
Artemus B. 12
46 Charles 12
Clarissa 19
47 David 12
99 Elias 19
Elizabeth 19
Elizabeth 84
Ellen 12
642 George P. 84
78 Harrison 16
Hezekiah 19
James M. 19
98 John 19
640 John 83
Madison 12

COLLINS (con't)

Madison	19
Mahala	13
Margaret	19
Martha	16
Martha J.	12
Martha J.	19
Mary	12
Mary A.	13
Mary E.	19
Merritt	19
Miranda J.	12
Mortimer T.	12
Nancy(Cur)	19
Nathan	13
Nathaniel	13
Patience	13
Polly J.	12
Rebecca B.	12
Ruth	13
Sylvie	13
Wesley D.	12
48 William	13
William	19
William	16

COMEN

Elizabeth	42
Johnny R.	42
Manutha	42
294 Michael	42
Stephen	42

CONLEY see Copley

CONNER

Abigail	79
Addison	108
Amanda	108
America	108
Amicetta	108
852 Andrew	108
Armilda	79
x923 Hetty	117
606 James	79
x923James W.	117
John M.	79
John W.	108
Joseph M.	108
Lavenia(H)	79
Lewis	79
Mary E.	79
Milly(Cha)	108
Permelia	108
Cornwesley	108
Samatha	79
Susannah	79
608 William	79
William W.	108

CONRAD

252 Catherine	37
Elizabeth	37
Francis M.	37
Joanna	37

COOBS

481 Abraham	64

COOCK(COCK-COOK)

Emmerine	21
Jemimiah	21
116 Tandy	21

COOK

699 Abner	90
Abner	91
Benjamin	91
Catherine	90
Eliza	90
Eliza	91
Elizabeth	91
x771 Elizabeth	99
Jane	90
700 John	91
John L.	91
Louisa	91
Martha V.	91
Mary	90
Mary A.	91
Nancy	90
Peter	91
Polly	90
707 Sarah	91
Sarah A.	91
Sarah J.	91
708 Solomon	91
709 Thomas C.	91

COOPER

Armilda	76
Catherine	76
Hudson	69
Lucinda C.	76
Lucy	69
Sarah	76
525 Silas	69
586 Thomas	76

CONLEY

348 Bailey	48
Adaline	48

CORNELL

63 Benjamin	14
Charles W.	15
Emma M.	14
Louisa	14
Margaret	15
Martin J.	14
Mary F.	15
Miranda S.	15
Nancy E.	15
Percilla	14
Pricilla A.	15
64 Samuel T.	15

COWENS

Henrietta	45
Hester	47
Hester A.	45
James	45
331 James	47
Mary	45

COWENS (CON'T)

Thomas J.	45
316 Thomas J.	47
Viney	45
Willis	45

COX

54 Andrew J.	13
George W.	13
Henrietta	13
James C.	13
John A.	13
Joseph	13
Margaret	13
Mary E.	13
Nelson	13
Sarah	13
54 William	13

CREMEANS

Abia C.	35
Alexander	35
Amanda	35
Asa L.S.	35
Bailey	35
118 Burton	21
Cathrin(Co)	22
Charles	34
Cynthia	22
Delila	34
Edissy	22
Elijah	34
Eliza J.	22
Elizabeth	34
236 Elizabeth	35
Fredrick	34
121 Hiram	22
Isaiah	34
John A.	35
John W.	34
Joicy	22
Joseph	22
x1008 Julia	127
Lewis	22
Louisa	34
Luther	34
x1008 Malinda	127
Marritha	34
Martha J.	34
Mary	34
Minta	21
Nancy	21
Nancy J.	35
222 Nathan	34
Parker	22
Polly C.	35
Ruben	22
231 Ruben	35
120 Sanders	22
Sarah	22
227 Sarah	34
Virginia	34
Wesley	35
Wesley	22

CREMEANS(con't)

William	22
William	35
226 Winget	34

CRUM

Elizabeth	14
61 James	14
Julian	14
Lucinda	14
Matilda	14
Penelope	14
Polly	14
Ruth	14

CRUMM(McCRUMM)

CRUMP

x929Elizabeth	118
Ellen	121
x929 George	118
956 Jesse	121
929 Isaac	118
Nancy	118

CURRY

Barbara	82
622 Benj.Frk.	81
Benjmin F.	82
Blackbourn	82
Elizabeth	81
George E.	82
Granville	82
627 Hiram	82
John C.	82
Martha A.	82
Mayberry	81
Permelia	82
Sarah A.	81
Sophia	81
Timothy	81
William H.	81

CURTIS

x322 Jane	45

CYRES-CYRUS

x743 Catherine	96
601 Elijah	79
602 James	79
John E.	79
x385 Joseph	53
Margart	79
Mary	79
Matilda	79
Nancy	79
Sarah	79
William	79

DAVIS

Adaline	90
Adison	31
Albert G.	27
Allen M.	90
America	10
Angeline	90

KENSOLVING(con't)
Louis W. 100
Walter S. 100

KEYSER
x627 Eli M. 82

KEYTON
Amanda 80
Andrew 80
Calvary 80
Emiletta 78
600 George 78
Henry 80
John 78
John 80
Lucinda 80
M.Harriet 78
Mary 80
Mary C. 78
Nancy 78
Preston 80
Recey 78
609 Ryland 80
Sandal 78
x433 Sarah 55
Susannah 80
William 80

KILE see KYLE

KILGORE
Elizabeth 40
279 George 40
Hetty(San) 40
James 40
Joseph C. 41
Malinda 40
Martha 40
Mary 40
Mary J. 41
Nancy 40
x281 Nancy 41
Sarah 40
278 Thomas 40
281 Thomas W. 41
William 40

KINCAID
Cynthia 70
Sarah 70
Simon 70
Wesley 70
538 William 70

KINDER
Elizabeth 71
Madison 71
Mary 71
Nancy 71
544 Samuel 71

KING
Absolum 28
Catherine 53
x796Elizabeth100
Elizabeth 28

KING(con't)
James 28
558 James 73
629 Jesse 82
390 John 53
John W. 28
Judy 82
Mary 73
Mary A. 53
Nancy 28
Nancy 82
Sampson 53
Sarah 73
169 William 28

KINNAIRD
x282 Ephraim 41
x282 William 41

KINNON
x481 A.M. 64

KITCHEN
364 Alonzo 50
Eliza 50
Margaret 50

KLENINGER
Catelia 29
Eustachia 29
172 John 28
Joseph P. 29
Margaret 28
Mary A. 29
Sarah E. 29
Thomas P. 29

KNIGHT
Abner 27
167 Abner 28
Adelia 26
America 26
Angeline 26
Ann 26
Ann 27
162 Ansel 27
Cathren 14
166 George W. 28
Hamilton 28
Harriet 27
56 Henry 14
Homer 26
164 James 27
James E. 26
James T. 89
John 28
John H. 14
Lafayette 14
Lenard 27
Lucinda 27
Margaret 14
Margaret 28
Mary 28
Mary J. 89
Matilda 27

KNIGHT(con't)
685 Matthew 89
Nancy 28
Nancy(Mor) 19
Nimrod 14
Partina 14
Pattina 28
Preston 28
Sarah 14
Sarah(Car) 26
Sarah 28
Susannah 28
Wayne W. 89
William 14
154 William 26
William H. 28
William W. 89

KOREUSZENSKI
Edward 33
212 John 33
Ludmilla 33
Matilda 33
Senon 33
Sophia 33
Wiadeston 33
Zophta 33

KRAUS
x737 Ann 95
737 Arnold 95
Herodias 95
x737Walter 95

KRYSZONOWSKI
215 Wiladislaw 33

KYLE-Kile
Ann 16
x912 Eliza 115
Elizabeth 12
x70 Elizabeth 15
Emily A. 92
George 12
Henrietta 92
Jane(Woods)16
72 John 16
Lewis 12
x70 Margaret 15
Martha T. 92
Mary(Pin) 92
Melieta 92
Missourie 12
x70 Peter 15
Phebe S. 92
x71 Polly 15
x70 Polly 15
Rebecca 12
x70 Rebecca 16
44 Robert 12
Sally 16
Samuel 15

KYLE(con't)
Sarah 12
Teresa 92
Thomas 16
717 Thomas 92
Virginia 12
x912 William 115

LACY
118 David B. 30
Eustacia 30
Charles 93
721 John 93
Milly M. 93
James W. 93
Mary E. 93

LAIDLEY
919 Albert 116
Alberta 116
Benjamin 116
Eliza M. 127
George S. 127
Herbert M.127
James H. 127
John 116
1011 John 127
John M. 127
Mary J. 127
Thomas M. 127
Vesta(Br) 116
William S.127

LAKE
Christopher68
Christophr126
1003 Daniel 126
Henry 68
519 Nicholas 68
Rachael 68
Robert A. 68
Sally 126

LANDES
x725 Adolphus 94

LARGE
Edford 116
Henry 116
Joseph 116
918 Nancy 116

LATTON
219 Charles 33
Daniel O. 33
Jane A. 33
Margaret E.33

LATULLE(Let)
Elloner 102
James L. 102
x455 John 61
Josephine 102
x455Lawrence 61
Louis Phi 102
Nancy 102
Sarah J. 102
797 Victor 102
Victoria 102

LAWRENCE		LUCAS(con't)		MALCOM		MAUPIN(con't)	
x576 Edward	75	Martha	63	Charles E.	86	Mary	87
x534 James	70	Mary	46	669 Edward	87	Mary E.	96
LAWSON		Mary E.	63	x669 Eliza	87	Matilda	7
x584 Lucinda	76	Miniriva	46	Jemima A.	86	Robert M.	125
LEGG		329 Parker	46	665 John	86	Thomas M.	7
Almeda	85	Rebecca	46	x669 Margaret	87	William	87
x246 Eda	36	Rebecca	63	Mary	86	993 William	125
Esther	36	Samuel H.	63	x669 Mary	87	**MAYAB**	
238 James	36	William P.	63	Nancy H.	86	Elizabeth	24
John H.	43	**LUCKWASKI-LUKOWSKU**		Robert	86	138 Milford	24
Nancy J.	85	Adolphus	33	x669 Robert	87	**MAY(S)**	
Rebecca(Ch)	43	213 Anna	33	William	86	Adaline	121
Thomas	36	Clemetina	33	**MANN**		Addison	79
Veletta	36	Wladisba	33	x774 Catherine	99	America	44
655 William	85	**LUNSFORD**		x710 Mary	92	Beverly J.	121
300 Willis	43	George W.	37	**MANUS**		Cathrin F.	44
LEONARD		John T.	56	x824 Jeanet	104	Celia E.	44
Cynthia	52	254 Joshua	37	**MARTIN**		307 Charles	44
Mary E.(We)	52	Martha	56	X637 Aaron	83	Clarenda	75
381 Rufus	52	Mary	56	24 Andrew	9	Cynthia	75
LEWIS		Nancy	56	Eliza	9	Dianna	118
x224 Fredrec	34	415 Richard	56	Nancy	78	Dicy A.	63
x224 Rebecca	34	Sarah(Wal)	37	Romaine A.	9	Elmira	75
LIONS		Susannah	37	William D.	78	Elizabeth	44
690 Abram	89	416 William	56	529 Zachariah	78	Emily J.	44
Eliza A.	89	**LUSHER**		**MATHER(S)**		Elvira	44
John	89	Charles	93	Ameretta	95	Franklin	79
Peggy	89	Frances	93	Arianna L.	94	George T.	42
Polly	89	Henry W.	93	Augusta J.	95	312 Hamilton	44
Sally	89	720 Irvin	93	x751 Elizabeth	96	Henry J.	121
Wilson	89	James M.	53	x735 John N.	95	Hezekiah S.	44
LONG		Jane	93	Laura A.	94	572 Jacob	75
Ann E.	94	John	95	x735 Mary	95	James	75
Laura	94	738 Johnson	95	726 Oscar W.	94	James B.	42
715 Orson	94	Lewis W.	93	741 Susan J.	95	958 James J.	121
LOVE		Lucy	95	Valcolon W.	94	Jane	42
Alphonse	127	Margaret	53	**MATHEWS**		John H.	42
Cynthia A.	127	Mary	93	x258 Elizabeth	38	John T.	44
Cynthia A.	10	Mary L.	53	George F.	36	John T.	121
1012 Daniel	127	387 Matthew	53	243 James	36	Joseph	44
Daniel A.	10	Morris	53	x829 James	103	Joseph	121
Elizabeth	10	Robert M.	93	James W.	36	Julius	121
Fanny	127	Sarah	53	x258 Mariah	38	290 Lewis	42
John E.	127	Taliaferro	53	Martha	36	Margaret	79
Leonidas	127	Winfield S.	95	Sarah	36	Margaret J.	42
Shelby	127	**MAHONE**		**MAUPIN**		Martha A.	118
22 William	10	Bennet D.	67	Adaline	87	Mary R.	118
William	127	Hellena	95	America	125	Matilda	44
LOVEJOY		742 James L.	95	668 Beverly W.	87	Malissa A.	44
954 David A.	121	Mahala F.	67	2 C.W.	7	935 Morgan	118
Jenetta	121	Mahala J.	95	Fanny C.	7	Nancy	44
John T.	121	Melitta U.	95	Henry	87	Nancy	118
LUCAS		x778 Nancy	98	745 Henry B.	96	Octavia	75
476 Calvin	63	Nancy(Car)	67	John	87	Susanna	63
Charles A.	46	Virgil H.	67	Lucy M.	7	Virginia T.	42
Cloa(Dial)	46	William	67	1 Margaret	7	607 William	118
David	46	513 William	95	Margaret	87	473 William	63
Daniel D.	63			Margaret	125	603 Willis	79
James	46					Winfried	121
John	46						

McMILLON(con't)							
Margaret	51						
Rebecca A.	51						
William	51						
McVICKER							
Almira	54						
394 Archibald	54						
Hiliry	54						
James	54						
John	54						
Pattie	54						
Permalia	54						
Rachael	54						
Rebecca	54						
Sarah A.	54						
McWARTER							
Albert	37						
249 Frances	37						
Floyd	37						
Henry	37						
James	37						
John	37						
William	37						
MEACHAM							
902 James	55						
Joanna	55						
Mary	55						
MEADOWS							
x851 James	108						
MEDLIN							
Bruno	113						
Dosia	113						
Hermma	113						
894 Henry	113						
John	113						
MERRITT							
Deborah	27						
Emily E.	125						
x1006 Eliza	127						
Eliza V.	27						
Eugenia	126						
Fanny	126						
George W.	12						
Harriet F.	125						
James S.	27						
Jane	125						
41 John	12						
989 John	125						
999 John A.	126						
John F.	27						
Joseph A.	125						
Mahala A.	125						
40 Margaret	12						
Margaret	126						
Martha J.	125						
Mary	123						
Mary W.	27						
991 Melchor	125						
Nancy J.	125						
Octavia	126						
Philip N.	27						
Sarah	126						

MERRITT(con't)							
Sarah E.	27						
Theresa	27						
1004 Thomas	126						
Thomas H.	126						
Thomas J.	125						
160 William	27						
William	126						
MESSINGER							
David	88						
Emily	61						
Emily	88						
Francis M.	88						
George W.	61						
Isaac	88						
John H.	61						
Mary	61						
Nancy	88						
458 Nicholas	61						
678 William	88						
MIDKIFF							
Abraham H.	64						
Adaline	15						
Adaline	64						
Albert	64						
Alexander	64						
America	25						
Cynthia A.	25						
Elizabeth	64						
Emily	25						
Emma	64						
Gordon C.	25						
Harriett	64						
Itha	17						
Itha J.	25						
John A.	64						
Joseph B.	64						
Julia	64						
480 Lewis	64						
Lucy	64						
Mary M.	64						
Sarah	64						
146 Solomon	25						
Solomon	64						
482 Spencer	64						
Vitura(McC)	64						
Waldon	64						
William B.	25						
MILLER							
Abigail	103						
Abigail	119						
Arabella	101						
Chapman C.	101						
Charles	94						
209 Charles W.	32						
Christian	96						
732 Christopher	90						
518 Cynthia	68						
Eliza	10						
Eliza	94						

MILLER(con't)							
Eliza	101						
Emily F.	10						
Eugenia	94						
Francis L.	94						
Frank	94						
Georgia	119						
George	103						
752 George F.	96						
x471 Guy	63						
Hannah C.	96						
Heber	103						
Henry	22						
140 Henry	24						
937 Henry	119						
792 Henry H.	101						
Hudene	24						
x471 Isham	63						
813 Jacob	103						
9 James	8						
James T.	10						
731 John G.	94						
21 John M.	10						
Joseph	94						
Josephine	119						
Leonora	101						
Luana	32						
Lucy	24						
Margaret	119						
Martha H.	119						
Martha J	10						
Mary	8						
Mary	96						
Mary(Blake)	90						
Mary J.	10						
Polly	24						
124 Rhodie	22						
Sarah	103						
Sarah	94						
Susannah	119						
Toysee(Cre)	24						
729 William C.	94						
MILLS							
716 John	92						
Mary	92						
Orsamus	92						
William E.	92						
MITCHELL							
Elizabeth G.	58						
John J.	58						
Lucy A.	58						
426 William B.	58						
MONTGOMERY							
Charlotte	52						
Elizabeth	52						
James	52						
377 Joseph	52						
Martha	52						
Mary	52						
Minerva	52						

MOOMAN							
x113 Sarah	21						
MOORAN							
x740 John	95						
MOORE							
x394 Albert	54						
Amira	76						
x394 Ann S.	54						
Charles M.	96						
x394 Cyrus	54						
Elizabeth	17						
Frances	17						
Granderson	73						
Granderson.	76						
x394 Helen H.	54						
Isaiah	73						
John T.	96						
x394 Lucinda	54						
81 Martin	17						
82 Martin Jr.	17						
Martin L.	73						
Mary	17						
x394 Mary Jane	96						
562 Nancy	73						
Nancy	76						
x394 Orson	54						
Rhoda	73						
Samuel	17						
Samuel	73						
Sarah	17						
Sarah	73						
Sarah	76						
583 William	76						
748 Wilson	96						
MORGAN							
Helen M.	115						
907 John	115						
Martha	115						
Orpheus	115						
Percy A.	115						
MORRIS							
x499 Benjamin	66						
676 Charles K.	88						
Edna E.	88						
Ellen	88						
Helen J.	41						
Helen M.	56						
424 James	56						
James J.	88						
272 John	41						
John A.	88						
Joseph W.	56						
Louisa	56						
Martha	88						
Mary	41						
Mary	88						
Moriah	56						
283 Sarah(Rus)	41						
x676 William	88						

MORRISON		NASH		NEWMAN(con/t)		NIXON	
Albert	44	Jane E.	86	Lucinda	52	Edwin S.	99
Angeline	88	663 John J.	86	Margaret	53	771 Edward	99
Anna	87	Joseph A.	86	Malinda	36	Edward H.	99
Calvin	44	Mary E.	86	Malinda L,	53	Mary A.	99
x272 David	39	Rebecca E.	86	Martha	36	Mary V	99
Eliza A.	20	Sarah	86	Mary(Jef)	66	NOEL	
Elizabeth	20	Sarah E.	86	Mary A.	68	Angeline	67
Elizabeth	44	NEFF		Mary J.	8	Emiline	67
Ellen	88	x949 David	120	Mary J.	126	Mary	67
Ellenar G.	44	NELSON		May	36	Mary J.	67
x677 Emeline	88	295 Fairfax W.	42	Milton	36	Matilda A.	67
Frances(Th)	88	Martha E.	42	x671 Morris	87	Nancy	67
Fredrick	88	Mary	42	Nancy	53	Wilks	67
575 George	75	Nancy L.	42	Nancy A.	8	512 Winston	67
Hannah M.	75	William L.	42	672 Peyton	87	NORRIS	
Henry	87	NEUBACKER		x671 Polly	87	x850 Benjamin	107
Henry	88	Anna	113	240 Russell	36	O'BRIEN	
681 James	86	Francis	113	Sarah(Elm)	8	Alice M.	110
James L.	20	893 Joseph	113	Sarah M.	53	873 Dennis	110
108 John	20	Ludwig	113	Sylvanus T.	53	Frances	110
John	44	Victor	113	12 Vincent	8	Jane	110
110 John	20	NEWLY		Virginia(Mc	126	Malinda J.	110
John	57	Abigail H.	81	Wesley	8	Thomas H.	110
418 John	75	620 Adophus	81	13 William	8	OLIVER	
Margaret	20	NEWMAN		William a.	52	George R.F.	32
Mariah	75	Addison	36	Winston	87	Griffin	32
Martha	88	Albert	36	NICELY		204 John	32
Martha A.	20	Albert	52	Elizabeth(S	18	Rebecca	32
Mary	88	671 Alexander	87	Elizabeth	25	ONG	
Mary A.	20	Amanda	36	Henry C.	18	Albina L.	98
Mary A.	44	America	87	93 James	18	Augusta V.	98
Mary E.	75	Anna E.	126	James A.	25	Ernest M	98
Matilda	87	Betsy	87	James H.	18	769 Isaac	98
Milly	87	Caroline	52	Lucinda	25	819 John	104
Nancy	20	Cyrus P.	52	148 Sacheryal	25	John	98
Nancy	57	Edna A.	36	Sarah E.	18	Margaret	104
Nancy	88	Eliza	36	NICHOLS		Susan	98
Patience W.	20	Eliza	87	x961 Georganna	122	OTT	
674 Patrick	87	Eliza A.	8	NICHOLAS		Catherine	76
Rachael	88	Elizabeth	52	Abaz H.	80	Elizabeth	76
Thomas	44	Elizabeth(Pe)	8	Calahill	80	Julia A.	76
309 Thompson	44	Emily	8	James B.	80	Michael	76
Valerie	44	Emily	87	611 John	80	Simson	76
109 Washington	20	Frances	126	John A.	80	581 William	76
308 William	44	Greenville	87	610 John S.	80	OWENS	
MURDOCK		Harrison D.	8	Louisa C.	80	Edward	111
Elizabeth	79	376 Harvey	52	Lucinda	80	576 Effy	111
604 John	79	Herman	9	Margarert	80	Eliza	111
Sarah	79	Henry A.	126	Preston T.	80	Elizabeth	111
William	79	995 James	126	NICHOOF		Henry	111
MURRAY		James L.	126	809 Fredrick	103	Jordan	111
782 John F.	100	Jasper	53	Margaret	103	Monroe	111
NANCE		John	9	NIPPS		Mary	111
Abraham	28	John	36	Charles	21	Saluda	111
Catherin	28	John M.	87	117 Nancy	21	William	111
Hannah	28	385 Joseph	53	Rosanna	21		
Mahala	28	Joseph	87	Samuel	21		
Malachai	28	Joseph A.	53	116 Tandy(Coock)	21		
171 Martin	28	Leroy	8				
Sarah	28						

PAINE
Ann 123
x382 Benjamin 52
Charles 46
Charles 123
Eliza A.M. 46
Elizabeth 123
Emma 123
Frances 123
323 Harrison 46
968 Henry B. 123
483 Jessie 64
x785 John 100
Joseph A. 46
Judith E. 46
Julia A. 46
Lucy A.(Mc)46
x304 Mary 43
Mary 46
Milly 64
Nancy D. 46
Polly 46
Sarah 123
328 Simon 46
325 Stephen 46
Velera 46
Virginia 123
972 William 123
PANDERLY
x397 Ann 54
x397 Andrew 54
PANNEL see Pennell
838 Abraham 106
Elizabeth 106
PARISH
Frances M. 96
Harriet J. 96
743 James 96
Julia 96
Martha A. 96
Mary C. 96
Nancy J. 96
PARKER
x919 Edmund 116
x919 Lillie 116
PARSONS=Person
Ballard 63
Cynthia 50
x476 David 63
471 Edward 63
Ehervel 50
Elizabeth 63
George 22
Hannah 50
x440 James 59
John 50
John 63
Lydia 62
Margaret 50
Nance J. 22
Rebecca 63

PARSONS(con't)
Robertson 50
358 Samuel 50
Susanna 22
Susannah 50
468 Thomas 62
Thurza 50
123 William 22
William 63
William R. 50
PARTLOW
Benjamin P.98
George T. 98
Henry L. 98
James L. 98
Mary 98
678 William 98
William A. 98
PATTON
Harriet 85
x650 Margaret 85
650 Robertson 85
PAUL
Amasiah 21
Goodwin 21
119 Jeremiah 21
Levren 21
Louisa 21
Susannah 21
PAYLY
Lafayette 75
Lamira 75
Mary 75
Serena 75
Sidney 75
572 Washington75
PEAS
x481 Elisha F.64
PENNEL=(Pinnel)
PERRY
Anne(Hage) 15
499 Benjamin 66
Eliza H. 66
Elizabeth 66
Haney F. 16
Jacob 16
John 32
John J. 66
Julia A. 66
Lucy 32
Martha J. 66
Melachu A. 16
Nancy 32
Peter F. 66
77 Polly(An 16
68 Richard A.15
Silas B. 66
Sarah A. 16
Thomas H. 66
William B. 66
William H. 16
206 William 32

PERSON=(Parsons)
Frances 70
Ida E. 70
626 Jane 82
x532 Lewis 70
x532 Malinda 70
Nancy 70
Nancy 82
Sarah 82
Sarah J. 70
536 Simon 70
535 William 82
PETERS
x950 Albert 120
Amecitta 120
Andrew J. 120
964Christoph 122
Cynthia 122
Eliza V. 120
x950Elizabeth120
Hannah 120
James M. 120
Lavenia 120
780 Lewis 100
x950 Louvicy 120
x950 Rufus 120
Virginia 100
951 William 120
PEYTON
Alexander 57
434 Archibald 59
419 Charles 57
Cynthia 45
Elisha 57
Eliza 56
x410 Elizabeth57
Elizabeth 57
Elizabeth 58
432 Harrison 58
Henriettta 58
320 Henry 45
410 John 56
462 John 61
479 John 64
Judith B. 64
Margaret 45
414 Mary 56
Mary 57
Milly 56
Perry 56
Sarah C. 59
x383 Sophia M.52
Susan 59
Susannah 56
William 56
William 57
William H. 64

PIATT
Andrew J. 114
Emily J. 114
890 James 114
James M 114
Robert 114
Tabitha 114
PILLOW
189 Edwin 30
Mariah 30
Mary A. 30
x187 May 30
Sarah A.L 30
Thomas J. 30
William T. 30
PINE
x909 Alexande115
x909 Byron H.115
x909 Clary 115
910 Floyd 115
George M. 81
Hester A. 115
x909 James E.115
John T. 81
x909 Julia 115
x909 Mary 115
621 Nancy 81
x909 Overton 115
x909 Rufus 115
Victoria 81
Virginia 115
William H. 81
PITTENZIL
x438 George 59
PLYBON(Plybourn)
Eliza A. 124
Elizabeth 124
Frances 124
986 Jacob 124
John 124
Josephine 124
Mary(Per) 124
x930 Rebecca 118
PLYBOURN(Plybon)
Elizabeth 111
Henry W. 111
Jacob 111
James C. 111
878 John 111
Lewis 111
Louisa 111
POAGE
Amelia 114
901 Ann 114
Calvin A. 41
Frances A 41
Fredrick .114
James H. 114
Jemina 114
x710 John 92
287 Josiah B 41
Lucretia 114
Mary J. 114

SMITH(con't)		
	Nancy	71
	Nancy	73
	Nancy	74
	Nancy	80
	Nancy	107
	Nancy V.	10
	Phebe Hilt	71
789	Percival	101
559	Peter	73
688	Peter	89
679	Ralph	88
	Rebecca	49
	Rebecca	89
	Rebecca	102
	Rhoda	73
	Richard P.	101
	Sally	89
566	Samuel	74
	Sarah	49
	Sarah	71
	Sarah	73
	Sarah A.	74
	Sarah E.	107
	Sarah M.	10
	Sarah P.	102
	Sinia	10
	Susannah	49
	Tennessee	49
246	Thomas	36
	Victoria	37
	Viley	88
	Wesley	88
	Whitcomb	102
350	William	49
612	William	80
	William	88
	William	89
847	William A.	107
	William H.	37
	William H.	73
	William J.	10
	William O.	49
	William P.	102

SNELL		
x310	Julia	44

SNODGRASS		
	George W.	68
	James	68
x520	James B.	68
520	James H.	68
	Joseph R.	68
	Mary A.	68
	Mildred	68
	Nancy A.	68
	Rebecca M.	68
	William A.	68

SOLOMON		
x850	Joel K.	107

SOWERY		
x282	William	41

SPEARS		
	Anna	48
341	Benjamin	48
	Henry	48
	John	48
	Rhoda	48
	Sally	48
342	William	48
	Willie	48

SPRECHER		
	Augusta	32
210	Henry	32

SPURLOCK		
578	Alexander	76
	Andrew	76
574	Burwell	75
202	Daniel	32
	Daniel E.	31
	Eliza	31
	Elizabeth	312
578	Harrison	76
	Jane A.	32
197	Jessee	31
	John H.	76
	Margaret	31
	Mary	76
	Nancy	75
	Rebecca	75
	Sarah	32
	Sarah E.	31
	Simon	31
203	Stephen	32
199	Thomas	31
	Thomas	75
	Thomas	76
	Thomas B.	31
	William	32

STAFFORD		
x465	William	62

STALY		
	Charles	122
	Eliza M.	122
	Elizabeth	122
	George A.	122
	Henrietta	122
	Jacob	122
967	Joseph	122
	Margaret	122
	Mary B.	122
966	Michael	122
	Susannah	122

STANDARD		
x961	Rebecca	122

STANLEY		
	Columbus M.	64
	Cynthia	56
x312	David	44
	Eliza J.	56
	Elizebeth	45
	Elizbeth	64
	George W.	56

STANLEY(con't)		
x312	Jane	44
	John	45
485	John	64
417	Joseph	56
	Margaret	56
	Robbins	45
	Samual	56
	William F.	64

STAPLETON		
X764	Cinderella	

STEVENS		
8	Abraham N	7
	Mary	7
	Sarah A.	7
	James W.	7
	William H	7

STEPHENSON		
	Abraham N.	8
	Adalene	50
	Amanda	50
	America	50
	America	104
936	Andrew J	119
356	Armstrong	50
	Calvary	110
941	Calvary	119
	Caroline	50
	Charles V.	119
	Christopher	50
	Daniel	110
X859	Eliza	109
	Elizabeth	119
	Elizabeth	121
	Georgia	119
366	George	50
933	George W.	118
	Gilbert	104
821	Gilbert	114
	Francis	50
940	Hannah	119
	Henry	119
	James	110
	Jeremiah	110
x576	John	75
	Joseph	110
	Lafayette	108
	Lucretia	108
	Malinda	50
957	Malinda	121
942	Mark	119
	Martha	119
	Mary	119
	Melissia	114
	Mary C.	110
	Nancy	50
	Nancy	108
	Nancy	114
	Rebecca	118
	Reuben	118
	Reuben	121

STEPHENSON(con t		
	Rutha	119
	Rutha A.	50
	Samuel	110
362	Thomas	50
	William	119
	William	121
870	William	110
	Willy	121

STEWART		
	Ann E.	105
810	Burgess	103
	Columbia	103
	Druzilla	105
x575	George	75
	Hamilton	103
	Hansford	103
814	James	103
	James	105
	Jedediah	103
	Joseph S.	103
	Mariah(Wi)	103
	Martha	105
	Nancy E.	105
833	Robert	105
x833	Sarah	105
	Sarah J.	103
	William F.	105

STONE		
	Elizabeth	101
790	Gracie	101

STROUP		
	Catherine	52
	Margaret	52
379	William	52

SULIVAN-(LL)		
945	Aaron	119
	Catherine	112
	Celia	112
x204	Clemens	32
817	David	111
	Elizabeth	112
	Ellenor	111
888	Henry	112
	Jacob	111
886	James	112
184	James M.	30
	John W.	30
	Lewis	111
	Malinda	111
	Margaret A.	30
	Martha Ton	30
	Mary	112
	Mary A.	111
	Polly	119
	Steven V.	30

SULZBACKER		
x145	Arnold	25

UNDERWOOD
Cynthia 92
712 Enrich 92
John M. 92
Mary E. 92

VALENTIN
X998 Bolomy 126

VANDERVER
791 James 101
Martha 101

VAUGHN
Andrew 45
322 John 45
Lucy A. 45

VERTIGANS
747 Edward 96
George S. 96
Mariah 96
Walter F. 96

VICKERS
California 85
Frances 85
George 85
Margaret 85
637 Thomas 85

WADE
Jacob 39
Jane 39
269 Jessee 39
Lucy 39
Samuel 39

WAGNER
x715 Jacob 92

WALKER
Adolphus 117
Eliza J. 117
Elizabeth 107
x925 Hannah 117
925 James H. 117
Jane E. 125
John W. 125
Mary M. 125
Mathew 125
Nancy 105
831 Nancy H. 125
986 Samuel A. 125
William 117

WALLACE
Amanda 38
230 Andrew 35
257 Benjamin 38
Caroline 42
Charles L. 38
Daniel 77
258 Edmund 38
Elizabeth 37
Elvira 35
Evira 37
588 Henry 77
Hugh M. 38
Jane A. 35

WALLACE(con't)
Jessee 38
John M. 37
John 77
Jonathan S. 37
Letty 38
Levi 77
Love C. 37
Margaret 38
Mary A. 37
Mary A.E. 38
Mary J. 77
May L. 35
Mount 37
Nancy 37
256 Parthena 38
255 Peter 37
305 Porter 43
Sarah 77
Sarah A. 37
Solomon 77
Susan 38
Susannah 77
Tabitha 38
250 Thomas C. 37
Washington 38
x795 William 101

WALTON see WHA

WALLET
Caroline 106
Comedore 106
842 Epimeter 106
John 106
Phebe 106

WALSH
249 Richard 37
Sarah 37

WARD
Adaline 105
Charles W. 105
CynthiaS 91
David 91
Eliza A. 91
Elizabeth 105
x1016 Isham 128
828 James W. 105
Joanna 117
702 John 91
924 John 117
John H. 91
Patrick 91
Susannah 91
703 Thomas 91

WARNER
x646 Mary 83
x646 Viletta 83

WARREN
384 Andrew 52
Augustus N. 52
Clark B. 52
John L. 52
Mary A. 52
Marion L. 52

WATSON
x383 Mary 52

WEBB
Betsy 125
Christina 125
Dicy 125
Elizabeth 68
Elizabeth L83
Hannah A. 83
Helen E. 83
516 James 68
Jane 83
John B. 83
992 Joseph 135
Nancy 135
Samuel 83
x790 Susan 101
635 William 83

WEISSACKER
x894 Julius 113

WELLINGTON
Charlotte 99
Elizabeth 99
774 Erastus 99
James 99
Lucinda 99
775 Noadiah 99
Sarah 99
Zachary T. 99

WENTWORTH
x777 Charles 99

WENTZ(Wintz)
Alexander 109
America 109
Elizabeth 52
Frances 109
Henry Clay 109
Isabella 18
x60 Jacob(Wen 14
John 109
John W. 52
380 Joseph 52
Lewis M. 52
Mary 52
Mary 109
Mary A. 18
x381 Mary E. 52
Matilda 109
91 Michael 18
Robert M. 18
Sarah A. 109
860 William 109
William L. 52
William W. 18

WESTOFF
x715 Arnold 92

WALTON see
455 Eli H. 61
Mary 61
Susan 61
Waldo W. 61

WHEELER
Alexander 76
Armand L. 100
580 Edward 76
582 Eli 76
Elizabeth 76
Frances S. 76
Henly 76
Illinois 100
579 James 76
Jane 76
Joseph 80
785 Joseph 100
Joseph C. 100
Leatha 76
Lucy A. 76
Malvina 80
Matilda 76
Mary 76
Mary 80
Mary D. 100
Reason 80
Rhoda 76
Venila 76
613 William 80
Zachariah 80

WHITE
Albert G. 117
Alice J. 117
Artemicia 117
Benjamin 29
177 Chapman M. 29
Ezra 117
George W. 117
Jacob E. 117
x183 James 30
James C. 29
John C. 29
John H. 117
Joseph C. 29
x784 Marie 100
Mary C. 25
Mary E. 117
Matilda C. 117
827 Overton 117
x397 Peter 54
Rebecca 29
Sarah J. 29
Virginia M. 29
William 117

WHITNEY
829 Alfred 125
Henry C. 125
Lucinda 125
Mary F. 125
Sarah J, 125

WHITTEN
Emmerine 95
Hetty S. 95
739 Littleton 95
Mary M. 95
Nancy E. 95
William N. 95

Heritage Books by the author:

1860 Census, Cabell County, West Virginia

1870 Census, Cabell County, West Virginia

An Atlas of Appalachian Trails to the Ohio River

An Atlas of German Migration and America

An Atlas of Northern Trails Westward from New England

*An Atlas of Settlement between the Appalachian Mountains
and the Mississippi/Missouri Valleys: 1760–1880*

An Atlas of the Southern Trails to the Mississippi

An Atlas of Trails West of the Mississippi River

*Cabell Cemeteries, Cabell County, West Virginia
Volume 1: Cemeteries North of US 60*

*Cabell Census Locator: Who and Where in Cabell County,
Virginia/West Virginia from 1810 to 1850 in One Volume*

Cabell County's Empire for Freedom

Cabell County, Virginia/West Virginia, Superior Court Records, 1843–1848

Etna Iron Works: Ledger Book - Expense Records, 1876–1878 (Final Ledger), Lawrence County, Ohio

*Looking at the Personal Diaries of William F. Dusenberry of Bloomingdale, (Cabell County),
Virginia/West Virginia, 1855 and 1856, Plus Parts of 1862, 1869, 1870, and 1871*

Minute Books: Cabell County, [West] Virginia Minute Book 1, 1809–1815

*Miscellaneous Cabell County, West Virginia Records: Order Book Overseers of the Poor, 1814–1861;
Fee Book, 1826–1839; 1857–1859 (Rule Book); Cabell Land for Tax Purposes, 1861–1865*

*Nicholas County, Kentucky Property Tax Lists, 1800–1811
with Indexes to Deed Books A & B (2), and C*

*Nicholas County, Kentucky Records: Stray Book 1, 1805–1811; Stray Book 2, 1813–1819;
Stray Book 3, 1820–1870; and Execution Book A, 1801–1878*

On the Frontier of Virginia and North Carolina

Owen County, Kentucky Stray Books 1 & 2: 1819–1830, 1830–1864

Torn Apart: How Cabell Countians Fought the Civil War

www.ingramcontent.com/pod-product-compliance
Lightning Source LLC
Chambersburg PA
CBHW081431270326
41932CB00019B/3163